FRIENDS FOR 350 YEARS

HOWARD H. BRINTON

"... through whom the Light shone."

FRIENDS FOR 350 YEARS

*The history and beliefs of the
Society of Friends since George Fox
started the Quaker movement*

by Howard H. Brinton

*with historical update and
page and line notes*

by Margaret Hope Bacon

PENDLE HILL PUBLICATIONS
WALLINGFORD, PENNSYLVANIA

FRIENDS FOR 350 YEARS
OCTOBER 2002: 7,000
a revised edition of

FRIENDS FOR 300 YEARS

FIRST PAPERBACK PRINTING: JULY 1965- 2,000
SECOND PRINTING: JUNE 1969-2,000
THIRD PRINTING: FEBRUARY 1972-2,000
FOURTH PRINTING: MAY 1974-2,000
FIFTH PRINTING: JULY 1976-3,000
SIXTH PRINTING: JUNE 1980-3,000
SEVENTH PRINTING: JULY 1983- 5,000
EIGHTH PRINTING: JANUARY 1988-3,500
NINTH PRINTING: APRIL 1991-3,000
TENTH PRINTING: JUNE 1994-3,000
ELEVENTH PRINTING: SEPTEMBER 1997-2,000

For information, write:
Pendle Hill Publications
Wallingford, Pennsylvania 19086

ISBN 0-87574-903-8
Library of Congress catalog card number: 52-5424
Printed in the United States of America

CONTENTS

Foreword by Margaret Hope Bacon   *vii*
Introduction by Howard Brinton   *xiii*

I.   "To Wait upon the Lord"   1

II.   The Light Within as Experienced   19

III.   The Light Within as Thought About   39

IV.   The Meeting for Worship   73

V.   Vocal Ministry   102

VI.   Reaching Decisions   121

VII.   The Meeting Community   143

VIII.   The Meeting and the World   176

IX.   The Four Periods of Quaker History   213

X.   Quaker Thought and the Present   245

An Historical Update by Margaret Hope Bacon   269

Page and Line Notes by Bacon   283

Appendix I: The Philadelphia Queries of 1946   291

Appendix II: The Philadelphia Queries of 2000   297

Index   311

Foreword

The decision to bring out a new edition of Howard Brinton's classic, *Friends for 300 Years*, in 2002, thus making it in effect, *Friends for 350 Fifty Years*, has not been easy. On the one hand, much that Brinton wrote fifty years ago remains timeless; on the other, some of the changes of the past half century need to be considered.

Howard Brinton's pioneering description of the birth of the Quaker movement as a form of group mysticism, the role of Quaker thought and belief and its place in the history of religious thought, the meaning of Quaker ministry, and the functioning of the Quaker meeting as both a worshiping group and a community, remain unique in the current literature on Quakerism. As one Quaker historian said. "We simply have nothing else that does the job." Fruit of his continuing studies of the journals of early Friends, Brinton's book speaks in many ways as clearly and simply to a new generation of Friends as it did fifty years ago.

But major changes have taken place in the past fifty years which need to be taken into account. The dramatic rise in Quaker scholarship and in the publication of books on Quaker history has brought to light some new material which must be considered in examining his text. This scholarship, under the leadership of Hugh Barbour and Geoffrey Nuttall, has discounted the assumption made first by Rufus Jones and his disciples, including Brinton, that Quaker mysticism had its roots in European mysticism, and has established the Quaker movement as originating in the left wing of the Puritan movement, with its own mystical side. Changes of attitude toward both women and persons of other races has led to changes in language which must be taken into account. Howard Brinton had a deep respect for women (he was married to a powerful Quaker minister) and for African-Americans, whom he encouraged to come to Pendle Hill, but in keeping with the custom of his day he used what we would now call "sexist" and "racist" language. He also illustrated his points with quotations primarily from the journals of Quaker men, since there had been less scholarship on the journals of Quaker women in 1950 than at present.

In his Introduction, Brinton claims to base his interpration of Quakerism mainly on George Fox's pastoral *Epistles* and Robert Barclay's *Apology*. He used editions now out of print; readers today are encouraged to consult John Nickall's edition of George Fox's *Journal* (Philadelphia Yearly Meeting and Quaker Home Service, 1997); T.C. Jones' edition of George Fox's pastoral epistles, *The Power of the Lord is Over All* (Friends United Press, 1990); and Dean Freiday's edition of Robert Barclay's *Apology in Modern English* (Barclay Press, 1991).

The past fifty years have seen major changes in the Religious Society of Friends, including a worldwide effort to overcome past differences and to come together as a religious society. It is no longer acceptable, as it perhaps was fifty years ago, to write the history of the Society of Friends exclusively from the point of view of one's own affiliation, as Brinton did from the view point of a member of the Wilburite-leaning Philadelphia Yearly Meeting. Belief in inclusiveness must be extended to inclusiveness of those who differ with us on points of theological interpretation. Soon the majority of Quakers worldwide will be from the Third World. Friends need to be mindful of the tendency to ethno-centricity in matters of race and class, as well as historical back-ground, in approaching the future of Quakerism in a new century.

Rather than make changes in the text itself, to reflect new understandings and new sensitivities, the Publications Committee has decided to indicate in page and line notes in the back of the book some places in the text where it is felt that Brinton would change the text himself if given the opportunity to rewrite it in terms of modern scholarship and modern sensibilities. We do so in the full knowledge that some of the changes we make today will be obsolete in another fifty years.

We want to thank Holley Webster for proofreading and updating Howard Brinton's index, providing publishing dates and specific editions where possible. Where more than ten editions are still extant, we have left Brinton's original reference.

A Short Sketch of Howard Brinton

For readers coming new to this book, we thought it well to include a short sketch of Howard Brinton, one of the most important figures in the Society of Friends in the first half of the twentieth century. Howard Brinton was co-director of Pendle Hill, the Quaker study center in Wallingford, Pennsylvania for almost twenty years and continued to live on campus after his retirement, influencing many generations of students there. It was at Pendle Hill that he wrote many of his ten books, and most of his pamphlets and articles on Quakerism. According to his unpublished memoir, he took just three weeks off from Pendle Hill to write *Friends for Three Hundred Years,* basing it on many years of lecturing on the subject and his wide knowledge of Quaker journals.

Howard Brinton was born on July 24, 1884, on a farm in Chester County, near the spot where his Quaker ancestors had settled nine generations earlier. He attended the Friends School in West Chester, graduated from the public high school, and went to Haverford College, where he majored in physics and studied philosophy under Rufus Jones, earning a B. A. in 1904 and becoming a member of Phi Beta Kappa. Following graduation he did additional scholarly work, earning an M.A. in philosophy from Haverford in 1905.

There followed a period of teaching, first at Friends Select School, next at Olney Boarding School in Barnesville (1909-1915), and then at Guilford College in North Carolina, (1915-1917) where he served as head of the department of mathematics and later as acting president (1917-1918). While at Guilford, he completed work for a Master's Degree from Harvard. It was during this time that he developed his lifelong devotion to Quaker education.

The American Friends Service Committee, formed in 1917 to provide "a service of love in wartime," next attracted his interest. He worked at the national headquarters in Philadelphia as Publicity Secretary before going abroad to participate in the child feeding in Germany and later in Poland. It was here he became acquainted with Anna Shipley Cox (1887-1969), from College Park, California, also a birthright Friend, scholar and teacher, and also working for the AFSC.

Just as Anna left Poland they became engaged and were married in College Park Friends Meeting, California in July, 1921. That fall the couple went to Earlham College in Indiana, where Howard taught physics and Anna, classics, and three of their four children were born. One of the Brinton legends was that Anna always managed to give birth over weekends so as not to interfere with her classes! While at Earlham, Howard completed his work for a Ph.D. from the University of California in physics and philosophy, earning the degree in 1925.

In 1928 the Brintons moved to Mills College in California, where Howard taught Bible and the history of religion and Anna archeology and art history. Here Howard published his first book, *The Mystic Will: A Study of the Philosophy of Jacob Boehme,* with the help of Anna's editing. In 1931 he gave the Swarthmore Lecture for British Friends, entitled *Creative Worship,* which became a Quaker classic.

While at Mills, the Brintons were active in the Berkeley Friends Meeting and the College Park Association. In April of 1931 they called together Friends from California, Oregon, and

Washington for a two-day meeting at their house. Here the Pacific Coast Association of Friends, forerunner of Pacific Yearly Meeting, was born.

The Brintons had been interested from the first in the development of Pendle Hill in Wallingford, Pennsylvania, as a center for adult religious education, similar to Woodbrooke in England and in 1936 they accepted an invitation to become joint directors of that institution which was still experiencing growing pains. Under their stewardship Pendle Hill flourished, Anna managing all the practical aspects of community life, Howard acting as the source of much spiritual and intellectual stimulation.

It was a time of close relations between Pendle Hill and AFSC; the Brintons jointly and separately accepted AFSC assignments during this period, helped with the orientation of AFSC workers going overseas, while Anna served on the AFSC board of directors. The Brintons were also active in the Friends World Committee, attending the world gatherings, and Howard gave many additional lectures, such as the William Penn Lecture, the Rufus Jones Lecture, the Ward Lecture, and the Shrewsbury Lecture, and earned several honorary degrees.

In 1946 Anna Brinton traveled widely in Asia for the AFSC, staying in Japan for some time. In 1949 she resigned from Pendle Hill and Howard took a leave of absence so that they could spend two years in Japan, Anna in charge of postwar relief in two centers, while Howard served as Quaker International Affairs Representative.

Returning to Pendle Hill, Howard, then seventy, requested retirement. The Board accepted reluctantly, urging the Brintons to continue to make their home at Pendle Hill, where Howard could continue to conduct courses and counsel students. One fruit of this period was Howard's book, *Quaker Journals: Varieties of Religious Experience Among Friends,* published by Pendle Hill Publications in 1972.

To the community of Pendle Hill and to their friends around the world, the Brintons were inseparable—Anna large, dynamic, witty; Howard, small, even wispy, quiet, a thinker and a dreamer.

When Anna died suddenly in 1969, it was hard to think how Howard would manage without her. But manage he did, with the help of his Japanese secretary, Yuki Takashashi. In 1972, he and Yuki were married, and in April of 1973, Howard died.

Of Howard Brinton in his final days, Elizabeth Gray Vining wrote: "With his white hair and frail, spare body, he was like a beautiful translucent shell through which the light shone."

—Margaret Hope Bacon

INTRODUCTION

THIS BOOK APPEARS AT THE TIME of the three hundredth anniversary of the beginning of the Quaker movement. As early as 1647 George Fox, the principal founder of Quakerism, had begun to preach, but though many were convinced of the truth of his teaching, Quakerism did not become a movement until 1652 when he came to the northwest of England. Here a large group of people known as Seekers found in his message that which they sought. From this stems the movement which the world called "Quaker" and which later called itself the Society of Friends.

These chapters record the history and attempt to assess the value of Quaker principles and practices as they have evolved through three centuries. An effort is made to describe the essential nature of the religion of the Society of Friends through the successive stages of its development. A secondary aim is to consider the past, present and future significance of the type of religion to which Quakerism belongs.

Quakerism is here defined as the type of faith and behavior which developed in the Society of Friends during its first century and a half. This type, allowing for cultural changes, still persists in many areas and is today experiencing a rebirth. The theory and practice of the Society of Friends during the later periods of its history can correctly be termed "Quakerism" in so far as the essential purpose is preserved.

The preservation of the original purpose is not the same as the preservation of the visible form in which that purpose was first expressed. As family life today presents an aspect different from family life in the seventeenth century, so Quakerism presents a different outward appearance. To revive the visible ways of primitive Quakerism would be impossible and inappropriate. But to revive that which was at the heart of the original awakening and the original witness is to meet a need as old as humanity, yet still fresh, essential and new.

It is sometimes implied that vital Quakerism ceased to exist after the seventeenth century. Modern Quaker historians maintain that the initial outburst was succeeded by a decline in the eighteenth century into a different faith, generally characterized as Quietism, and that, after the period of Quietism, a revival occurred in the nineteenth century. A different pattern of development is envisaged in this book. The second period is portrayed as exhibiting no change in intention. The faith of the Society of Friends remained what its founders had set forth. The only change was in the form in which the original message was expressed, a form determined by the fact that this was a period of conservation and consolidation. During the nineteenth century changes occurred not only in the form but in the actual intention. That which finally appeared in some large areas of Quakerism was not a revival of the original faith, but a movement strongly colored by a different type of religion with a different method and basis. Today increased awareness of Quaker thought and history is leading many Friends to reaffirm the original emphasis. As the earlier purpose is preserved or regained, the movement may properly be called Quaker even though the intention may be inadequately realized.

Though the word "Quaker" is an old word, the word "Quakerism" has only recently come into use. The primitive Quakers called their doctrine the Truth. A Quaker was defined as one who "professes the Truth." This book is an effort to state how much of original Quakerism still lives, how much is dead, and to what extent Quakerism today can be called the Truth. The first great Quaker apologist, Robert Barclay (1648-90), evaluated his religion in terms of the thought of his day. If Quakerism is to remain a vital religion it must come to terms with the thought of each succeeding epoch.

In interpreting early Quakerism the present writer has depended mainly on George Fox's pastoral *Epistles* and Robert Barclay's *Apology* or defense of the Quaker position. The first portrays Quakerism as *felt*, the second affords the most complete interpretation that we have of Quakerism as *thought about*.

Writers on Quakerism in the early years of the twentieth century—John William Graham, William Charles Braithwaite, Edward Grubb, A. Neave Brayshaw, John Wilhelm Rowntree, Rufus M. Jones and others—performed an inestimable service in reinterpreting Quakerism in the language and thought of their own time. Their work resulted in a great renewal of interest in Quaker thought and history. Without them Quakerism might not have cleared the hurdle set up by modern science and Biblical criticism. In different ways and to different degrees they were influenced by the idealistic Neo-Hegelian philosophy which colored theological thinking in the later decades of the nineteenth century. This resulted in an optimistic view of human life and a high opinion of man as akin to God. Since then two world wars and their results in the form of totalitarian states have afforded a grim revelation of the evil that men can perpetrate. As a consequence, pessimistic trends have appeared in religious thinking. These tendencies come close to Calvinistic theology which emphasizes human depravity and insists that salvation is the miracle of God's grace in which man, as man, because of the evil of his nature, can perform no part. The position of Robert Barclay, who set the pattern for early Quaker thought, was intermediate between the two poles of Hegelian idealism and Neo-Calvinism. Barclay was pessimistic regarding what he called "natural" man's present condition, but optimistic in respect to man's capacity for regeneration and union with God even in this life. He thought that with divine help, man might, as God's creation, become perfected here and now. The present writer sympathizes with Barclay's position, while rejecting much of his terminology. Idealism identifies too closely the divine and the human and runs the risk of eliminating the reality of evil; Calvinism tends to make impossible the attainment of the good.

The Society of Friends has attracted attention by its continuous and widespread efforts to remove the causes and effects of war through education, mediation and relief. But this activity, important though it is as the world becomes increasingly warlike, is a limited aspect of Quakerism. Quaker peace principles and philanthropic ideals which have resulted in social pioneering can best be understood in terms of doctrines and methods more fundamental than their results in terms of activity. It may, therefore, be worthwhile for these doctrines and methods to be better understood, especially by Quakers themselves, who are frequently unaware of the roots, and fix their attention mainly on the plant above ground.

There are at least two additional reasons for writing about the Society of Friends. These have no relation to the recent attention which has been focused on relief work. The first is the position of Quakerism as an explicit and developed manifestation of one of the three main forms of Christianity, the other two being Catholicism and Protestantism* The form which I designate as Quaker, though not confined to the Society of Friends, has not received the attention it deserves. The second reason for writing arises from an impression that the time is ripe for the emergence of this third form of Christianity into greater influence and power. This may occur through or within the Society of Friends or in some other context. If a need is realized, the time may be ripe for that need to be met, but it does not necessarily follow that the need will be met.

*In speaking of Protestantism in this book reference is usually made to the earlier Protestantism. Modern Protestantism has assumed such a vast variety of forms that it is difficult to generalize about it.

The relation of Quakerism to the special needs of today is explained in the concluding chapter.

The precedent for characterizing the faith and practice of the Society of Friends as a third form of Christianity was set by Quakers of the seventeenth century. In controversial books written to refute opponents, they draw a clear distinction between themselves, the Roman Catholics and the Protestants. This is particularly true in Barclay's *Apology** which early became the accepted exposition of Quaker theory and practice. A large part of this treatise is devoted to a comparison of the three positions. Sometimes, for the sake of completeness, Barclay also brings in a fourth position which he calls the *Socinian,* representing the rationalistic point of view. Thus in the section defending the Quaker doctrine of immediate revelation through the Spirit, Barclay answers his opponents who argue that the leading of the Spirit cannot be trusted as a certain guide to truth, by saying, "neither tradition, nor the scriptures, nor reason which the Papists, Protestants and Socinians do respectively make the rule of their faith are in any whit more certain."[1] The Catholics, he says, disagree about tradition; the Protestants about the meaning of Scriptures; and the Socinians about the conclusions of reason. He then points out that in the last resort they all depend on the Spirit which produced all three, the Church tradition, the Scriptures and also the assumptions of reason. Similarly, Barclay compares Catholic, Protestant and Quaker doctrines of the nature of the Church, the call and ordination of ministers,[2] justification by faith[3] and the other major subjects of seventeenth-century religious controversy. Under the term Protestants, he includes Lutherans, Calvinists, Presbyterians, Independents

---

* Complete title *An Apology for the True Christian Divinity, being an Explanation and Vindication of the Principles and Doctrines of the People called Quakers,* first published in Latin, 1676; in English in 1678. All references to *The Apology* will be to the seventh edition in English, 1765.

(Congregationalists) and Baptists. The Church of England in that day occupied an intermediate position between the Catholic and Protestant positions. In 1660, after Cromwell, it resumed its function as the Established Church. The Anglicans became the persecutors of all dissenters, but the chief theological opponents of Quakerism came mainly from the nonconformist sects.

The Reformation was closer to Quakerism at the outset than it was later. In defense of their position the Quakers often quoted the early Reformers.[4] But, though the Reformation began in a highly spiritual revolt against old forms and authorities, it quickly developed its own forms and authorities. Its leaders feared a religion based purely on the Spirit and insisted that such a religion laid open a broad road toward anarchy. The new churches sought alliance with the state to supplement their own authority. The German Reformation crushed the Anabaptists, who represented an inward type of religion. The English Reformation tried to crush the Quakers.

In some respects Quakerism represented the extreme left wing of the English Reformation. It originated as a part of the religious revolution which accompanied the political revolution under Cromwell. In that sense the Society of Friends might be called Puritanism carried to its logical conclusion. But, though one ancestor of Quakerism is the English Protestant Reformation, especially in its early stages, another ancestor can be traced in the mystical trend which has always been present in the Christian Church, producing saints and martyrs.[5] Mysticism is a religion based on the spiritual search for an inward, immediate experience of the divine. Whenever and wherever religion becomes too formal and institutional, too dependent on external expression, the mystic rises up in protest and points the way to a religion which is internal, independent of outward forms or organization and centered in the direct apprehension of God. This experience requires no intermediary of church, priest or book. The history of all religion is a chronicle of the tension between the mystic or prophet, whose religion is inwardly grounded in experience, and the priest or theologian, whose religion is expressed through doctrine and symbol.

It is difficult, perhaps impossible, to trace any direct connection between Quaker thought and the mystics and mystical movements of the Middle Ages. The mystical groups of the fourteenth century in the Rhineland, such as the Friends of God and the Brethren of the Common Life, had much in common with the Society of Friends. It is probable that their doctrines, through a series of stages and transitions, eventually reached England by means of refugees from persecution on the Continent. Mysticism in a variety of forms was certainly in the English air just prior to the rise of Quakerism. In the Commonwealth period, England enjoyed for the first time a large measure of religious freedom. Bishops had been to a great extent eliminated and the new Presbyterian system had not yet succeeded in duplicating their authority. The prevailing form of Protestant religious doctrine was Calvinism, but England was swarming with a variety of small radical religious groups. Lists of their opinions compiled by scandalized Puritan divines show that many of these were unbalanced manifestations on the fringe of a great movement. But some were based on sound mystical concepts derived from the New Testament, particularly the writings of Paul and John. Christianity itself was born of the Spirit of Pentecost. For the mystical forebears of Quakerism we need go no further than the Bible, which was then for the first time becoming widely known in England, and the inevitable mystical influence which accompanies every great reform in religion. Out of a mist of undefined tendencies Quakerism was precipitated.

But if Quakerism were only mysticism, it could not be classified as the third form of Christianity. Mysticism exists in all religions; every great world religion has its mystical sect or groups. What the Quakers, as mystics, are to Christianity, the Zen (or Chan) sect is to Buddhism, the Yogis are to Hinduism, the Sufis to Mohammedanism and the Taoists to the religion of China. But Oriental mysticism, like Oriental religion in general, is individualistic. Congregational worship can hardly be said to exist, unless it be in Mohammedanism, which is strongly influenced by its Jewish and Christian origins. Quakerism is peculiar in being a group mysticism, grounded in Christian concepts. If it had been what might be called pure mysticism, it would not belong to any particular religion, nor could it exist as a movement or sect. Pure mysticism is too subjective to provide a bond of union.

There has always been a temptation to express the characteristics of mystical religion in a general rather than a particular frame of reference. To do so might create a wider appeal. Many persons shy away from the suggestion of sectarianism. In their opinion, organization kills the spirit. But religion is as it does. It may begin in the thought and imagination of some seer or prophet, but its full implications are demonstrated only in the course of historical development within a group of human beings who live according to its precepts. If religious truths do not become embodied in a movement, they lose their vitality and their power of propagation.

The endeavor in this book is not to produce a history of Quakerism, but, by means of historical illustrations, to examine a method; just as a writer on science might interpret science by explaining and illustrating the development of the scientific method through successive periods. Quakerism is primarily a method, just as science is primarily a method. Quakerism includes also a certain body of beliefs, as does science, but in both cases these beliefs are accepted because they have been arrived at by experts using the proper method. They can be modified by further use of the same method by which they were arrived at in the first place. The scientific method is directed toward the outer world. This is true, even in the case of psychology, which depends as far as possible on laboratory methods. But the Quaker method differs from the scientific method in that it is dealing with what can neither be measured nor weighed. It is directed to the inner life, the response to moral claims and religious insights. Since both Quakerism and science are based primarily on experience, rather than on reason or authority, they have nothing to fear from the results of discovery or research.

Every vital method is inevitably based on accepted facts regarding the objective world. The scientific method assumes that the universe is a cosmos not a chaos, that the same results will follow from the same conditions, that man can, by means of his senses, learn some truth about the physical universe and by a process of reasoning deduce further truth not revealed to the senses. This, and more, must be accepted by scientific faith and intuition.

Similarly, Quakerism, though primarily directed toward the inner life, accepts objective historical events. Chief among them is the central event in the history of Christianity, the revelation of God in human terms through Jesus of Nazareth. If God had not revealed Himself both outwardly in history and inwardly in experience, the outward revelation would have lacked power and meaning and the inward revelation would remain formless and vague. Only as the outward eye of time and the inward eye of eternity are focused on a single fact does that fact attain the three-dimensional quality of Truth.

Much has been written about mysticism as an individual phenomenon exhibited by certain great personalities in religious history, but mysticism as a group phenomenon has received less attention, especially from a philosophical and psychological standpoint. Rufus M. Jones is distinguished as the scholar who has devoted most attention to mystical groups. To him the present writer, who was his student, owes a deep and permanent debt.

Quakerism represents a form of group mysticism which has persisted longer than any other instance in literate times. In the course of three centuries it has shown both the strength and the weakness of a religion of this type. The central fact of such a religion is the uniting power of the divine Spirit integrating the group as an organic whole. This is the main theme of this book. Examples drawn from the records of a single religious movement serve to show how religion as such possesses an important social function in creating social organisms. It is also evident that the divine Spirit performs the function of producing unity within the individual as well as within the group. If not resisted, the same Spirit is able to overcome all disunity everywhere among and within men, and between man and God.

—Howard H. Brinton

Notes

1. Robert Barclay, *Apology*, 7th edition in English, 1765, p. 55. See complete title on page xvii of the Introduction. All following references will be to this edition.

2. Barclay, *Apology*, pp. 271-343.

3. Barclay, *Apology*, pp. 196-241.

4. See such passages in Barclay, *Apology*, as pp. 22, 44, 69, 223, 236, 284, 823, 350, 505.

5. Rufus M. Jones, *Studies in Mystical Religion, The Flowering of Mysticism,* and other works.

CHAPTER I

"To Wait Upon The Lord"

IN OLIVER CROMWELL'S ENGLAND during the Puritan Revolution, in the years 1652-56, a religious movement began which was different from any that had preceded it. Small groups of men and women gathered in town and country homes and sat together in silence "to wait upon the Lord." In their countenances and bearing there was awe and reverence, as if they were gathered, not in a simple living room, but in a holy temple. Expectancy pervaded the group like that felt by those who await the coming of a great person or the occurrence of an important event, yet it was obvious from the expression of their faces that attention was directed not without but within. Some heads were bowed in wordless prayer, others uplifted as if gazing at supernal light. At times, unpredictably, the silence was broken by a voice pleading for submission to the divine Will or by words of supplication to God.

In these first Quaker meetings new life was stirring; new, yet as old as mankind, releasing power which was again to challenge conventional forms of life and thought. Beginning in the northwest of England on the fells and in the dales of Westmorland and Lancashire, the movement spread to London and the south. To hundreds of towns and villages the Quaker message came with a double impact. By some it was embraced with unbounded fervor as the way to God and His Kingdom; by others it was dreaded and feared as an evil capable of overthrowing all established order and

1

belief. Those "who embraced the Truth for the love of it" found
themselves possessed of a spiritual vitality and holy energy which
sent them to all accessible lands to tell others of their great discovery and to endure, with inward serenity and peace, years of relentless and cruel persecution.

This new outburst of spiritual power, which sometimes caused
its possessors to tremble with fervor, was labeled "Quaker" by its
opponents, though its adherents called themselves "people of God"
or "children of the Light" (I Thess. 5:5, Eph. 5:8), or "Friends"
(John 15:15) and eventually the Society of Friends. At first there
was no desire to organize a new sect, but only to tell others of what
they themselves had found. This they called "the Truth" and truth
is beyond and above all sects and opinions. This Truth was not so
much a new doctrine as a new life. It gave a feeling of heightened
power and insight, an uplift of the soul to a higher existence, which
in some mysterious way was generated in the group waiting in
silence upon the Lord.

Though there had never before been anything just like a Quaker
meeting for worship, there was nothing new about the feeling of
strength resulting from time spent in the divine Presence. The
prophets of Israel and the writers of the Psalms were well aware
of it. "They that wait upon the Lord shall renew their strength,
they shall mount up with wings as eagles" (Isa. 40:31).

> I waited patiently for the Lord; and he inclined unto me
> and heard my cry. He brought me up also out of an hor-
> rible pit, out of the miry clay, and set my feet upon a rock
> (Ps. 40:1, 2).

"Wait on the Lord . . . and he shall strengthen thine heart" (Ps.
27:14). The book of Psalms is a collection of hymns which give
expression to the feelings and aspirations of worshipers waiting in
the Presence of the Lord in the temple at Jerusalem.[1] It was only
there, according to the book of Deuteronomy, that God could be

worshipped. When the Jews migrated to other parts of the world, synagogue worship was substituted for temple worship. In the synagogue God was talked about and prayers were addressed to Him. The ancient scrolls were read telling of what God had once said through his prophets, but there was no longer the same intimate sense of His living Presence on the Mercy Seat. Protestant worship, as compared with Catholic worship or Quaker worship, is more like that of the synagogue than that of the temple.

Emergence of life and power in the worshipping group, giving rise to a sense of what the Psalmist calls being "lifted up," is a phenomenon particularly characteristic of early Christianity. In Christianity the exaltation was first experienced at Pentecost, possibly in the temple. The Disciples, being all of them Jews, naturally assumed that the Presence of God was there. The first Christian century affords many records of the descent of the Spirit on worshipping groups meeting in Christian homes. On an occasion described in the Acts of the Apostles, "the place in which they were gathered together was shaken; and they were all filled with the Holy Spirit" (4:81).* This descent of the Spirit to create a living unity between God and man, and man and man, was the most important, the unique feature in early Christian history. Without this, Christianity might never have become a world religion. This Spirit which the early Friends, like the early Christians, sometimes thought of as the living Christ, brought life and power to the group as a soul gives life and power to a body, to use Paul's favorite figure. Sometimes Paul used another image and spoke of the little gathering of worshipers in the home as growing "into a holy temple in the Lord; in whom you also are built into it for a dwelling place of God in the Spirit" (Eph. 2:21, 22).

* All quotations from the New Testament are taken from the Revised Standard Version, copyrighted, 1946, by the International Council of Religious Education.

The saying in Matthew, "Where two or three are gathered in my name, there am I in the midst of them" (18:20), might never have become part of the Gospel canon had it not described a central fact of early Christian experience. When Christian worship lost its spontaneity and became organized and mechanized, with human leadership more apparent than divine leadership, this living presence in the midst was no longer felt so strongly, although by a priestly miracle it could still be realized on the altar.

Catholic worship is a form of temple worship in the sense that Divinity is felt to be present at a particular time and place. At the elevation of the Host, when the miracle of transubstantiation is completed and the bread and wine transformed into the body and blood of Christ, there is a brief period of silent waiting, the only conduct appropriate in the very presence of the Divine. For the same reason the Reserved Sacrament is worshipped in silence. Catholic worship resembles Quaker worship in this fact that Divinity is felt to be present.

Such a group mysticism as Quakerism is different from the solitary seeking cultivated by many of the great Catholic contemplatives. Medieval Christian mystics for the most part followed Plotinus in thinking of the approach to God as "the flight of the alone to the Alone." Lonely seekers for God were more at home in a monastic cell than in the toil and struggle of family or business life. Their aspirations are directed toward God alone, rather than toward man. The mysticism of the Quakers is directed both toward God and toward the group. The vertical relation to God and the horizontal relation to man are like two co-ordinates used to plot a curve; without both the position of the curve could not be determined.

The Catholic Church retained the ancient Christian doctrine of the Church as the Body of Christ. This meant that Christ's saving grace was inherent in the Church and could be disseminated through the sacraments. The Church felt that power was committed to it to save sinners. Because this power was abused and commercialized, Protestants arose and denied it to the Church, holding that salvation was a transaction between man and God alone. There was much in early Protestantism which upheld a religion based on the Spirit within, but by the middle of the seventeenth century the early vitality had somewhat ebbed. God, according to Protestantism, had withdrawn from His world, leaving the Holy Book to explain His plan of salvation and the Holy Spirit to interpret the Book. The Christian Church again tended to become dry and formal. Its leaders were more interested in politics than in religion. The time was ripe for rediscovery of the divine Presence in the midst of the worshipping group and the advent of a religion which satisfied man's longing to go beyond words about God, to God Himself.

The heart and soul of Quakerism as it first appeared in England is not so clearly revealed in the vast sum of pamphlets and books written to convince the unconvinced or to defend Quaker principles against attacks by opponents,[2] as in what the Quakers wrote for one another, particularly their letters and autobiographies. These express a spontaneous upspringing of feeling and thought out of the living heart of the movement-flashes of insight rather than of argument. The collection of documents issued under the title *First Publishers of Truth,* to which reference will frequently be made, gives a graphic account by eye witnesses of the way in which the Truth was first proclaimed in England in the various communities where regular Friends meetings became established.

At the time when the early participants in the movement were beginning to pass from the scene, the Yearly Meeting, the central executive body of the Society of Friends, asked each Quaker meeting to send up to London a report of the way in which Truth first came to that community. Meetings were slow to respond, some reporting as much as thirty years later, in 1720. These reports remained unused and almost forgotten until 1907, when they were printed in all their quaint simplicity and sometimes crude but forceful expression. In the following quotations the spelling is modernized.

> Thomas Stacy, Thomas Stubbs and several more . . . first published the Truth in Upper Side . . . and some soon after convinced met together, when but five or six in number, to wait upon God in silence and the Lord blessed us with his presence and gave us the spirit of discerning.[3]

> By this time we were pretty many gathered in this place (Cornwall) to sit down in silence and wait upon the Lord and we had many good and comfortable seasons and meetings at this time where we felt the alone Teacher nigh us administering to our spiritual wants.[4]

> And John Wilkinson, staying some days with us, advised to settle a meeting, though there was none to speak words, to wait upon the Lord, which was done and for a time kept in Christopher Story's house in an upper room until it was too little.[5]

As Friends thus were diligent in the inward exercise of true silence, the Lord was pleased in his own time to fill the hearts of many as with new wine, insomuch that several Friends could not contain but spoke forth a few words that their spirits might be eased. Great was the tenderness and brokenness of heart in those days for the Lord was witnessed to be near at hand by his living presence from whence refreshment comes.[6]

They [William Caton and John Stubbs, preaching in Kent] sought to settle and establish meetings and to bring them that were convinced to assemble and sit together to wait upon the Lord in silence, in the measure of that Light of Life in themselves which they turned them unto to the end that they might come gradually to feel, possess and enjoy the living substance of what they had long professed.[7]

These passages, written by persons who had witnessed that which they were writing about, describe in the simplest possible terms the essence of the Quaker exercise of religion. This was the source from which came all activity, whether in preaching the Truth or engaging in social service. The small group which met in silence to "wait upon the Lord" was the dynamo which generated light and power in the Quaker movement. Like a dynamo, this generator drew on Power beyond itself. When these meetings became large and more dependent on preaching and human leadership, the generator degenerated, the light was dimmed and the power weakened. "Friends grew as the Garden of the Lord," writes one eyewitness,[8] but this very growth resulted in a new danger. Large meetings have an important and indispensable function of their own, but they are not so likely to "grow into a temple of the living God" as are smaller, more intimate gatherings.

Writers of Friends *Journals* often describe meetings in which they participated in a way to reflect the fervor and power which was often realized in them. For example, Richard Davies has this to say of a meeting in 1657:

> Though it was silent from words, yet the Word of the Lord God was among us; it was as a hammer and a fire; it was sharper than any two-edged sword; it pierced through our inward parts; it melted and brought us into tears that there was scarcely a dry eye among us. The Lord's blessed power overshadowed our meeting and I could have said that God alone was Master of that assembly.[9]

We find the following account by Thomas Story of a meeting held in a ship's cabin:

> And being together in the great cabin, the good presence of the Lord commanded deep and inward silence before Him, and the Comforter of the Just broke in upon us by

His irresistible power, and greatly tendered us together in
His heavenly love, whereby we were melted into many tears.
Glorious was this appearance to the humbling of us all,
and admiration (astonishment) of some there who did not
understand it.[10]

The following passage describes a meeting in a Boston jail held by
the prisoners with two Friends, Robinson and Stephenson, who
were to be executed on the following day:

During this time though the hearts of the ignorant were
hardened against us to shut us up in a dark, solitary place,
we sat together waiting upon the Lord . . . and this was a
time of love for as the world hated us and despitefully used
us, so the Lord was pleased in a wonderful manner to manifest his supporting love and kindness to us in our innocent
suffering. And especially the two worthies who had now
nearly finished their course . . . many sweet and heavenly
sayings they gave us, being themselves filled with comfort.[11]

In the *First Publishers of Truth* the names of two hundred and five
men and women are recorded "who first raised the witness of God"
in some particular place. Among those who became Friends, whose
names are mentioned in this book, fifty-six different callings are
represented. Twelve are former justices of the peace and nine had
been ordained ministers. "Many shepherds and husbandmen came
out of the north," says a writer from London. Among them George
Fox emerged as the organizing genius of the movement. He was
the greatest "public Friend," a title given to those who went about
preaching to any who would listen in market place, farmhouse,
tavern, on dale or moor, often in a church after the sermon. Sometimes they interrupted the minister and were violently dealt with
by the congregation. When they succeeded in convincing hearers,
they sent them to a silent meeting in the neighborhood, or, if none

existed, they brought them together to form such a meeting. Convincement was only the first stage. Conversion, or change of character, often required a long, slow struggle, worked out in the silence of the meeting for worship. By inward discipline the human will was gradually humbled and brought into submission to the will of God. Meetings held by public Friends occasionally consisted of thousands of hearers. They were called "threshing meetings" because the speaker endeavored to separate the wheat in his audience from the chaff. Sometimes this exercise was described as "ploughing," which meant that the hard ground was broken up that the divine Seed within might grow. Howgill and Burrough, two of the greatest of the public Friends, write to Margaret Fell, mistress of Swarthmore Hall:

> George [Fox] was that day in private with Friends; and we two were in the general meeting place among the rude world, threshing and plowing. [12]

"Thresh out the corn," writes Fox to Howgil and Burrough, "that the Wind may scatter the Chaff, that the corn may be gathered into the Barn."[13] The "Barn" was the meeting for worship to which the threshing meeting served as an invitation. The public work of these Friends was important as the first stage in the history of many Friends meetings. The meeting for worship was less spectacular, but it contained the real life and power of the movement. A public Friend would retire exhausted by his ministry to a silent meeting to become recharged for further service.

Howgill and Burrough describe their work in London in these terms:

> We have thus ordered it since we came, we get Friends on the First days to meet together in several places out of the rude multitude and we two go to the great meeting place which will hold a thousand people, which is always nearly

filled, to thresh among the world; and we stay till twelve or
one o'clock, and then pass away, the one to one place and
the other to another place, where Friends are met in private; and stay till four or five o'clock.[14]

George Fox, at the age of twenty-eight, after four years of searching, five years of preaching and two imprisonments, came to the
northwest of England where he convinced large numbers and initiated Quakerism as a movement. His visit to Preston Patrick in
Westmorland is described in these words by an eye witness:

John Audland would have had George [Fox] to have gone
into the place or pew where usually he and the preacher
did sit, but he refused and took a back seat near the door,
and John Camm sat down by him, where he sat silent waiting upon God about half an hour, in which time of silence
Francis Howgill seemed uneasy and pulled out his Bible,
and opened it and stood up several times, sitting down again
and closing his book, a dread and fear being upon him yet
he dared not begin to preach. After the said silence and
waiting, George stood up in the mighty power of God and
in the demonstration thereof was his mouth opened to
preach Christ Jesus, the Light of Life and the way to God ,
and Saviour of all that believe and obey him, which was
delivered in that power and Authority that most of the au-
ditory which were several hundreds, were effectually
reached to the heart, and convinced of the truth that very
day, for it was the day of God 's power.

A notable day, indeed, never to be forgotten by me, Thomas Camm, who, with some other brethren, by the Quarterly Meeting is appointed to collect the matters herein
mentioned, I being then present at that meeting, a school
boy but about 12 years of age, yet, I bless the Lord for his

mercy, then religiously inclined, and do still remember that blessed and glorious day, in which my soul, by that living Testimony then borne in the demonstration of God's power was effectually opened, reached and convinced, with many more, who are seals of that powerful ministry that attended this faithful servant of the Lord Jesus Christ, and by which we were convinced and turned from darkness to light and from Satan's power to the power of God.[15]

This congregation was ripe for Fox's message. They were an unorganized, fluid group of Seekers, persons who had departed from all established forms to seek for something better. Sometimes these Seeker congregations had already discovered the value of waiting on the Lord in silence. For them the step into Quakerism was a short one, as is shown by the experience of the group at Wigton:

About the year 1653, a few people were gathered together from the public worship of the nation and oftentimes sat together in silence. Some of the persons that were so separated were William Pearson and his wife, James Adamson, Senior, John Seanhouse, in whose hearts the Lord raised good desires after himself.

About which time, it pleased the Lord to send his faithful servants, George Fox, William Dewsbury, James Lancaster and Robert Withers, who came to the house of William Pearson's (of Tiffinwhate, near Wigton), whose heart the Lord had opened to receive these messengers of God into his house, where they had a meeting with these separated people, who were by them turned to Christ their teacher and lived and died in the faith.[16]

A similar group met at Ross:

In the beginning of the twelfth month, in the year 1655, Thomas Goodayer, a yeoman inhabiting in Yorkshire, and

George Scaff came afoot to Ross on a week day to James
Merrick's house, a tanner, where they were first received;
where, after a little stay, they went to the steeple house,
where a great many people were met together (they having
notice of the above friends coming), many of whom were
desirous and in expectation to hear Truth declared, who
had for some time before separated themselves from the
public worship of the world, who did see the end of the
priests' teachings, who did often before meet together by
themselves and would many times sit in silence, and no
particular person appointed to speak or preach among
them, but each of them did speak by way of exhortation as
had freedom, so that the Lord's power was mightily at work
in their hearts and great openings there were amongst
them.[17]

These were Quakers before the rise of the Society of Friends.
The same phenomenon appeared in New England.[18] A number of
Quaker autobiographies indicate that the writers had reached what
was essentially the Quaker position independently.

The extreme simplicity of this act of waiting upon the Lord reduces worship to its essential universal elements, stripped of all
accidental additions. This was the logical fruition of a historical
evolution. From the days of Henry VIII the Bible was becoming
increasingly known in England. By the time of the revolution under Cromwell it was so widely committed to memory that long
passages could be quoted as authority by almost any religiously
minded person. When, because of this familiarity with the New
Testament, the Christianity of the time could be compared with
the Christianity of the first century, a number of radical differences were noted. It was obvious that much had been added in the
course of Christian history which was not there in the beginning.
It was assumed, moreover, that at the outset Christianity existed in

its purest form. The Puritans set out to "purify" the inherited religion of extraneous elements which had been added in the course of its history, but there was a wide difference of opinion as to how far such purification could or should be carried. The first Puritans subtracted the Pope, the Mass, images and five of the seven sacraments, thus creating the Church of England. Presbyterianism, which was the second wave of Puritanism, originating in Calvin, subtracted the rule of bishops and substituted the authority of presbyters or elders. For this they found sound precedent in the New Testament. Then came the more radical Independents or Congregationalists, who subtracted the centralized form of church government which had not existed in New Testament times and substituted a decentralized and more democratic procedure. The Baptists were still more radical. They subtracted infant baptism and made church membership dependent on conversion and the gift of the Spirit as described in the New Testament. Finally arose the Quakers. They subtracted all ritual, all programmed arrangement in worship and the professional ministry, allowing for no outward expression except the prophetic voice which had been heard in the New Testament Church at the beginning. They endowed no officials with religious or administrative duties. Worship and administration were considered the responsibility of the local group or meeting as a whole. Elders and overseers, it is true, existed in the primitive church and the Quakers eventually made use of both. They exercised an advisory function, not over the meeting, but *under* it as the instruments of its will.

This account of the progressive "purification" of the historic church in England is too brief to be accurate, but it suggests in general terms the main direction of the current of change which eventually produced Quakerism. This was a movement from a conservative religious right toward a radical, religious left, whose stages can be labeled Catholicism, Anglicanism, Presbyterianism, Congregationalism, the Baptists and the Quakers. This movement in all its stages produced fundamental changes which extended from religion into politics, science, literature and every phase of life.

Quakerism was, however, one step removed from the most extreme form of seventeenth-century religious radicalism. Furthest to the left was the tendency called "Ranterism" or "anti-nomianism." Today's label would be "anarchism." A movement like Quakerism, depending in its worship on pure inwardness, would inevitably tend to become anarchistic in the absence of all outward rules and restraints. But the meeting for worship, free as it was from outward form, was by no means the whole structure of Quakerism. The steps by which the Society of Friends avoided anarchism constitute the most critical process in its early history.

Quaker *Journals,* or autobiographies, of the initial period show that some converts went through all the stages in moving from the Catholic right and proceeding through Presbyterianism, Independency, the Baptist or some Anabaptist sect and finally finding rest in Quakerism.

One example will suffice. John Gratton (1641-1712) records the stages in his *Journal:*

> I cried unto the Lord that he would tell me what he would have me do, and that he would shew me, who were his people that worshipped him aright.[19]

> I was not satisfied with their doctrine of election and reprobation which put me into deep trouble.[20]

> When the people sang Psalms in the steeple-house I durst not sing the same lines or sayings of David, it would have been a lie in my mouth.[21]

> The Presbyterian priests, whom I had so much esteemed and admired, made their farewell sermons and left us (at the command of the government at the Restoration)

... They ought not to be silent at man's command if the Lord had sent and commanded them to preach.... So I left them.[22]

The Episcopalian Priests came in their white surplices and read common-prayers.... I saw they had the form without the power ... their worship to be in ceremony and outward things without life.[23]

I went to Chesterfield to seek out and meet those people called Independents for I liked the name, seeing nothing at all in man as man to depend on, but they depended only upon the death and sufferings of Christ in his own body and did not come to see him nor his appearance in themselves to be their life, so they were dead professors and dry trees not bringing forth fruit, for I read the Scripture and saw "if any man hath not the Spirit of Christ, he is none of his.[24]

I found a people called Anabaptists.... I thought they came nearest the Scriptures of any I had yet tried.... After they came out of the water ... I saw no appearance of the spirit of newness of life or power.. their baptism being only with water which can only wash away the filth of the flesh.[25]

After trying out a strange sect called Muggletonians, he writes:

After some time I heard of a [Friends] meeting at Exton at one widow Farney's house. I went to it and found divers Friends were come many miles; and when I came I was confirmed that they were in that truth whereof I had been convinced, though they were so much derided by the world.

There was little said in that meeting but I sat still in it, and was bowed in spirit before the Lord, and felt him with me

and with Friends, and saw that they had their minds retired, and waited to feel his presence and power to operate in their hearts and that they were spiritual worshipers
who worship God in Spirit and in truth and I was sensible
that they felt and tasted of the Lord's goodness as at that
time I did, and though few words were spoken, yet I was
well satisfied with the meeting. And there arose a sweet
melody that went through the meeting and the presence
of the Lord was in the midst of us and more true comfort,
refreshment and satisfaction did I meet with from the Lord
in that meeting than ever I had in any meeting in all my
life before.[26]

This ended John Gratton's long search. He had come to his
religious position independently, except for the Scriptures. He
knew exactly what he was looking for before he found it. He was
first drawn to the Quakers by hearing that they were holding their
meetings openly, in spite of the Conventicle Act which forbade all
religious worship except that of the Established Church of England, while other sects were meeting in secret.

These people were despised, persecuted and suffered
deeply beyond others, for others could flee from sufferings and conform a little sometimes; but these abode and
stood though the winds blew, and the rains fell and the
floods beat upon them .[27]

The Quakers, when he found them, had little more to teach
him regarding the inward Christ whom he had himself already
found. But there was a vital difference between the lonely listener
to the divine voice within and the member of a gathered meeting
into which there flowed through many separate channels the con-
verging currents of spiritual life. The story of John Gratton runs
parallel to that of many others who joined the new movement. For

them Quakerism added something new, whereas Puritanism had resulted largely from a process of subtraction. This new element was a doctrine about an experience of the one root out of which all else grew. The energizing Center of the whole movement was the Inward Light, the Inward Christ, that of God in every man, the Power of God, the Witness of God, the Seed of the Kingdom, the pure Wisdom which is from above (James 3:17). The Society of Friends escaped anarchism because its members realized that this Light was a superindividual Light which created peace and unity among all persons who responded to it or "answered it in one another," to use an expression which often appears in George Fox's letters. It was this doctrine of the Light as the unifying principle which made Quakerism something more than just another protesting sect which carried the Protestant principle of individuality and private judgment further than its predecessors had done. The presence of the Light of Christ enabled the meeting to become the Body of Christ-a principle in essence closer to Catholic than to Protestant doctrine.

Notes

1. For a waiting worship see also Psalms 25:3, 5, 21; 37:7, 9, 84; 39:7; 59:9; 69:3, 6; 123:2; 130:5.

2. A Quaker book or pamphlet appeared on an average of once a week during the seventeenth century. Arnold Lloyd, *Quaker Social History,* 1950, p. 147.

3. *First Publishers of Truth,* edited by Norman Penney, 1907, p. 6; henceforth abbreviated F.P.T.

4. F.P.T., p. 22.

5. F.P.T., p. 63.

6. F.P.T., p. 75.

7. F.P.T., p. 135.

8. F.P.T., p. 145.

9. Richard Davies, *Journal,* 1752, p. 35.

10. Thomas Story, *Journal,* 1747, p. 150.

11. Gould's relation in George Bishop, *New England Judged,* p. 316, Phila. ed. undated.

12. *Letters Etc. of Early Friends,* edited by Abram Rawlinson Barclay, 1841, p. 26.

13. George Fox, *Epistle* 114, 1656.

14. *Letters,* p. 27.

15. F.P.T., pp. 244-45.

16. F.P.T., p. 52.

17. F.P.T., p. 124.

18. Rufus M. Jones, *Quakers in the American Colonies,* 1923, Chap. I.

19. John Cratton, *Journal,* p. 34.

20. Cratton, *Journal,* p. 35.

21. Cratton, *Journal,* p. 36.

22. Cratton, *Journal,* p. 89.

23. Cratton, *Journal,* pp. 44-46.

24. Cratton, *Journal,* p. 49.

25. Cratton, *Journal,* pp. 64-66.

26. Cratton, *Journal,* pp. 86, 87.

27. Cratton, *Journal,* pp. 82, 83.

CHAPTER II

The Light Within as Experienced

WHEN A SO-CALLED "PUBLIC FRIEND" stood up to convince his hearers of the Truth, his objective was to persuade them to wait upon the Lord, to experience directly and immediately the life and power of God brought to bear upon their souls. This was the objective of the Friends meeting for worship to which he directed his hearers. The speaker pointed out the emptiness of outward forms, rituals, creeds, hymns, sacred books and sermons when they were not immediate and sincere embodiments of an inward spirit. These forms, when prescribed in advance and independent of the inward spirit, become a second-hand religion, that is, a religion based on the experience of others. An example of the type of preaching which created the Society of Friends is found in Margaret Fell's account of her convincement by George Fox who came to the church which she was attending:

> The next day being a lecture, or a fast-day, he [Fox] went to Ulverstone steeple-house, but came not in till people were gathered; I and my children had been a long time there before. And when they were singing before the sermon, he came in; and when they had done singing, he stood up upon a seat or form, and desired that he might have liberty to speak; and he that was in the pulpit said he might. And the first words that he spoke were as followeth:

"He is not a Jew that is one outward; neither is that circumcision which is outward; but he is Jew that is one inward;
and that is circumcision which is of the heart. And so he
went on, and said, how that Christ was the Light of the
world, and lighteth every man that cometh into the world;
and that by this light they might be gathered to God, &c. I
stood up in my pew and wondered at his doctrine; for I
had never heard such before And then he went on, and
opened the Scriptures, and said, "the Scriptures were the
prophets' words, and Christ's and the apostle words and
what, as they spoke, they enjoyed and possessed, and had
it from the Lord": and said, "then what had any to do with
the Scriptures, but as they came to the Spirit that gave them
forth? You will say, Christ saith this, and the apostles say
this; but what canst thou say? Art thou a child of Light, and
hast thou walked in the Light, and what thou speakest, is it
inwardly from God?" &c. This opened me so, that it cut me
to the heart; and then I saw clearly we were all wrong. So I
sat down in my pew again, and cried bitterly: and I cried in
my spirit, to the Lord, "We are all thieves; we are all thieves;
we have taken the Scriptures in words, and know nothing
of them in ourselves." So that served me, that I cannot well
tell what he spoke afterwards; but he went on in declaring
against the false prophets, and priests, and deceivers of
the people.[1]

In other words, the writers of the Scriptures possessed what they
professed. Why do we lean on them when we might have the same
experience for ourselves, when we might experience Christ himself who is the Light of the world? It is he who shines in our hearts.

The Protestants rejected the authority of the Church. Instead
they set up the authority of the Bible as the source of religious
truth. Over and gone, they believed, were the days of prophets

and apostles, when God spoke directly to man. Religious worship consisted of hearing what God had said long ago and of expositions of the inspired written word. The Protestant preacher exhorted the congregation to have faith in the truth of the Bible and to obey its commands. The service was essentially pedagogical, a kind of sacred school where a lecture was delivered on God's plan of salvation for men. Assurance was given that if that plan were accepted through faith, salvation would follow.

The Quakers had a different conception. The Spirit of God which gave forth the Scriptures was still at work, as they believed, in the human heart. It was more important to hear what He was saying directly to them than what He once said centuries ago. Worship consisted in waiting upon the Lord to hear His voice and to feel His power. Rituals, books, words and songs which were at one time vital expressions no longer for the most part retained their vitality. They were not necessarily expressions of the experience of the worshiper. Quaker worship was designed to prevent the substitution of form for Spirit by omitting forms established in advance of the time of worship and presenting an opportunity, in the silence of waiting, for the Spirit to appear in whatever form it chose to take. What that form would be no one could predict. "The wind blows where it wills and you hear the sound of it, but you do not know whence it comes or whither it goes, so it is with everyone who is born of the Spirit" (John 3:8).

The public Friend, in addressing those of his hearers who were waiting on him and not on the Lord, could not appeal to an experience which they had not achieved. He could, however, appeal to the Scriptures which they for the most part accepted as supreme authority in matters of religion. There he could find much which was suited to his purpose. Both the religion of the prophets of the Old Testament and the religion of the early Christian Church were based, not on form and tradition, but, in the case of the prophets, on immediate experience of the voice of God in the soul, or, in the case of the early Church, on the renewing and resurrecting power of the Christ Within. "The new man, Christ Within," was the central concept and experience which created the early Church. Whatever the first Christians may have believed about Christ's second coming in the flesh, the feeling that he continued with them in Spirit was the vitalizing, energizing factor which gave them life and power. It was to John and Paul that the Quaker preachers most often turned. John's doctrine that Christ is the Word of God by which the world was created, the Light that lighteth every man, the Bread of Life which comes down from heaven, the Way, the Truth and the Life, the well of water within springing up into Eternal Life, the Vine of which we are all branches, the Resurrection and the Life, these figures fitted perfectly into the Quaker theme. True religion is Life, not blind adherence to a particular doctrine or a special form. Paul's language was equally apposite; "walk as children of light"* (Eph. 5:8), or his word to the Thessalonians, "Ye are all the children of light" (I Thess. 5:5), gave the Quakers one of their names. "If any man have not the spirit of Christ, he is none of his" (Rom. 8:9). "Because you are sons, God hath sent forth the spirit of his Son into your hearts" (Gal. 4:6). "When it pleased God . . . to reveal his Son in me" (Gal. 1:15, 16). These texts were frequently used. Paul thought of this Inward Light as God or Christ or Spirit, not just one person in a Trinity. "Ye are the temple of the living God" (II Cor. 6:16). "God who commanded the Light to shine out of darkness hath shined in our hearts" (II Cor. 4:6). "If so be that the Spirit of God dwell in you" (Rom. 8:9). "The manifestation of the spirit is given to every man to profit withal" (I Cor. 12:7).

There is no single New Testament doctrine which designates just what this experience of Christ within, or God within, or Spirit

---

* The following quotations are taken from the King James Version as being in the form in which the Quakers used them.

within, meant in terms of systematic theology or philosophy. There are differences in the conceptions of John, Paul, the writer of the Epistle to the Hebrews, the Synoptic Gospels, James, and the writers of the Epistles of Peter. Similar differences appear in the writings of the early Friends. They were not Trinitarians in the usual sense of that word. The word "Trinity" seldom occurs in their writings, except when they remark that it is not a word which is found in the Bible. In their thought God was not divided; God is One. He becomes manifest in various ways. In the Old Testament He appeared as Father, in the Gospels as Son and since the Gospel days as Spirit, revealing His will in the hearts of those who heed His voice. As Light Within He manifests Himself as Father, Son and Spirit. Barclay says:

> By this seed, grace, and word of God and light wherewith we say everyone is enlightened . . . we understand a spiritual, heavenly, invisible principle in which God as Father, Son and Spirit dwells, a measure of which divine and glorious life is in all men as a seed which of its own nature draws, invites and inclines to God.[2]

Barclay's chapter on "The Universal and Saving Light" is an evidence of real scholarship. He draws not only on the Bible, but also on the Church Fathers and early leaders of the Reformation. As a treatise it is too analytical and systematic to give a full impression of how this Light was actually felt when it dawned upon Friends as they waited upon the Lord in silence. For them it was not an intellectual, theological concept, but a living experience. It was inevitable and necessary that in defending themselves against their enemies who left nothing untried to strangle the new movement, the early Quakers should have rationalized their experience and made an effort to explain it, but in writing to one another they spoke as they felt. Fox's pastoral epistles contain a convincing account of what the Light first meant to Friends.

All Friends everywhere in the Power of God dwell . . . for
that brings all your souls into peace, into oneness, into God.
[Ep. 104, 1655]

Keep in the Power and know the Power of God in one another that out of all dryness and barrenness ye may be
brought. . . . And when ye are met together in the Light,
hearken to it that ye may feel the Power of God in every
one of you . . . ye that feel the Power of God, ye feel Christ
for Christ is the Power of God. [Ep. 130, 1656]

It is this Power, Fox shows, which creates the Fellowship.

The Mystery of the Fellowship is known which is in the
Power. . . . For want of the Power, the Gospel, in which is
the Fellowship, hath Christendom been in heaps . . . and
ye who are in the Power of God, ye are in the Mystery of
the Fellowship. [Ep. 169, 1658]

In the Power of God is the Fellowship of the Cross which
keeps over all the Fellowships in the world. [Ep. 216, 1662]

And to all Nations of mankind the Everlasting Gospel, the
Power of God is to be preached, through which Life and
Immortality shall come to Light, in which Power is the Fellowship. Therefore, this is the Word of the Lord God to
you all. Those that are convinced by the Power of the Lord
God and the Light, let them dwell in it, in which they may
have unity. [Ep. 189, 1659]

Abuse not the Power, in which is the Gospel-Fellowship
which will keep all in Unity. [Ep. 228, 1663]

And wait in the Light for Power to remove the earthly
part . . . that with the Light your minds may be kept up to

> God, who is Pure, and in it ye may all have unity who in the
> Light of Life do walk. [Ep. 49, 1658]

These passages reveal the secret at the heart of the early Quaker
movement. In the group "standing still in the Light" (Ep. 10, 1652),
there emerged fellowship, unity and power. As when carbon and
oxygen are brought together and the temperature sufficiently
raised, there is a sudden unification of the two and a great increase in energy, so in the gathered worshiping group when hearts
were opened toward the Primal Source of unity, the members became fused together. There was a heightened sense of life, fellowship and power. The gifts of the Spirit, the charismata, are poured
out upon the group which is able to realize the divine Presence.
The Inward Christ is the unifying power. "In Him all things hold
together" (Col. 1:17). "He is our peace who . . . hath broken down
the middle wall of partition" (Eph. 2:14). Fox is never tired of
repeating that in the Light there is Unity and out of the Light
there is strife, discord and "jangling," to quote a favorite word.

> [The Light is] the Word of Life, the Word of Peace, the
> Word of Reconciliation which makes of twain one new man
> and if ye do abide there, there is no division but unity in
> the life. . . . Therefore, in the Light wait where the Unity
> is, where the peace is, where the Oneness with the Father
> and Son is, where there is no Rent nor Division. [Ep. 115,
> 1656]

This is the whole basis of the peace doctrine of the Society of
Friends, peace within the individual and peace in society.

In these Epistles of Fox we find many names for the Light. It is
the Witness of God (Ep. 208), the Bread of Life (Ep. 211), the
Royal Seed (Ep. 211), The Vine (Ep. 215), the Wisdom, sweet,
cool and pure (Ep. 242), the Springs of Life opened to you (Ep.
38), the Truth's Voice (Ep. 222), your Habitation in the Power of

the Lord God (Ep. 246), that of God in every one (Ep. 182), that of God in all consciences (Ep. 114), The Heavenly Dignity (Ep. 313), that Love which bears all things (Ep. 336), Truth in the inward parts (Ep. 186)—the list could be extended indefinitely.

The variety of these designations shows that George Fox had no consistent system of philosophy or theology into which he could fit his doctrine of the Light Within. Surprisingly enough, nevertheless, he had more of a philosophy than a theology, though his philosophy was arrived at by feeling and intuition rather than by systematic thinking. To Fox, the universe apparently consisted of two kinds of existences, variously designated —Substance and Shadow, Eternity and Time, Unity and Multiplicity, or Life and Form. The object of religion was to bring men out of the second into the first, or "up to" the first, as Fox usually expressed it. The Light was the Life which went out of Substance, Eternity, Unity down into Shadow, Time, Multiplicity and by its uplifting Power drew men to the higher type of Being which existed before the lower type of Being existed and which would continue to be after the lower had disappeared. There is much in Fox's letters and other writings to indicate that he was master of some such philosophical view of the universe. As prophet, Fox followed the Hebrew tradition, bearing witness to the personal God whose prophets are instruments through which He utters his voice and works His will. As philosopher, Fox followed the Hellenic tradition, apprehending the inner Unity which exists beyond time and space, *Real* as compared with the phenomenal world, *One* as contrasted with the multiplicity recognized by the senses. It is this inner Unity which generates in the outer world of strife and disunity whatever there is of peace and harmony. When Fox first declared in 1650 that he lived in the virtue of that life and power that takes away the occasion of all wars,[3] he meant that his life was centered in this Eternal Being:

> And central Peace subsisting at the Heart
> Of endless agitation.

So established, he was clear of the world of haste, struggle and contention.

In his early letters Fox speaks of the Light as that "which guides out of many things into one Spirit," advising his friends "to keep in the Oneness . . . to guide and preserve all in the Unity of the Spirit and the Bond of Peace" (Ep. 24, 1652). "The Light of God is but one" (Ep. 25, 1653). Friends never used the term "spark" for the Inward Light as some other mystics have done. Spark or Sparkle might imply that the Light was divided, a part being in one person and part in another. There was but one Light. The nearer all come to it, the nearer they come to one another, like radii of a circle when they approach the center, to use a figure from Plotinus. Fox writes in his *Journal* for the year 1648, near the beginning of his ministry:

> Great things did the Lord lead me into and wonderful depths were opened unto me beyond what can by words be declared; but as people come into subjection to the Spirit of God and grow up in the image and power of the Almighty, they may receive the Word of Wisdom that opens all things and come to know the hidden unity in the Eternal Being.[4]

Coming to know this "hidden unity" is to come into the state in which Adam was before he fell. The fall of Adam was a fall from unity to multiplicity. As for George Fox, he felt that he had come to know "a more steadfast state than Adam's innocency," even the "state in Christ that should never fall." Adam's sinless state was based on innocency. When he was tempted he fell. But Christ's sinless state was based on resistance to temptation. This, therefore, remains stable. To reach that state Fox had come "up in the

Spirit through the flaming sword into the paradise of God." He had reached the center of things from which he says, "The creation was opened unto me."

This "unity in the Eternal Being" is substance as compared with the external changing world of shadow.

> See if you do find something in your understandings made manifest, which is Eternal, to guide your minds out of all external things which wither away and fade. [Ep. 19, 1652]

> In that dwell which doth bring out of the Shadows, types, traditions. [Ep. 72,1654]

> So over all the world ye may stand in the Light which doth it comprehend and condemn, and with it ye may witness to the end of shadows. [Ep. 73,1654]

> All Friends take heed of running on in a form lest ye do lose the Power, but keep in the Power and Seed of God, in which ye will live in the Substance. [Ep. 173, 1659]

> All know one another in Him who is the Substance. [Ep. 166, 1658]

> And so ye living in the unchangeable Life and Light, ye see Christ, that does not change, but ends all changeable things, types, figures, shadows . . . . Therefore in the Power of the Lord God . . . live in which is the perfect fellowship which was before imperfection was. [Ep. 221, 1662]

In the inner world there is an eternal and changeless aspect to life, mind and spirit.

> In that live that doth not change, the unchangeable Life, the unchangeable Mind, the unchangeable Spirit and

Wisdom, and the unchangeable worship and church of which Christ is the unchangeable head. [Ep. 200, 1661]

This existed before our changeable world of strife and shadow and will exist after it. Fox seldom mentions the Light without bringing out its priority in time to the created world. It was the Light or Word by which the world was created (John 1:1).

> Stand fast in the Unchangeable Life and Seed of God which was before all changings and alterings were and which will remain when all that is gone. [Ep. 76, 1654]

> Ye that be turned to the Light walk in the Light . . . that never changeth, ye may come to see that which was in the beginning before the world was, where there is no shadow nor darkness. [Ep. 105, 1655]

> For this Light was before Time and is in Time. [Ep. 111, 1656]

> Receive the living food from God to nourish you in time with that which was before time. [Ep. 122, 1656]

> In that live which was before enmity was. [Ep. 147, 1657]

> Keep your minds in the strength of the Almighty and not in Weakness nor in the infirmities but in the Lord's Power which was before weakness and infirmities were. [Ep. 159, 1658]

Out of such passages we can construct a fairly consistent philosophy of the Inward Light. No other early Quaker writer is so explicit, unless perhaps Isaac Penington, who also compares the Light to substance as contrasted with shadow.[5] At the heart of things there is a Being whose characteristics are Unity, Substance, Life, Peace, Power, Light, and who is eternal and changeless. From Him there streams into this temporal world of shadow, strife, multiplicity and change His own Unity, Life, Peace, Power, Light (to use but a few of the names) in order to transform this lower world into His own likeness. Christ is this "Power of God" (Ep. 184, 186), this "Wisdom of God" (Ep. 247), the Way, the Truth and the Life, which continually goes out from God to create and redeem this world. This became fully embodied in Jesus of Nazareth.

> He is your prophet, your shepherd, your bishop, your priest in the midst of you to open to you and to sanctify you and to feed you with Life and to quicken you with Life. [Ep. 288, 16721

These are the main outlines of the picture as it seems to have existed in the mind of George Fox, but something more must be emphasized to complete the delineation. The Dark World is beneath the World of Light. This Dark World does not lack reality, as is the case in some systems of thought which bear a certain resemblance to the system which Fox worked out, but which may be said to be less realistic. The phrase "shadow world" might be used, but, as Penington points out, "the shadow is a real shadow" and no illusion of the mind. Throughout Fox's writings there appears a constant reference to that which is contrary to the Light, a real opposing power which man is free to choose instead of choosing the Power which comes from God.

> All ye whose Minds are turned with the Light towards Jesus Christ, from whence it comes, in it wait that with it ye may all see Jesus and all that condemned which is contrary to it. [Ep. 90, 1655]

> My dear hearts in the Seed dwell . . . that all the contrary may be kept under. [Ep. 95, 16551

> Beware of striving in thy own will against Eternal Providence and Power which is now working invisibly, cross and contrary to all the Powers of Darkness. [Ep. 97, 1655]

In which Seed shine, answering the Witness of God in every one which bruises the earthly part under . . . and all the contrary. [Ep. 109, 1656]

All men's and women's strength is in the Power of God which goes over the Power of Darkness. [Ep. 208, 1661]

In His Life wait to receive Power to bind and chain all down which is contrary to Truth. [Ep. 156, 1658]

Therefore, keep in the Power of the Lord which will keep all the contrary down and out. [Ep. 180, 1659]

A word often used by Friends for this "contrary" was "Deceit," because it was contrary to truth.

Confound the Deceit and bring the Truth over the heads of the heathen. [Ep. 87, 1655]

That the dread and terror of the Lord may be among you and Deceit confounded. [Ep. 96, 1655]

And ye all walking in this Light, it will bring you to all plainness and singleness of speech which will make the Deceit to tremble. [Ep. 111, 1656]

The Lord God of Power give thee Wisdom, Courage, Manhood and Boldness to thresh down all Deceit. [Ep. 113, 1656]

That . . . ye may be carried along to minister to all the Spirits imprisoned by the Deceit. [Ep. 114, 1656]

Gervase Benson writing to George Fox from London in 1653 says:

Pray to the Lord for me, that I may be kept in all faithfulness; with boldness to bear witness to the Truth against all deceits.[6]

The nature of Deceit is also made clear in a letter from Anthony Pearson:

> I find my heart is full of deceit, and I exceedingly fear to be beguiled (as I have been) and to be seduced into a form without power, into a profession before I possess the Truth.[7]

Deceit is a state of form without power. The Quakers believed that the Christian Church of the seventeenth century had slipped into that condition. To be dependent on outward forms—baptism, communion, singing, "preaching by the clock," and the formal acceptance of creeds as a condition of salvation, was to remain in the shadow world of time, change and all that is contrary to the Light. This world of form was a real world, but it was a "deceit" in the sense that the form did not represent what it professed to represent. The common Quaker designation of Christians who did not wait upon the Light was "professor" in contrast to "possessor."

This contrast is an ancient, ever-continuing differentiation made by prophet, mystic and reformer who lay the emphasis on the inward life rather than on the outward form. "To obey is better than sacrifice and to hearken than the fat of rams" (I Sam. 15:22); "Incense is an abomination unto me" (Isa. 1:13) are examples of a cry which goes out from the prophets all through the Old Testament. And Christ's complaint of the Pharisees as whited sepulchers inwardly filled with dead men's bones renews the same indictment. The world of appearance and the world of reality, however we may distinguish between them from a metaphysical point of view, are different. Deceit arises when appearance *takes the place* of reality instead of being a genuine and sincere expression of it. In preaching this doctrine, the Quakers were delivering no new message. What was new was the creation of a religious practice in which the form was more unlikely than usual to take the place of the reality. To wait upon the Lord in silence can, of course, become formal, but silent waiting commits no one to any action or expression which is not a sincere outcome of inward life and thought. If silent waiting becomes a form, the participant generally knows it, especially if, as sometimes happens even in the best Quaker meetings, he should fall asleep. As Barclay says of Quaker worshiping:

> It is impossible for the enemy, namely the devil, to counterfeit it so as for any soul to be deceived or deluded by him in the exercise thereof . . . . He can accompany the priest to the altar, the preacher to the pulpit, the zealot to his prayers, yea, the doctor and professor of divinity to his study . . . when the soul comes to this silence and as it were is brought to nothingness as to her own workings, then the devil is shut out.[8]

Barclay admits that the devil "is not wanting to come to our assemblies" but he has a more difficult task in a Quaker meeting than elsewhere, for there is no set form of activity which can be gone through in a routine way and so take the place of inspired activity.

The phrase "up to" or "on top of" which Fox often uses in speaking of the Inward Light, refers, not to any position in space, but rather to the Light as highest in nature, value and power. In one of his earliest openings he says:

> I saw . . . there was an ocean of darkness and death, but an infinite ocean of light and love which flowed over the ocean of darkness.[9]

A few quotations from the *Epistles* will indicate this quality of the Light as being "over" or guiding "up to."

Wait in the measure of the Spirit of God to guide you up to God, and keep you all in peace and unity. [Ep. 70, 1654]

That which is new, that mind to guide all your minds up to the living God. [Ep. 77, 1654]

Walk in the Truth and the love of it up to God. [Ep. 79, 1654]

Keep a-top of that which will cumber the mind. [Ep. 86, 1655]

Take heed of being hurried with many thoughts but live in that which goes over them all. [Ep. 95, 1655]

As the Life of God doth arise, it will lead you up to God. [Ep. 114, 1656]

Keep your feet upon the top of the mountains and sound deep to the witness of God in every man. [Ep. 195, 1660]

Mind the Light and dwell in it and it will keep you a-top of all the world. [Ep. 203, 1661]

Let your minds and souls and hearts be kept above all outward and visible things. [Ep. 283, 1670]

In Fox's *Journal,* whenever he encountered an obstacle his effort was to get "a-top of it." This sense of the Light as an elevating, uplifting Power was primary. Frequently it is referred to as the Topstone (Ep. 84, 109, 121, 164).

Another characteristic of the Light is its bestowal on each man "in a measure." This does not mean that the whole Truth is not accessible to every person, but rather the obvious fact that some persons apprehend more of the Truth than do others. Returning to Fox's letters as our primary source, we find such expressions as the following:

Mind the pure Life of God in you according to your measures to guide you up to God. [Ep. 69, 1654]

All Friends wait in the measure of the Spirit of God to guide you up to God. [Ep. 70, 1654]

Friends in the measure of the Life of God wait to guide your minds up to the Father of Life where there is no shadow or changing. [Ep. 77, 1654]

Wait in the measure of the Life of God, in it to grow up in Love, in Virtue and in Immortality, in that which doth not fade, which joins and unites your hearts together. [Ep. 77, 1654]

Dwell in the measure which God hath given you of himself, in which is no Strife but unity. [Ep. 94, 1655]

Let no Friends go beyond their own measure given them of God, nor rejoice in another man's line made ready to their hands. [Ep. 118, 1656]

If we are faithful to our measure of Light, we shall be guided up toward God, and up to a greater measure of the Truth. To go beyond our measure and imitate persons who have a greater measure than we have, is to be deceitful and to represent ourselves as something more than we are.

To take a specific example of the use of this conception, the Quakers have all along considered participation in war to be unchristian. Nevertheless, if a man feels that his conscience urges him to fight, he must be faithful to the measure of Light he has, however small this may be. If he is really faithful and if he waits upon the Lord so as to sensitize himself to the reception of more Light, a greater measure will be given him. He will eventually come to see the error of all fighting. In his first state he would be a coward if he did not fight; in his second state he would be a coward if he did fight.

Another characteristic of the Light, which is realized more by actual experience than by any theory about it, is indicated by the use of the word "answering," which often occurs in Fox's writings. To Friends in Barbadoes he writes:

> Be faithful and spread the Truth abroad and walk in the Wisdom of God answering that of God in every one. [Ep. 186, 1659]

Elsewhere, he encourages "Friends beyond the Seas":

> Do the work of the Lord faithfully and ye will feel it prosper, answering that of God in every one. [Ep. 182, 1659]

And to Friends in New England who had opportunities to preach to the Indians:

> Answer the Witness of God in every man, whether they are the heathen that do not profess Christ, or whether they are such as do profess Christ that have the form of godliness and be out of the Power. [Ep. 292, 1672]

The most famous passage in which this concept occurs is found in a letter written from prison to "Friends in the ministry":

> This is the word of the Lord God to you all and a charge to you all in the presence of the living God: be patterns, be examples in all countries, places, islands, nations, wherever you come; that your carriage and life may preach among all sorts of people, and to them; then you will come to walk cheerfully over the world, answering that of God in every one.[10]

It was the responsibility of the Quaker preachers to "answer that of God in every one," that is, to appeal to the same Light of God in their hearers which they felt in themselves, confident that this Light would lead them to the same Truth. Fox says of his ministry that "he took them to their guide and left them there." For him, preaching was to bring "people to the end of all preaching."[11] According to the Quaker theory, it would be impossible to convince anyone of the Truth unless he already had the divine Seed of Truth within him. That of God in the hearer must answer that of God in the speaker. If this does not occur, the response of the hearer is "in the form but not in the power."

This "answering that of God in every one" is the basis, not only of the Quakers' welfare work in general, but of their whole theory of social behavior. We cannot "answer that of God in every one" by any form of violence, physical or psychological, for violence moves only the external flesh and not the internal spirit. But if we feel that even in the most evil of men there is that of God, we can appeal to it, and we may, though we are never sure of success, reach it and set in motion a process of transformation from within.

Fox's epistles, formless, and rhapsodical though they often are, present a reasonably consistent theory of the nature of the Light and the way in which it operates in man, a theory obviously derived from experience rather than from any process of logical reasoning. The Light, as experienced in personal form, may appear as Father, Son or Holy Spirit—God is not divided. In a less personal form it appears as Truth, Substance, Life, Power, as opposed to Deceit, Shadow, Form without Power. As Truth and Substance, it shines down from a world higher than our world of Deceit and Shadow, and guides us up toward itself. This higher world is eternal. It existed before our world of time and will outlast it. The higher world is a world of unity and peace as compared to our lower world of multiplicity and strife. The Light is a principle of unity which creates the fellowship of those who expose themselves to it. More than that, the Light, in proportion to the measure of it which is granted, is a source of Power by which those who follow it may create unity, not only in their own fellowship, but by "answering that of God in every one."

Notes

1. Testimony of Margaret Fox, *Journal of George Fox,* II, 1891, 512. BiCentenary ed. All future references to the *Journal* are to this edition, except where otherwise noted.

2. Robert Barclay, *Apology,* pp. 137-38.

3. William Penn, *Journal,* I, 68.

4. Penn, *Journal,* I, 29.

5. See, for example, Isaac Penington's essay entitled *The Jew Outward,* 1659.

6. *Letters Etc. of Early Friends,* edited by Abram Rawlinson Barclay, 1841, p. 2.

7. *Letters,* p. 12.

8. Barclay, *Apology,* pp. 370, 871.

9. Penn, *Journal,* I, 19.

10. Penn, *Journal,* Cambridge, 1911, I, 321.

CHAPTER III

The Light Within as Thought About

THAT THE LIGHT FIRST APPEARED TO FRIENDS in terms of feeling and experience is best shown in George Fox's epistles. It was inevitable and necessary that, before long, this experience should be rationalized and fitted in with other accepted beliefs. What relation has the Light to Scripture, conscience, reason, the historic Christ, the Fall of Man, and his salvation? The task of rationalization fell mainly on two of the younger converts, Robert Barclay and William Penn. Both had been trained in theology in France. Both could bring to the defense of Quakerism a wide knowledge of Christian thought and history. Barclay was the more systematic thinker in the realm of theology, while Penn excelled in political thought and government. Both insisted that thinking about religion was far less important than immediate experience of it. To take two examples of this attitude, Barclay writes in his treatise called Universal Love:

> Friends were not gathered together by unity of opinion or by a tedious and particular disquisition of notions and opinions, requiring an assent to them, and binding themselves by Leagues and Covenants thereto; but the manner of their gathering was by a secret want, which many truly tender and serious souls in divers and sundry sects found in themselves which put each sect in search of something beyond all opinion which might satisfy their weary souls.

39

William Penn writes similarly in *A Key Opening the Way:*

> It is not Opinion or Speculation or Notions of what is true;
> or assent to or Subscription of Articles or Propositions,
> though never so soundly worded, that . . . makes a man a
> true believer or a true Christian.

Yet, in spite of assigning a secondary role to doctrine, Barclay
and Penn were fully aware of the importance of a consistent
system of ideas, without which religion is vague, and incapable of
propagating itself. The Inward Christ is not only the Power of God,
but also the Light of God, and Light is knowledge.

The following outline of Quaker thought is, in some of its parts,
an interpretation as well as an exposition. The conflicts of the nineteenth century were produced by some extreme positions which
are not described in this chapter.

The Scriptures

The relation between the Light Within and the Scriptures was a
matter of continued debate between Quakers and Protestants. For
the Protestants, the Scriptures were primary and the Holy Spirit
secondary as an aid to their understanding. The Bible was *the* Word
of God. Nothing could be added to it nor subtracted from it by
any further revelation of religious truth. For the Quakers the Light
Within or the Spirit was primary and the Scriptures *a* word of God,
that is, secondary, confirming and clarifying the revelations of the
Light Within.

According to Quaker doctrine, the Light or the Christ Within
was, as in John's Gospel, *the* Word of God which could reveal further truth according to the words of Jesus: "When the Spirit of
Truth comes, he will guide you into all the truth" (John 16:13).
Revelations through the Spirit are progressive in scope according

to man's ability to receive them. The Old Testament cannot be accepted now as a full revelation of Truth for, though it came from the Spirit, it reveals only what man was prepared for according to his measure, at a time when he was emerging out of the ways and thoughts of primitive life. No Christian accepts all of it. We accept "Thou shalt not steal" but we do not accept "Neither shall a garment mingled of linen and woolen come upon thee" (Lev. 19:19). Did not Jesus himself have one message for the multitude and a deeper, though not a different, message for the inner circle of his disciples? God speaks through symbols and figures, and the parable which the multitude takes literally reveals to the enlightened soul a profound spiritual truth. If, as all Christians agree, the Bible was produced by the Spirit of God, could not the same Spirit be trusted as a source of Truth today? Friends might tend to agree with the commentator on the *Bhagavadgita,* "To the illumined one who hath known the Indweller all the Sacred books are as useless as a reservoir in time of flood."[1]

Barclay points out that the Bible we now have was produced by a process of selection on a basis of spiritual discernment subsequent to the writing of the various books. How did it come about, he asks, that we have this particular selection of canonical books rather than a different selection, or these particular renderings of Greek and Hebrew texts rather than others, except for the spiritual insight of those who made the selection? What is there in the Epistle of James, for instance, to indicate that it is authentic? Does it not contradict Paul on the primacy of faith? Nowhere in the Scriptures is it declared that the canon is complete. It is not a new gospel we plead for, says Barclay,[2] but a new revelation of the old gospel. "As for the Scriptures being a filled canon, I see no necessity in believing it."[3] Samuel Fisher wrote several hundred pages to show that all versions of the Bible were corrupt and uncertain.[4] Such a critical view of the Scriptures is common today, but it was a bold innovation in the seventeenth century.

To the Protestants of that time this doctrine of the primacy of the Spirit over the Scriptures appeared dangerous and anarchical, opening the way for almost any heresy or idiosyncrasy to be proclaimed as divine truth. But the Quaker logic was irrefutable. How, they asked, is any Truth sincerely accepted except on the basis of an inward willingness to accept? If there is no such inward acceptance, inspired by the Spirit of Truth, then acceptance is formal and may be hypocritical. Isaac Penington writes:

> If I receive a truth before the Lord by his Spirit makes it manifest to me, I lose my guide and follow but the counsel of the flesh, which is exceedingly greedy of receiving truths and running into religious practices without the Spirit.[5]

Yet the Quakers were fully aware of the dangers of pure individualism and subjectivism. As we shall see, apparent revelations of the Light need to be checked and rechecked by the Scriptures, by revelations to other persons, and by the writings of authors who are accepted as sincere lovers of the Truth.

There are three ways of dealing with Biblical events and doctrines which often follow one another in personal experience in three consecutive stages. The first is a naïve, uncritical acceptance of every statement at its face value. This may be followed by a critical appraisal in the light of scientific facts and historical research. The result of such an analysis is usually a rejection of parts of the Bible and sometimes an attitude of complete skepticism regarding Biblical religion in general. A third stage may then follow which, while retaining the critical attitude, makes possible a return to belief with an understanding of the deeper meanings inherent in the words of the Bible. At this stage we are not so much concerned with historical validity or rational consistency with our scientific or philosophical outlook as we are with the inner significance of history, myth and symbol. Symbol is a language of religion but it must never be a substitute for religion. All living theology grows out of personal experience. Accordingly, each Biblical text, to be of real value, must have spiritual relevance to the inner religious experience of the reader or hearer. This third stage may be understood as interpretation of the Bible through the Light Within. The importance of this to Friends is illustrated by Catherine Phillips in her account of a sermon which she heard on shipboard while on her way to America in 1758:

> The parson, observing that in our ministry we spoke extempore, told me that he could preach extempore and we should hear him if we pleased the next Sunday. Accordingly, when the day came we were all seated in the great cabin and he preached without notes. His subject was the transfiguration of Christ which he found a wonder (miracle), expatiated upon it as a wonder—and left it a wonder; without entering into the spirituality of the text; indeed I doubt he did not understand it.

Conscience

The Light Within is not to be identified with conscience. Conscience is not the Light in its fullness but "the measure of Light given us." The Light illumines conscience and seeks to transform an impure conscience into its own pure likeness. Conscience is partly a product of the Light which shines into it and partly a product of social environment. Therefore conscience is fallible. But conscience must always be obeyed because it reflects whatever measure of Light we have by which to form our moral judgments. This measure of Light in the conscience may be increased; as this occurs conscience becomes more sensitive to moral Truth.

Spiritual growth was often described by Friends as a process of becoming more "tender." The word "sensitive" did not then bear its modern connotation. One object of the meeting for worship was to make the conscience more tender, or sensitive. As the measure of Light in the conscience increases, we are, in Fox's words, "guided up to God." We become more and more able to see Truth with the eyes of God.

To use an analogy from science, the physical world is not known to us completely, but, as our scientific instruments become increasingly sensitive, we can learn more and more about it; similarly, moral truth may not be known to us completely, but as our consciences become sensitive, we can learn more about it. The Light is the Absolute to which man's relative conscience gradually approaches as the physical world is the Absolute to which our relative scientific knowledge gradually approaches.

Reason

The same considerations hold in respect to the relation between the Light and reason. As conscience gives us our judgments about good and evil, so reason gives us our judgments about truth and error. Friends did not give attention to the relation between the Light and aesthetic judgments. Probably the same considerations would hold true in this realm as in the case of conscience and reason. There is an illuminated reason and a darkened reason. Barclay shows[6] that the worst persecutions in Christian history were based on careful reasoning.

Reason must start with certain premises which it does not itself produce. If these premises are bad and are carried to their logical conclusions, the worst evils result. An example can be drawn from the doctrine of the supremacy of the state as carried out by Hitler. An enlightened reason as contrasted with a darkened one will start with the right premises, and the Light itself, being the Truth, will guide reason into further truth. As Barclay says, "Because the Spirit of God is the fountain of all truth and sound reason, therefore, we have well said that it cannot contradict either the testimony of Scripture or right reason."[7]

A great deal is said in Quaker writings about the inability of reason to reach religious truths unless the Light, or the Scriptures or other writings inspired by the Light, furnish it with the right premises on which to work. The same is true in science. Scientific truths are not produced by reason alone, but by reason operating on physical facts previously ascertained through experiment.

The Universality of the Light

No Quaker belief aroused more opposition than the doctrine that the Light of Christ has been given to all men everywhere, since the beginning of the human race. This concept was especially repugnant to those Protestants who believed that only the elect would be saved. Fox, writing in his *Journal* for the year 1656, makes this comment: "Great opposition did the priests and professors make about this time against the Light of Christ Jesus, denying it to be universally given." He puts out a leaflet showing that the prophecy is being fulfilled: "I will pour out my Spirit upon *all* Flesh and your sons and your daughters shall prophesy." (Joel, quoted by Peter in Acts 2:17). A wealth of Biblical texts follows, including these favorite Quaker quotations: "For the Grace of God has appeared for the salvation of *all* men" (Tit. 2:11). "I will also give thee for a Light to the Gentiles that thou mayest be my salvation unto the end of the earth" (Isa. 49:6). This Light is the inward gospel "preached to every creature under heaven" (Col. 1:23), a statement clearly untrue of the outward gospel. Paul, who did not know Christ "after the flesh," was converted by the Inward Christ. The same possibility is open to every man. Paul clearly held that the Eternal Christ was known long before the historical Christ. He says of the Israelites in their wilderness journey, "For they drank from the supernatural Rock which followed them, and the Rock was Christ" (I Cor. 10:4).

To the objection of opponents that "there is no other name under heaven given among men by which we must be saved" (Acts 4:12), Barclay replies: "I confess there is no other name to be saved by, but salvation lieth not in the literal but the experimental knowledge."[8] He goes on to show that many persons who have never heard of the historic Christ have had experimental knowledge of the Christ Within. William Penn goes furthest in defending this doctrine which was sometimes referred to as "Gentile Divinity." In his *Advice* to his children Penn concludes with the words:

> That blessed principle the Eternal Word . . . by which all things were at first made and man enlightened to salvation is Pythagoras' great light and salt of ages; Anaxagoras' divine mind; Socrates' good spirit; Timaeus' unbegotten principle and author of all light; Hieron's God in man; Plato's eternal, ineffable and perfect principle of truth; Zeno's maker and father of all; Plotinus' root of the soul; . . . the divine power and reason, the infallible, immortal law in the minds of men, says Philo; the law and living rule of the mind, the interior guide of the soul and everlasting foundation of virtue, says Plutarch.

Penn holds that, with Christ's coming, "The Spirit that was more sparingly communicated in former dispensations began to be poured forth upon all Flesh."[9]

This principle of universality was undoubtedly derived, not only from Scriptures, but also from the tender sensibilities of persons who could not endure the thought that any man should be condemned by a God of love because of unavoidable ignorance. Were not the Protestants hardhearted and inconsistent in attributing Adam's sin to every man, even though many had never heard of Adam, while failing to attribute Christ's saving grace to every man, even though many had never heard of Christ? It was not difficult for Quaker writers to find in pre-Christian writings many statements about an inner, divine Guide and much that supported the chief Christian virtues. Barclay[10] quotes Justin Martyr, Clement and Augustine to show that they believed in a pre-Christian Christianity. History clearly shows that the measure of Light given to men was greatly increased after the coming of Christ, but it also shows that the great men of antiquity were not without some measure of it, as can be ascertained from their writings. What we recognize in the case of those who were articulate must also have been true of the unlettered faithful.

This doctrine of the universality of the Light was also based on Quaker experiences with non-Christians. Josiah Coale writes, "We found these Indians more sober and Christian-like toward us than the Christians so-called."[11] Fox, by questioning an Indian, proved to the governor of an American colony that the Indian possessed the "Light and Spirit of God."[12] Elizabeth Newport, in visiting the Indians in the Cataraugus Reservation, found them divided into "Christians" and "Pagans." The "Pagans believed," she said, "in Quaker worship and the guidance of the Spirit while the Christians seek information of the missionaries."[13]

The Biblical concept of God as Creator was in itself sufficient to support the universality of His Light. In the Bible there are two accounts of creation. In Genesis it is written, "The Spirit of God moved upon the face of the waters," and John's Gospel begins with the Word through which all things were made. This Word is God Himself as Creator. "The Word was with God and the Word was God." As Creator, God is also "the true Light which lighteth every man that cometh into the world."* (John 1:9). Barclay calls this "the Quaker text." Taking the chapter as a whole, even in a

---

*The Standard Revised Version reads, "The true light that enlightens every man was coming into the world."

more modern translation, it is still possible to use this verse in defending the universality of the Light. The Light which enlightens *every man*, since it is the creative principle in the Universe, was coming into the world personified in Jesus Christ. It is fair to comment that the theology of the Society of Friends is essentially Johannine theology. As Creator, God is the Spirit through which man is born again so that in reality a new Life is created in him (John 3:3). But before Christ came, the full nature of this Creative Word was not known. "He was in the world and the world was made through him, yet the world knew him not" (1:10). And then, says John (1:14), "the Word became flesh and dwelt among us full of grace and truth. We have beheld His Glory." The world process reached its goal when the Word became fully revealed in a person, though it had been partially revealed since the beginning in every creative act.

The Eternal Christ and the Historic Jesus

Taking the Bible as a whole, we can detect three main stages in the creative or evolutionary process through which God gradually reveals Himself. When "the Spirit of God moved upon the face of the waters," the world of nature came into being; when God breathed his Spirit into Adam, man came into being; and when the "Word became flesh," there was then and there a new mutation, a new dispensation of the Spirit which lifted man up to a higher level of life. Christ is, therefore, more than a revelation of the nature of God, more than a teacher, more than an example for us to follow. He is a source of saving power. The history of mankind since his coming shows that "to all who received him . . . he gave power to become children of God." (1:12).

But even before Christ's coming, God had never been without a witness. He has appeared in nature—"ever since the creation of the world his invisible nature, namely his eternal power and deity has been clearly perceived in the things that have been made" (Rom. 1:20). He has appeared in man, as is shown by the great insights into Truth in the pre-Christian philosophers and the writers of the Old Testament. Finally, He has appeared, as the consummation of this long process of ascending revelation and the release of new creative power, in Christ Jesus.

It was largely through the Gospel of John and the later Epistles of Paul which resemble it in their theology, that the Friends worked out their conceptions of the relation between the person, Jesus, and the Eternal Christ, the Inward Light, God as engaged in creative activity directed toward this world of space and time. The problem which seemed so difficult to early Christian thinkers and which occupied the best thought of theologians for more than five centuries—how can the divine nature and the human nature of Jesus exist together in a single person?—did not trouble the early generations of the Society of Friends. They knew by experience how the divine Light was related to their own human consciousness. They conceived of the relation between the divine Spirit and the human mind in Jesus as following the same principle, except for this important difference: "God giveth not the Spirit by measure unto Him" (John 3:34). Fox quotes this verse in his long letter defending the universality of the Light.[14] This was as near as the early Quakers came to an explicit theory regarding the difference in nature between Christ and themselves. It was a simple Christology based on experience. Because they had themselves experienced a measure of the Spirit they realized what it might be to experience the Spirit without measure, that is, completely. If they, like the Greeks, had attempted to think in terms of metaphysical substance, they would have encountered the same difficulties as did the early Christian theologians who were under Greek influence. How can two different substances, a divine and a human substance, exist together in one person? But, like the Hebrews, the Quakers usually thought in terms of will. They knew from experience that sometimes their own wills were united with God's will and at other times their wills were opposed to God's will. It was not difficult to go from that perception to the realization that the will of Jesus was wholly the will of God, not parallel to the will of Cod but the very will of God.

Jesus was completely human, he "was tempted like as we are," otherwise the incarnation would have been an appearance and not a reality. He was also completely divine because he resisted temptation and permitted the divine Spirit to possess him entirely. The Light is one. It is not divided so that part is in one person and part in another. When the Light shone in Jesus completely it was not withdrawn from other men. It can, therefore, be said that since Jesus possessed the Light without measure he was the Light. The Light Within is the Christ Within. This does not mean that Jesus differs from other persons in degree. Persons do not differ from one another in degree. Every person is unique. That is a primary characteristic of personality as such. The uniqueness of Jesus, according to the Christian faith, consists in the fact that he was the supreme revelation of God in human terms. Since the Light Within is God revealing Himself to man, Jesus of Nazareth was God revealing Himself in history. Without the historical revelation the inner revelation would be incomplete. Each revelation requires the other for its fulfillment. The timeless requires the temporal and the temporal requires the timeless.

The Atonement

The Word or Light proceeding continually from God to create whatever is good in the world dwelt fully in Christ and by measure in men as human beings. For this reason the Quakers did not take pains to distinguish between the Eternal Christ and the historic Jesus. It is often difficult to tell of which they are speaking. Every event has its inward and its outward, its eternal and its temporal aspect. The same can be said of the life of Christ on earth, including his sacrifice on the cross for the sins of the whole world. That sacrifice has both a temporal and an eternal significance. Each is incomplete without the other. Eternally, Christ is the "Lamb slain" in the book "written before the foundation of the world" (Rev. 13:8). It is the very nature of God eternally to sacrifice Himself for His children, paying the penalty for their sins and receiving them back to Himself as the father in the parable received his prodigal son. This had been going on before the sacrifice of Jesus as is declared by the prophet Hosea, who, speaking for Jehovah, says, "I drew them [the erring Israelites] with bands of love" (Hos. 11:4).

In the sacrifice of Jesus we have, as it were, a temporal transverse section of an eternal process, an emergence into time and space of the Heart of God, eternally pierced for His children. This sacrifice was not made simply to show men on earth the way to reconciliation with God, though that was part of the meaning. It occurred also as an essential part of the eternal process itself.

In itself, as history shows, the crucifixion possesses a saving and redeeming power. As one might look through an aperture into a furnace in which iron is melted to be molded into new forms, so the crucifixion serves as a cleft through which we behold the molten center of existence. There, through pain and sacrifice, a new and higher form of life is molded.

The Quakers did not apply to the sacrifice of Christ the Old Testament concept of a blood sacrifice offered to appease an angry God. The blood sacrifice commanded by the Mosaic law was for them an external form belonging to the old dispensation. They believed that the word "blood" was used metaphorically in the New Testament as a figure of speech natural in view of the cultural background of the Hebrew people, but not one which could have the same meaning for themselves. They more characteristically considered the "Blood of Christ" to be the Light Within in its redeeming and sanctifying capacity.

George Fox in 1648 writes at the beginning of his ministry:

> Soon after there was another great meeting of professors,
> and a captain, whose name was Amor Stoddard, came in.
> They were discoursing of the blood of Christ; and as they
> were discoursing of it, I saw, through the immediate open-
> ing of the Invisible Spirit, the blood of Christ. And I cried
> out among them, and said, "Do ye not see the blood of
> Christ? See it in your hearts, to sprinkle your hearts and
> consciences from dead works, to serve the living God": for
> I saw it, the blood of the New Covenant, how it came into
> the heart. This startled the professors, who would have the
> blood only without them, and not in them."[15]

This is the usual Quaker emphasis on the inward life rather than
on the outward event.

In his letters Fox sometimes refers to the Light Within as "blood"
when he speaks of it as a cleansing power. After speaking of the
Light as a Spring of Water "which waters the plants and causeth
them to grow up in the Lord, from whom the pure living Springs
come," he goes on to speak of it as performing another function:

> And here is the water which is the Witness in the earth,
> which doth wash; and here comes the Spirit to be known,
> the Witness which doth baptize and the Witness, the Blood,
> which doth cleanse. [Ep. 155, 1657]

The Light as blood is also life.

> And now, being gathered in the name of Jesus . . . whose
> blood you have drunk, yea, even of the heavenly man's,
> which is his life. [Ep. 279, 1670]

This identification of blood and life indicates that we are regen-
erated, not so much by the death of Christ, as by his life in our
hearts. Here we may have a clue as to what Christ meant when he

said at the Last Supper, "This cup is the new covenant in my blood" (I Cor. 11:25). The mention of the new covenant brought to the minds of the disciples the ancient covenant which, as Jews, they knew so well, the covenant between Jehovah and Israel in the wilderness of Sinai. Here was sealed a contract by which the people of Israel adopted Jehovah as their God and Jehovah adopted Israel as His people. That contract was sealed by Moses in an age-old ritual (Exod. 24). The people stood before Jehovah who was represented by an altar. Animals were sacrificed and their blood poured into bowls. Part of the blood was sprinkled over the altar and part over the people with the words, "Behold the blood of the covenant."

In its symbolic meaning blood represented life (Lev. 17:11, 14). Two parties formerly independent of each other were united into a single living organism by sharing the same blood or life. A blood kinship was thus established between Jehovah and Israel, like that within a tribe or a family. To seal this relationship, the life of a living creature was sacrificed in order that its blood, imparted to others, might unite them into a single life. Other Semitic tribes felt themselves united to their deity by ties of lineage. These people were not chosen by their god, nor had they chosen him. In the case of the Israelites the union was a deliberate choice, sealed by the blood of a third life in order that an organic relationship might be established.

What was more natural than that Jesus, knowing that his own blood would be shed on the morrow, should refer to the blood of the new covenant foretold by Jeremiah (Jer. 31:31) which was written in the heart. Like the blood of the old covenant, his blood would create a living bond between God and man. His was to be that third life which would bridge the gap between the divine and the human, overcoming the isolation and estrangement of the human individual. This would be an at-one-ment, a uniting of that which had been separated.

So Paul writes: "But now in Christ Jesus you who once were far off have been brought near in the blood of Christ. For he is our peace who has made us both one, and broken down the dividing wall of hostility" (Eph. 2:13, 14). This is the peace-creating and uniting power of the Eternal Christ, the Light of the World, the only Christ that Paul knew.

More explicitly,

> God is Light. . . . If we walk in the Light as he is in the Light, we have fellowship with one another and the blood of Jesus, his Son, cleanses us from all sin (I John 1:5, 7).

This verse may appear to present a *non sequitur*. What is the connection between Light, fellowship and blood? But if we identify blood and life as the Hebrews did, the meaning becomes clear. Fellowship is created by Light or Life (John identifies the two, John 1:4), which, like the life of the lamb sacrificed by Moses, is a third life uniting two separated lives into one. The Light Within not only unites man with God, but also, as we have seen so explicitly expressed in George Fox's epistles, it unites men with one another in a fellowship of the Spirit.

For this reason we seldom find the Friends referring to the unifying power of the Light without indicating that it unites them both to God and to one another. "This," says Barclay, "is that cement whereby we are joined as to the Lord, so to one another."[16]

John Burnyeat writes:

> . . . the openings of the power that was daily amongst us and wrought sweetly in our hearts, which still united us more and more unto God and knit us together in the perfect bond of love, of fellowship and membership, so that we became a body compact.[17]

The union with God becomes a union of men with one another, the branches become united in the Vine and the prayer of Christ becomes fulfilled "that they may all be one; even as thou, Father, art in me and I in thee, that they also may be in us" (John 17:21).

Man's Responsibility for Good and Evil

On two important religious doctrines the Quakers differed from their Protestant opponents and were closer to the Catholics. They believed that righteousness could not be imputed to man by God unless man was actually righteous, while the Protestants believed that God, because of the sacrifice of Christ, could impute Christ's righteousness to man even though he continued to sin. The Quakers also believed that perfection and freedom from sin was possible in this world, while the Protestants believed that all men, even the saints, continue to sin in "thought, word and deed." These two doctrines are still subjects of acute controversy in religious thought and have important practical consequences in terms of behavior.

Catholicism was a preindividual religion, existing long before the Renaissance tendency to individualism. According to such a religion, lives closely united with one another can share in one another's righteousness and guilt in some such way as the head suffers for the sins of the stomach or profits by its accomplishments. This conception, based on the close interrelatedness of men in a tribal society, is characteristic of all early religions including the religion of the Hebrews up to the time of the exile. In Catholic doctrine a member of the Church shares in its supernatural righteousness and in its store of grace, accumulated particularly by the sufferings and death of Christ, but also by all the martyrs and by the prayers and penitence of all the devout in all ages. Accordingly, a person who by the nature of his duties in life is compelled to become involved in what is evil, as a soldier for example is compelled to kill, can make up for his lack of goodness by sharing in the accumulated goodness of the Church. This is not an imputed goodness, but a real goodness, affecting man internally through his organic relationship to the Church and through the Church to Christ.

But Protestantism did away with this organic interrelatedness and substituted an individualistic, almost a mechanistic, conception. It was no accident that Protestantism and modern mechanistic science arose at the same time. Imputed righteousness became accepted as the only possible means of salvation for a sinner. Since on this evil and depraved earth there was no store of righteousness on which the sinner could draw, he had to receive his righteousness through a supernatural transaction. This was envisaged in terms of an act carried out long ago, with which man, as an individual, had nothing to do. As this transaction was external to himself, it did not affect him internally. Even the willingness to accept it as a means of salvation came from without, as a gift of grace. God could, however, account man to be good, just as a judge might remove the penalty for a crime, while leaving the criminal as much a criminal in character as he was before.

The Quakers revived the Catholic principle of interrelatedness, but in a different way. As is shown by Barclay,[18] man, by uniting himself, not with the Church, but with the Eternal Christ, shared vicariously in God's goodness and suffering for sin. The whole work of redemption, as once performed in Judea, must be repeated in each human heart if it is to be effective.[19] Man must be crucified with Christ, as Paul said, and be raised with Christ to newness of life. By this means man might acquire undeserved goodness, but it was a real internal virtue, not an imputed goodness which might even countenance further sin.

The Old Testament ends with an impasse. It cannot answer the question, Why do the righteous suffer? Slowly through a thousand years the religious insight of the Hebrews had become clarified until Jehovah, first known as the primitive tribal war god, was realized as absolute ruler of the universe. Then the Deity, who had in earlier times appeared as a God jealous of other gods, could say through the mouth of his prophet, the Second Isaiah, to a people in exile, "I am the Lord and there is none else. I form the light and create darkness. I make peace and create evil" (Isa. 45:6, 7). The religion of ancient Israel here reaches its climax. Exaltation of Deity can go no further.

Israel returned from exile, but not to freedom. Persian, Greek and Roman ruled and persecuted. Prophet, seer and priest inquired, "How can these things be when God is both just and omnipotent?" In the book of Job the solution of the problem is placed beyond man's finite mind though it is felt to be somehow solved in God's infinite wisdom. The writer of Ecclesiastes gives up in pessimism. The author of Daniel prophesies that God will intervene by a catastrophic act through which those who suffer unjustly shall receive their recompense. But these answers fail to satisfy the agonized cry of the soul, "Why hast thou made me suffer?"

The answer is attained by one of those strange spiral movements of history through which man returns to an earlier belief but on a new and higher level. The primitive sacrificial system of Israel was built upon the doctrine that an innocent victim could be offered and accepted for the people's sin. The account of Abraham's attempted sacrifice of Isaac indicates that this victim, who had once been the first-born son, was now replaced by a symbolic offering. To ancient Israel such vicarious suffering appeared reasonable. Early man is not individualized. To him all life appears bound together in a living whole. But, as Israel became more civilized, the tribal blood brotherhood dissolved. In its stead we have a swarm of individuals. Now, as Jeremiah and Ezekiel declared, each man must suffer for his own sin. "The soul that sinneth *it* shall die" (Ezek. 18:20). On such an individual basis the problem of suffering is insoluble. Job was right. There is no reason why a righteous individual should be the innocent victim who suffers for the sins of others.

In the New Testament the ancient drama of sacrifice is reen-
acted, not within a tribal setting, but on a cosmic scale. The Son of
God offers himself for the sins of the whole world. To modern
individualistic thinking such a doctrine appears impossible, perhaps absurd, or it is mechanically construed according to some
legalistic scheme, such as the doctrine that Christ allows himself
to be punished by an angry God as a substitute for man. But to
those who become aware of the unity of all life in God the doctrine of Atonement is pregnant with meaning. Because He has
made Himself one with them, God must needs suffer for men's
sins. The tribal concept of the interrelatedness of life within the
tribe is replaced by the doctrine that all life is one in God whose
suffering for sin is redemptive and creative.

But not all suffering is redemptive and creative. Pain and loss
and want may be degrading and destructive. So it was for one
of the three who hung on the crosses outside Jerusalem. But for
Another there was resurrection and a new incarnation in His
church. So all suffering is sacrificial in so far as it becomes one
with the suffering of the Eternal Christ seeking to draw mankind
into a living and related whole.

Is the suffering of our time redemptive and creative? When
Abigail met the outlaw David she said, "The soul of my lord shall
be bound in the bundle of life with the Lord thy God and the
souls of thine enemies them shall He sling out" (I Sam. 25:29).
This "bundle of life" with God did not then include enemies. But
in the New Testament enemies also are included. Even the Samari-
tans, between whom and the Israelites there existed a racial tension, were singled out by Jesus as neighbors whom we should love
as ourselves. If the suffering of the world today is to be creative
and bring redemption, it must be suffering in behalf of all without
exception. So it was on the day of the crucifixion which released
among men the power of resurrection.

Perfectionism

The Quakers believed that this process of redemption and regeneration might go so far as sometimes to free man completely from sin and leave him at least temporarily in a state of perfection. It is easy to misunderstand this doctrine. Perfection is not a static state of self-satisfaction. It not only permits growth, it requires growth. Did not Christ grow in wisdom and stature (Luke 2:52)? As Barclay says, a perfect boy can become a perfect man and he is not a perfect boy unless he is on the way to becoming a man. The man who had one talent in the parable was nearer perfection than the man who had five because his talent was growing through interest.[20] Perfection means simply living up to the measure of light that is given, (our one talent),[21] and if we are faithful to that, we shall be given more. Job Scott writes in his *Journal,* "If we attain all that we can we are perfect, for nothing which we cannot is required . . . by our God."[22] This doctrine is important because it made an inner state of peace and serenity possible, even in this imperfect world, provided man made full use of whatever talents he had. The Protestant of that time was continually disturbed by an inner sense of guilt and original sin. His life was a series of choices between sins. This is essentially the position taken by some prominent theologians today. They are right in holding that we are organically united to an evil society, but this does not make all our acts evil. We are also organically united to Eternal Goodness.

For the Quaker the doctrine that complete freedom from sin was impossible was pure defeatism. George Fox, in arguing with some who "pleaded for sin," said, "If your faith be true, it will give you victory over sin and the devil and purify your hearts and consciences";[23] and to others who said, "We must always be striving," he replied, "It is a sad and comfortless sort of striving to strive with a belief that we should never overcome." In the *First Publishers of*

Truth we find it recorded that the Independents, finding happiness and peace not possible in life, "gave up to sit down short."[24] Of course, the state of "perfection," in the Quaker sense, may be lost as well as gained.

The presence of inner peace was the main Quaker test of right guidance. It had nothing to do with the results of an action. The outcome was in God's hands. Peace comes to him who lives up to the divine requirement, even though that requirement may not take him very far at first. Where there is no fear of failure and no sense of compromise, the soul is at peace. Man can be internally free and at peace even though God may lay upon him the burden of the world's suffering.[25] He may, as Fox often expressed in his epistles, "keep his head above the waters . . . in which there is a tempest," even though the rest of him be caught in the storm.

The problem of consistency and compromise faces every thoughtful man. The soldier feels compelled to do many things contrary to the code of morals which he has accepted from childhood. The pacifist finds it impossible to extricate himself from all connection with war. Each is uneasy. For both there is a sense of frustration and failure.

The problem may be stated in this way: Should men try to live up to the highest they know, squarely facing the probability of failure? or, Should they direct their efforts toward a lower goal with some likelihood of attainment? Most persons accept the second alternative, believing that some gain is better than none at all.

Yet, in accepting the lower and more attainable standard, there are few who do not preserve some area in life in which they can pay homage to the highest. This is especially true of adherents to the great religious faiths which all began by repudiating compromise, though, as the number and variety of their members increased, they gradually came to accept it. Even so they tried to retain a way by which consistency could be somewhere saved in spite of general compromise.

The Catholic Church has its priests, its monks, its nuns who strive to fulfill literally Christ's commands in regard to hate and strife and love of possessions. Their merits help to redeem those who are involved in compromise. Historic Protestantism believed that in this world all must sin, but, through a miracle of grace, perfection would be attained, at least by some, hereafter. The Hindu view of life tolerates compromise in the earlier stages of a man's career. After he has fulfilled his duties as householder he may in old age realize the detachment which opens a way to the ultimate goal. The Buddhist admits compromise because of ignorance, but sometime, in a future incarnation, every individual will achieve enlightenment. This epitome is too brief to be truly representative, but it shows that in no one of the great religions is there complete surrender to compromise.

The Quaker is charged with Utopian tendencies and is called a perfectionist because he does not limit freedom from hatred and strife to a special professional class or to a future state in this life or the next. He is, indeed, a perfectionist in the sense that he believes that every man has within him the possibility and the duty to be wholly obedient to the will of God as inwardly revealed, but even such complete obedience does not mean that the goal of life has been reached. The divine Light is a principle of growth. In this Light the perfect seed grows into the perfect sprout, which in turn develops into the perfect plant. Compromise consists in deliberate failure to choose the way which leads toward the highest.

The Fall of Man

The story of the Fall of Man belongs to the class of myths which record in highly symbolic form a genuine occurrence in human history.[26]

The early Friends were influenced by the doctrine of the Fall but, as was the case with the Catholics, the Fall was not as com-

plete for them as it was for the Calvinists. Man was not a total
ruin. There was still left in him a Seed of the divine which in the
end would bruise the serpent's head (Gen. 3:15). Although it is
easy to be misled by figures of speech, yet sometimes we have no
other recourse but to use them. A common form of the doctrine
of the Light Within seems to have been envisaged in such a way
that the divine Light appeared to shine in from above man causing the divine Seed in man to germinate and grow. The Seed will
grow if it is not too heavily overlaid with hard earth. But the ground
can be tilled and watered by the preaching of the Truth and by
worship and prayer. "Natural" man, like all other natural things, is
the creation of God. There remains in him, however low he falls,
something of that divine Word by which all things were created
and are being created.

Man's fall from the superhuman to the human can be partially
understood, Barclay believes, by comparing it to a further fall from
the human to the subhuman. In the first case man falls from life in
the Spirit to dependence on law and reason, and in the second
case he falls from dependence on law and reason to a condition of
sensuality. He distinguishes the three realms by saying:

> As nothing below the spirit of man (as the spirit of brutes
> or any other creatures) can properly reach unto or com-
> prehend the things of a man, as being of a... higher na-
> ture, so neither can the spirit of man, of the natural man...
> receive nor discern the things of God.[27]

> Which enlightened reason, in those that obey and follow
> this true light, we confess may be useful to man even in
> spiritual things as it is still subservient and subject to the
> other; even as the animal life in man, regulated and or-
> dered by his reason helps him in going about things that
> are rational.[28]

This brings us to the heart of Quaker theology as it grew out of actual experience. Man finds himself in the twilight zone of reason, poised between two worlds, an upper world of Light, and a lower world of Darkness, a Spiritual world which is superhuman and a material world which is subhuman. He is free to center his life in one of the three; he can live by the Light, he can live by human reason, or he can live at the mercy of his sensual cravings. His body is animal, his mind rational and the Light Within him is divine. He is never without all three, though the three are so intimately related that it is impossible to distinguish between them sharply. Much depends on their relationship. The Light of Truth should be a guide to reason and reason should help instinct in a properly ordered life. This is a simple empirical theology, but it sums up much of early Quaker thought. It is considered further in the final chapter.

The Relation Between the Divine and the Human

The Quakers did not concern themselves to interpret the metaphysical character of the relationship between God and man. It was to be felt rather than understood. There have, however, been variations of thought and attitude upon it which have had important results in Quaker history. Quaker Quietism, the conflicts and divisions of the nineteenth century, and the revolution in Quaker thought which took place about the beginning of the twentieth century, are all concerned directly or indirectly with this problem.

About the beginning of the twentieth century nearly all Quaker writers were critical of Barclay's *Apology* which had up to that time largely expressed the character of Quaker thought. William Charles Braithwaite, for example, in *The Second Period of Quakerism* accuses Barclay of dualism in too sharply separating the Light as divine and the human mind as natural. This, he says, not only makes inexplicable the union of the divine and human in Christ, but leaves no trace of goodness in man by which he can reach out toward God. According to Barclay, man, after Adam's fall, is "natural" and depraved. All he can do is to wait passively for the coming of the Light which is wholly other and avoid resisting it when it comes. In such a system man has no positive part in his own salvation. He has only the passive function of not resisting the saving power of the Light.

This sharp separation of the divine and human Braithwaite attributes to the influence of Calvinism on Barclay, who was brought up in the atmosphere of Scotch Presbyterianism. It was, he maintains, one of the causes of the later decline of Quakerism,[29] for it led the Quakers to wait for divine guidance rather than to seek for it actively. Today, says Braithwaite, we think of the divine and human as akin to each other. "We seek expression for the truth in terms of life unified in God."[30] "The spiritual belongs of right to our natures."[31] "The blue heaven of the larger life may seem beyond our present reach, yet its very air is on our faces."[32]

Here we have before us a fundamental issue which has been debated throughout Christian history. It first appeared in the controversy between the Greek and Latin forms of Christianity, and it has reappeared today in the debate between liberal theology influenced by Hegelianism and the various forms of NeoCalvinism or Barthianism. It appears in another form in the long and never-ending philosophical debate between those who see the universe in terms of internal organic relations and those who see it in terms of external mechanistic relations. In the first view the divine is an essential internal element in man, a constituent part of human personality. In the second, the divine and human are wholly separate, yet able to interact, as it were, externally.

If the dualism between the "natural" man and the Light were as absolute as Barclay appears sometimes to make it, man would hardly have enough goodness even to accept the Light. Yet Barclay's distinction is moral and practical rather than metaphysical. At the beginning of his religious journey, the human being must look on God as wholly other. If man does not realize that he is himself unregenerate he cannot be reborn into a higher life. The first function of the Light, as Fox so often points out, is to reveal sin. Man, thinking of himself as akin to God, may be so puffed up in his own estimation that he will never seek regeneration. Yet Barclay's dualism is provisional. It can be overcome. The Light, which at first sight appears external, may eventually become harmonized with the human will in genuine organic union with God.

Barclay's critics take his figures of speech too literally. A. Neave Brayshaw says[33] in reference to *Apology*, page 147 (italics his):

> This Principle or Light in man was compared to a candle in a lantern illuminating it for a time, *but leaving its essential nature unchanged.*

Rufus M. Jones says[34] in reference to *Apology*, page 140:

> The supernatural Seed lies as a 'real substance' hidden away and dormant in the natural soul as naked grain lies in barren stony ground.

The lantern is a mechanistic figure which is not wholly applicable to a living organism, but it does help to illustrate the difference between the Light and conscience by comparing the latter to a lantern. The figure of the Seed is probably taken from the parable of the Sower. The Seed of the Kingdom may lie in ground so stony that it never takes root, but it may also lie in fertile ground and grow. Barclay says that it lies "many times" in stony ground, implying that it may sometimes lie elsewhere.

Barclay's *Apology* was written mainly to refute Calvinism and particularly *The Westminster Confession of Faith*. Its author concedes to his opponents in order to find a common ground from which to win them over, but the externalism of the Calvinistic theory finds no place in the internalism of Barclay's Quakerism. Barclay op-

poses the doctrine of election as attributing sin to God. Man is
"natural" as contrasted with "supernatural" (words for which, for-
tunately, we have little use today), but he is capable of making a
choice between accepting or rejecting the "supernatural." If he
accepts it, the dualism between God and man begins to be overcome with the ultimate result of union, or at-one-ment. Thus
Barclay speaks of the possibility of becoming one with the Seed;[35]
"union" is "the manner of Christ's being in the saints" but not as
he is in all men:[36]

> as man is wrought upon, there is a will raised in him, by
> which he comes to be a co-worker with the grace; for ac-
> cording to (the doctrine) of Augustine, "He that made us
> without us, will not save us without us."[37]

> By this also comes that communication of the goods of
> Christ unto us by which we come to be partakers of the
> divine nature, as saith Peter (II Peter 1:4), and are made
> one with him, as the branches with the vine, and have a
> title and right to what he hath done and suffered for us; so
> that his obedience becomes ours, his righteousness ours,
> his death and sufferings ours.[38]

This is far from Calvinism, which leaves man so depraved and so
far outside of all that is divine that he is wholly dependent on that
which is done for him toward his regeneration.

The fundamental question, "Is man by nature in union with
God or does he attain union as the goal of a long upward climb on
a mystical ladder toward perfection?" has important consequences
in terms of behavior. Some assume that "the practice of the Presence of God" is always possible provided we simply realize that
God is continually in us and around us. This is called the "sacrament of life." Every action according to this view is really sacramental and we need only become aware of this fact in order that,

for us, it may be valid. In such a view there is no real difference between the religious and the secular; there only appears to be a difference due to our lack of insight. The other view holds that the continual practice of the Presence of God, being difficult of attainment, becomes possible only to persons of saintly character after a long period of preparation through spiritual exercises. The well-known case of Brother Lawrence, who felt in the kitchen the same degree of God's nearness that he felt in the presence of the holy sacraments, is explained by the fact that he had attained to this state by a life of search and endeavor. Life as a whole can be sacramental, but this is the goal of the spiritual journey not a stage on the way. According to the first view, that which is religious is brought to the level of that which is secular; according to the second view, the secular is slowly and by striving raised up to the level of the religious. The Quakers have, for the most part, taken the second point of view. The authors of the *Journals,* who write from immediate experience, have all gone through a struggle from darkness up to the world of Light. They have never remained wholly and continually in the Light. They experience periods of dryness. Yet for most of their lives, once the self-centered will is by a great struggle subdued, there is a continued consciousness of the guiding hand of God.

In the history of Christian thought divergence in the answers to this problem of the relationship of man to God are not only due to psychological differences in men but they are also inherent in Christianity's two roots, the one in Hebrew religion, the other in Greek philosophy. Christianity originated in Palestine. It spread rapidly into the Graeco-Roman world absorbing much of the thought pattern which was Platonic in origin. This is evident in the New Testament. The Synoptic Gospels are Hebraic and strongly ethical. They are concerned primarily with good action. The writings of Paul and John, although also largely Hebraic, show the emphasis of Greek thought and are concerned to a greater degree with understanding the philosophical and theological significance of the Incarnation. In the Hebrew religion the relations between God and man are like the relations between one person and another, separated to be sure in space and time. But sometimes the Spirit of God may seize upon a man and use him to convey a special message to other men. Such a man is a prophet who speaks as a mouthpiece for God. This emergence of the divine in the human is temporary. It has occurred in order to accomplish a particular divine purpose. At other times the prophet speaks for himself. The Spirit may descend on any person at any time. Man must be careful to make the most of these times of visitation not knowing when they may occur again.

In Greek philosophy of the type we are here considering, the union of God and man is not a temporary circumstance to carry out a particular purpose but a continuing condition due to the very nature of human existence. Man's sin consists in ignoring this unity; his virtue consists in realizing it. God is the ground and source of all Being and can, if searched for, always be found in the depths of the soul. God is Eternal Goodness, all else is evil. God is Eternal Reality, all else is appearance.

In the Hebrew conception man is saved by doing; in the Greek, he is saved by being. In the Hebrew, the goal is obedience to the divine will; in the Greek, the goal is right knowledge—"You will know the Truth and the Truth will make you free" (John 8:32). The Hebrew, therefore, seeks for a change of will; the Greek, for a change of nature. As the Hebrew emphasizes action in this world in obedience to God's will, so the Greek emphasizes contemplation and withdrawal from this world as the way to Eternal Life. For the Hebrew, unity with God results from an act of God the Creator in time; for the Greek, unity with God is a timeless fact to be realized as eternal Truth. For the Hebrew, the perfect divine-human society, the Kingdom of God, will come at a certain time in human history in this world; for the Greek, the Kingdom is already in our hearts in a spiritual world different from our material existence. For the Hebrew type of mind the Incarnation is a miracle. It is not to be understood. For the Greek, it is a natural and inevitable culmination of the long process of divine revelation. For the Hebrew, the Messiah appears in history to introduce a new social order; for the Greek, the Son of God is eternally being born and seeks continually to become incarnate against the resistance of the flesh. For the Hebrew, inspiration is occasional and to be waited for; for the Greek, inspiration is continuous and to be searched for. For the Hebrew, evil is real and results from the acts of persons opposed to God; for the Greek, evil is less real than goodness and results from the nature of the lower world of sensuous desire as contrasted with the higher world of spiritual life. For the Hebrew, religion is this-worldly; for the Greek, other-worldly.

This comparison could be carried further—the subject is a large one—but perhaps enough has been said to indicate the nature of these two distinct sources of Christian thought. The Christian theologian, by confining himself to one or the other, can arrive at a fairly consistent system of theology. However, difficulties arise when, as in Paul's case, both are followed to some degree. In general and with many exceptions it may be said that Catholicism tends toward the Greek concept and Protestantism toward the Hebrew. Plato and Aristotle strongly influenced the religious thought of the Catholic Middle Ages. The theology of Thomas Aquinas, which became ascendant in Catholicism, tended to be Aristotelian. Protestantism was an attempt to get back to a more Hebraic form of Christianity. Luther and Calvin regarded Plato and Aristotle as heathens to be avoided and refuted.

Quakerism might be said to combine the two concepts but without any attempt to work out a consistent system. The distinctions between Substance and Shadow, Power and Form, Reality and Deceit made by Fox and Penington tend to be Greek in character. So is the doctrine of the Universality of the Light Within as an

essential element in all human beings. The admonition heard in
Quaker meetings to "center down," to "dig deep," to seek for the
revelations of the Light in the depths of the soul is characteristic of
the great mystics of the Church who followed the path earlier
explored by Plato and Plotinus. The silent waiting in the divine Presence of the meeting for worship and the cultivation of contemplation and sensitivity to inward leading is more Greek than Hebrew.

On the other hand, the ministry in Quaker meetings stems
from Hebrew prophetism rather than from Greek mysticism. The
first Quakers thought of themselves as prophets in the Hebrew
sense. Sometimes they imitated the Hebrew prophets in word and
act. The Quaker emphasis on action as a necessary and inevitable
consequence of inward revelation is more Hebrew than Greek.
Quakers today are known more for their works than for the depth
of their spiritual life; more for doing than for being. For many
Quakers worship and contemplation are valuable, not in themselves, but as the means to right action.

That Quakerism has not worked out a consistent system of theology is not an important criticism, for its ancestry is both Greek
and Hebrew, contemplative and active. Logical consistency tends
toward a static system of ideas which can easily become a fixed
creed and a formal test of membership in a church or a political
movement. Logical inconsistency tends toward growth, development, new revelations of truth which approximate the one consistent system of ideas which is Truth. No fixed creed is therefore
possible; the indispensable factor is a sincere search for truth.

In Quakerism there are two complementary movements, withdrawal to an inward Source of Truth and return to action in the
world. The first is Greek in its religious emphasis, the second,
Hebrew. Quakerism is both contemplative and active, both metaphysical and ethical, not because it has combined the two in a
consistent system of thought but because it has combined them
through experience.

Notes

1. Commentary on *Bhagavadgita*, 1882, II, 46.
2. Robert Barclay, *Apology*, p. 91.
3. Barclay, *Apology*, p. 92.
4. Samuel Fisher, *The Testimony of Truth Exalted*, 1666, p. 197.
5. Isaac Penington, *Works*, p. 239.
6. Barclay, *Apology*, pp. 58-62.
7. Barclay, *Apology*, p. 62.
8. Barclay, *Apology*, p. 184.
9. Penington, *Works*, 1771, p. 759.
10. Barclay, *Apology*, pp. 192-93.
11. James Bowden, *The History of the Society of Friends in America*, 1850, I, 125.
12. William Penn, *Journal*, II, 185.
13. Elizabeth Newport, *Memoirs*, compiled by Ann A. Townsend, 1878, p. 99.
14. Penn, *Journal*, I, 350.
15. Penn, *Journal*, I, 24.
16. Barclay, *Apology*, p. 357.
17. John Burnyeat, *Works*, 1691, p. 11.
18. Barclay, *Apology*, p. 206.
19. Barclay, *Apology*, p. 256.
20. Barclay, *Apology*, p. 243.
21. Burnyeat, *Works*, p. 11.
22. Job Scott, *Journal*, p. 116.

23. George Fox, *Journal,* I, 56.

24. *First Publishers of Truth,* edited by Norman Penney, 1907, henceforth abbreviated F.P.T., p. 332.

25. That the early Christians were perfectionists can be shown by many quotations from the New Testament, including Matt. 5:48, 19:21, Eph. 4:13, Phil. 3:15, Col. 1:28, 4:12, 11 Tim. 3:17, Heb. 12:23, Jas. 1:4.

26. See Howard H. Brinton, *Divine-Human Society,* Chap. II, "The Fall of Man," 1938.

27. Barclay, *Apology,* p. 29.

28. Barclay, *Apology,* p. 145.

29. William C. Braithwaite, *Second Period of Quakerism,* 1921, p. 635.

30. Braithwaite, *Second Period,* p. 396.

31. Braithwaite, *Second Period,* p. 397.

32. Braithwaite, *Second Period,* p. 398.

33. Brayshaw, A. Neave, *The Quakers, Their Story and Message,* p. 52.

34. Braithwaite, *Second Period,* Introduction, p. xxxviii.

35. Barclay, *Apology,* p. 141.

36. Barclay, *Apology,* p. 143.

37. Barclay, *Apology,* p. 149.

38. Barclay, *Apology,* p. 206.

CHAPTER IV

The Meeting for Worship

THE DISCOVERY OF THE LIGHT WITHIN was followed by a
determined and uncompromising effort to act in accordance
with the discovery. It was in realizing the revolutionary character
of their religious experiences that the Quakers were unique. That
God reveals Himself directly within man is accepted in most
branches of Christianity and in some sects of all religions of the
world. The Quaker meeting in its waiting upon the Lord in silence carries this doctrine to its logical conclusion. If God reveals
Himself, then worship can be nothing less than reverent waiting
in His Presence. If He speaks to man, then it is man's highest
privilege to listen.

As Catholic worship is centered in the altar and Protestant
worship in the sermon, worship for the Society of Friends attempts
to realize as its center the divine Presence revealed within. In a
Catholic church the altar is placed so as to become the focus of
adoration; in a typical Protestant church the pulpit localizes attention; while in a Friends Meeting House there is no visible point of
concentration, worship being here directed neither toward the
actions nor the words of others, but toward the inward experience
of the gathered group.

These three types may be compared to three ways of teaching
science: the lecture-demonstration method, the lecture method,

and the laboratory method. In the lecture-demonstration method, the teacher presents before his pupils the facts which he desires to convey by performing experiments in which those facts are illustrated. Similarly, the priest at the altar not only speaks of the divine, but he also reveals the divine to the attentive congregation in the Sacrament. In the lecture method the teacher expounds by means of words the reality which he is presenting. In some such fashion the Protestant preacher makes known by means of Scripture, hymn and sermon the nature of the divine. He proclaims the way of salvation rather than the present fact of salvation. The sacramental may sometimes be present, but it is subsidiary. The primary purpose is the proclamation of the Word of God as witnessed to in the Scriptures. In a scientific laboratory an opportunity is offered for the student to experience scientific events. Some guidance may be, and generally is, offered, but this guidance is for beginners, it suggests the way to the desired result and the mistakes which are to be avoided. The more advanced arrive at the result for themselves. They may fail or they may succeed. They may even discover something different from what is expected. Similarly, in a Quaker meeting an opportunity is offered for each individual to practice the presence of God as an experience of his own. Some guidance may be offered by vocal ministry which suggests the way to this experience or expresses cautions regarding obstacles and difficulties, such as sins and temptations. Such guidance is knowledge *about.* It is not that direct knowledge of acquaintance to which the worshiper must himself attain.

Workers in a laboratory are not always separate searchers. One may aid another, especially if all are working on a common project. So it is in a Quaker meeting; individual seekers are not searching independently of one another. Their search is a group search in which those who are further advanced help those who have not gone so far.

Withdrawal and Return

While no figure of speech is adequate, the figure of the scientific laboratory may be carried a little further. The laboratory worker withdraws from the routine business of the world to contemplate and experience fundamental truths in a small interior, shielded from outside interference. He emerges from the laboratory to apply to the outer world the truth he has discovered. Such truth has a value of its own independent of practical application. Pure science, or science for its own sake, has always been honored as worthwhile. But even pure science sooner or later becomes applied or practical as the history of science abundantly illustrates. The searcher withdraws from the world but eventually he returns to it to apply what he has found to the affairs of life.

This process of *withdrawal and return,* to use a phrase made familiar by Arnold J. Toynbee, is characteristic of all life. If we are building a house, we withdraw from time to time, study the blueprint and return more completely aware of the desired result. If we are on a journey, we stop to scrutinize a map to make sure of our sense of direction, then go forward with greater confidence.

If action is simply action and nothing more, it becomes meaningless. Out of action alone there will sooner or later arise a sense of futility because action as such requires the centering of attention on a limited field. But, in focusing attention in order to act, I cut off attention from all other objects. Thus I may deprive my own act of meaning, for meaning arises out of the relation of one object to other objects and particularly out of the relation of the part to the whole. For instance, if I examine the stamen of a flower by itself, it may have little meaning. Its meaning exists in its relation to the flower and more fully to the plant. Action in building a brick house requires attention to one brick at a time, and yet one brick by itself is meaningless. In order that the brick may acquire significance, I must consider the structure as a whole. Pure action concerns a part which is meaningless if detached from the whole. Only contemplation of the whole will disclose meaning.

It is for reasons such as these that a sense of futility is so widespread today. The emphasis in modern life is on action and more action. But in order to act, the man of action has necessarily limited his attention to so small an area that his action may have become meaningless. Sooner or later he begins to wonder whether or not what he is doing is worth doing, since he cannot see its relation to the whole. A purely active life may be compared to the activity of a man on an assembly line in a factory. His whole responsibility may be to turn a single screw in each element as it passes by. Since he does not see the completed machine, his action may become meaningless for him. The same futility may be felt by the man who buys the article. If it is an automobile, it may take him swiftly and smoothly to no destination of importance.

If a life of pure action is futile, a life of pure contemplation may be equally meaningless. The builder who spends his time gazing at a blueprint, the traveler who only stares at maps, the musician who ponders his score and never strikes a note, does not make a free choice. Therefore, he loses his freedom. He becomes absorbed in what he contemplates and is dominated by it. The person who is exclusively active loses his sense of the value of his action and becomes a mechanism. On the other hand, he who is wholly absorbed in the source or goal of action, ceases to be a free individual because he makes no choices. *Withdrawal* and *return* are both essential; each without the other is inadequate. The negative way takes us back to the source of meaning and value; the positive way takes us forward to the embodiment of meaning and value in the routine of life.

Since both are found in most aspects of human life, it ought not to surprise us to discover that both appear in our religion. Worship can be looked upon as withdrawal in order to experience the divine Source of value and meaning. It is a purification of self-centered desires in order to discover and obey the will of God.

In withdrawing into the presence of God, man seeks to perceive the whole as it is seen by God. Adherence to the part—to a particular individual, nation, race or class—may be overcome by communion with the Father of *all* being. Even adherence to private possessions is weakened by knowing Him who possesses all. Hatred of a wrongdoer may be overcome by union with the will of Him who "sends His rain on the just and the unjust." By withdrawing from particular creations to the Creator of all, we can place ourselves nearer the creative Heart of the Universe, the Spring out of which all being flows. Similarly, we may observe a variety of acts of an individual and from them judge of his character, but we do not really know the person until we commune with him at the center of his being, which is the spring of his will. Such knowledge of other persons is not reached through thought, but through love, the love which seeks not to possess, but to be possessed.

Outward arrangements and procedures in a Friends meeting conduce to the cultivation of this withdrawal. At first sight, it might appear that the meeting can only be described by negatives—there is no altar, no liturgy, no pulpit, no sermon, no organ, no choir, no sacrament, and no person in authority. No external object of attention prevents the worshiper from turning inward and there finding the revelation of the divine Will. Whatever is outward in worship must come as a direct result of what is inward—otherwise, it will be form without power. There must first be withdrawal to the source of power and then a return with power. This alternation between withdrawal and return is never so sharp and complete that one state is entirely given up when the other is realized. As spiritual life progresses it may be that the two gradually merge until in the lives of those who are most advanced the two become one.

Friends have never opposed activity, but they have opposed what they used to call "creaturely activity," that is, uninspired activity,

activity which is not based on divine motivation. Creaturely activity is the performance of a form, or ritual, which is not at the time it is performed the sincere expression of an inward state, or it is an act of service to humanity which is not at the time it is performed the result of a genuine concern.

The history of Christian mysticism, and particularly of Oriental mysticism, shows that supreme emphasis is sometimes placed on a wholly negative withdrawal in which there is no temptation to become absorbed in the outer world. The hermit retired to a cave. He possessed no worldly goods, no family, few, if any, pleasures of the body. Sometimes the flesh was mortified to keep it in subjection. On the assumption that contemplation of the Eternal Reality behind and sustaining this temporal world is the highest possible human experience, everything became subordinated to that. Nothing else was deemed of consequence.

There are some resemblances between Quakerism and this more extreme form of negative mysticism. The Quakers believe in withdrawal to obtain an experience of God. They also believe that this experience, being the highest of all human experiences, has value in itself independent of any results in terms of action or transformation of character. To evaluate it as a means to something beyond itself would be to subordinate the higher to the lower. The modem tendency to estimate everything in pragmatic terms, that is, in terms of results rather than of intrinsic worth, is not characteristic of essential Quakerism. This nonpragmatic attitude applies not only to the supreme religious experience, but also to all acts performed because they are felt to be good. The results both of worship and of social activity are in the hands of God. Only God can know what these results will be in the whole course of time.

Yet the history of the Society of Friends shows that acceptance of the principle of withdrawal in worship has not resulted in any attempt at a final or complete withdrawal. The negative journey to the Light was invariably followed by the positive journey to the

needy, but good world. The Light is God in His capacity as
Creator and Redeemer, as is suggested in the first chapter of John's
Gospel. To live in the Light is to become God's agent in the process of creation and redemption. But the Light is also Substance
as contrasted with shadow, Reality as contrasted with deceit, Unity
as contrasted with multiplicity, Peace as contrasted with strife, the
Eternal as contrasted with the temporal. To live in the Light is to
deny the world. Here Quakerism agrees with the negative mystics.
But Quakerism is both world-denying and world-affirming:
world-denying in order to seek God, the ultimate Life, Truth and
Love at the basis of all existence; and world-affirming in its return
to active life through the creative power of God the Person, Christ
the Word, to enter into the process of redemption by which the
world is reconciled with God. There must be fruits of the Spirit
and these are, as Paul enumerates them, "love, joy, peace,
patience, kindness, goodness, faithfulness, gentleness, self-control"
(Gal. 5:22).

The negative road implies a sharp dualism between God and
the world. God is first felt to be transcendent, separated from the
world, wholly-other than man. But on further experience, this is
found to be but an incomplete view. The world is not separated
from God, but estranged from Him by evil. Estrangement implies
continuing kinship, like that between the prodigal son and his
father. Estrangement is never complete separation. God can perhaps be found only by man's withdrawing from the world, but the
worshiper must take the positive road back to the world fulfilling
his responsibility as a child of God in order that, through him, the
world may be reconciled to God. But the words "through him" do
not mean that man accomplishes this entirely in his own strength.
He achieves it in so far as he is helped by the wisdom and power of
Christ within, "the Power of God and the Wisdom of God" (I Cor.
1:24). This is atonement, the reconciliation of God and His world.
"God was in Christ reconciling the world to Himself," and to man

God has given this ministry of reconciliation (II Cor. 5:19). This is vicarious suffering, suffering by one person in behalf of another. The worshiper, in returning to the world, must take upon himself the burden of the world's sufferings. This is also Incarnation. In re-entering the world, man, in so far as he is filled with the spirit of Christ, must seek to incarnate Christ's spirit.

The leading Quakers have generally been fathers and mothers, often of large families, supporting themselves by a variety of occupations. There is no record of a recluse among them. They were frequently engaged in long journeys, visiting meetings and families and preaching to Quaker and non-Quaker gatherings. Barclay comments on this characteristic:

> God hath . . . produced effectually in many that mortification and abstraction from the love and cares of this world who daily are conversing (conducting themselves) in this world, but inwardly redeemed out of it, both in wedlock and in their lawful employments, which was judged only could be obtained by such as were shut up in cloisters and monasteries.[1]

The following passage from William Penn illustrates how the negative, quietistic way qualifies the worshiper for a life of service:

> When you come to your meetings . . . what do you do? Do you then gather together bodily only, and kindle a fire, compassing yourselves about with the sparks of your own kindling, and so please yourselves, and walk in the "Light of your own fire, and in the sparks which you have kindled" . . . ? Or rather, do you sit down in True Silence, resting from your own Will and Workings, and waiting upon the Lord, with your minds fixed in that Light wherewith Christ has enlightened you, until the Lord breathes life in you, refresheth you, and prepares you, and your spirits

and souls, to make you fit for his service, that you may
offer unto him a pure and spiritual sacrifice?[2]

Both the passive and the active phases of worship are again and
again illustrated in the Bible. In the Old Testament the command,
"Be still and know that I am God" (Ps. 46:10), is balanced by,
"Son of man, stand upon thy feet and I will speak unto thee"
(Ezek. 2:1). And in the New Testament Christ not only says, "My
peace I give unto you" (John 14:27), but also, "I have not come to
bring peace, but a sword" (Matt. 10:34).

The condition of being inwardly detached from the world,
yet outwardly engaged in its activities, has led to many misunder-
standings. The Quakers from about 1700 to 1850, particularly those
of the eighteenth century, have been frequently spoken of as
quietists. Quietism is the doctrine that every self-centered trait or
activity must be suppressed or quieted in order that the divine
may find unopposed entrance to the soul. "God is most where
man is least," is Whittier's sympathetic expression of this attitude
in his poem, "The Meeting." For the quietist, the search for God
begins in removing obstructions, such as self-will and worldly desires, greed, pride and lust, so that the inner room may be ready
for the divine guest if He should enter. This is not the extreme
form of negative mysticism which eliminates the soul. The room is
the human soul. The soul is waiting expectantly for God. "Soul"
is used here rather than "mind" because mind implies thought,
and the whole inner man, the psyche or soul, possesses feelings,
intuitions and sensations as well as thoughts. The objective of Christianity is to regenerate the soul, not to eliminate it.

As thus interpreted, the application of the term "Quietism" to
the Society of Friends is not without some justification. Much
Quaker preaching and writing emphasized removing all that was
worldly, temporal and external in order that the soul might be
open to the inner world, and, to use George Fox's words, "Stand

still in the Light" (Ep. 10, 1652). The following passage from a sermon of Elias Hicks illustrates the kind of guidance along this negative road which is sometimes offered in a Quaker meeting:

> I felt nothing when I came into this meeting, nor had I a desire after anything but to center down into abasement and nothingness; and in this situation I remained for a while, till I found something was stirring and rising in my spirit. And this was what I labored after . . . to be empty, to know nothing, to call for nothing, and to desire to do nothing.[3]

It is important not to misunderstand such "emptiness." Elias Hicks was a farmer with a wife and children. He was engaged in an active life, both in the ministry and in social reforms, including the antislavery movement. Yet he realized that complete self-surrender to whatever God might reveal within him was the true basis of divinely motivated activity as contrasted with "creaturely activity." The self-centered will must be given up if God is to become active in and through a human life.

This surrender of human claims upon the will in order that the will may be centered in God is not generally accompanied by a great emotional upheaval such as that which takes place in a revival meeting. To wait, free from the heat of passion and desire, expectantly, silently in the Light is the normal experience. George Fox advises in his letters, "Dwell in the Cool, Sweet, Holy Power of God" (Ep. 131). "Dwell in the Endless Power of the Lord . . . that hath the Wisdom which is sweet and cool and pure" (Ep. 242). "Be still and cool in thy own mind and spirit" (*Journal,* I, 432). Such an experience may be accompanied by deep feeling, but not often by emotional outbursts which frequently have their source in powerful self-interest, sometimes in the fear of eternal punishment. Violent reactions tend to have few permanent results. Friends have usually heeded the words of the prophet, "In returning and rest shall ye be saved, in quietness and in confidence shall be your strength" (Isa. 30:15). "He that believeth shall not make haste" (literally, "shall not fuss") (Isa. 28:16).

"The Society of Friends," says Evelyn Underhill, "has produced no great contemplative."[4] This is true if, by a great contemplative, we mean a person primarily engaged in contemplation. The Quakers set aside regular times for contemplation, both individual retirement and public meetings, but contemplation has always been for them the inner side of a complete action, which to be whole must represent perfect balance of inner and outer. Real experience of the divine Presence had the result of sensitizing the conscience so that the worshiper could rise from quiet waiting with the feeling that a new and sometimes very difficult task had been laid upon him.

Without a deep awareness of the divine Spirit by which the world is united from within, social reformers can only prescribe external remedies. Modern society is disintegrating because the sense of an inner, uniting Life has been lost. We exist in a world of multiplicity and our unity in that world has become that of a mechanical aggregate produced by forces acting upon us externally. "If a man does not abide in me, he is cast forth as a branch and withers" (John 15:6). Only worship can restore that sense of inner unity which makes an organic social order possible.

The word "pure" was formerly much used by Friends to designate the Inward Light, Life and Power, cleared of all accidental or conventional additions. John Woolman, one of the greatest of all quietists and social reformers, calls the Light "Pure Wisdom," a designation probably derived from a verse in the Epistle of James.

The significance of this negative word "pure" as used by Woolman is well illustrated in the following passage:

> There is a principle which is pure, placed in the human mind, which in different places and ages hath had differ-

ent names, it is however pure and proceeds from God. It is deep and inward, confined to no forms of religion nor excluded from any, where the heart stands in perfect sincerity. In whomsoever this takes root and grows, of what nation so ever, they become brethren, in the best sense of the expression. Using ourselves to take ways which appear most easy to us, when inconsistent with that Purity which is without beginning, we thereby set up a government of our own and deny obedience to Him whose service is true liberty.[5]

From this we see the connection between the Pure Principle, free of worldly taint, and social action. The Pure Principle is "deep and inward," yet it produces brotherhood. It is not excluded from any heart standing in perfect sincerity. Its purity consists in the removal of insincere and easy ways which arise out of a "government of our own," that is, egoism or self-centeredness. Woolman connects insincerity and selfishness. The true self is that which is in union with God, not the false, self-centered ego. The service of God is "true liberty," for liberty results from detachment from bondage to the world. It is an inward liberty, which man can feel even in prison, not a physical, outward liberty.

As we read further in Woolman's essay, we find that purity consists also in the removal of all that is simply conventional. Speaking of the children of slaveowners, he says:

The customs of their parents, their neighbors and the people with whom they converse working upon their minds and they from thence conceiving ideas of things and modes of conduct, the entrance into their hearts becomes in a great measure shut up against the gentle movings of uncreated Purity.[6]

By this he means that the conventional view that slavery is admissible stands in the way of the movings of that Principle which, when purified of conventionality, would cause a realization that slavery is evil.

The negative way, therefore, consists in the removal of all that is insincere, false, egocentric and conventional. It opens the way for a corresponding effort to face directly and freshly the naked Truth purified of all that is contrary to it. To wait upon the Lord is such an exercise and it is easy to see why it resulted in social pioneering. The conventional, the insincere, the self-centered will seldom desire a change for the better. Only the will which "centers down" to the deeper, more genuine, more universal Life which unites us from within, can feel that Truth which is not yet embodied in the world of flesh. To know the central Unity at the heart of existence is to seek to embody it in a greater degree of human brotherhood. Fox writes:

> Mind that which is pure in one another which joins you together, for nothing will join or make fit but what is pure, nor unite nor build but what is pure. [Ep. 13, 1652]

The absence of the outward sacraments in a Friends meeting for worship is one evidence of the negative path. There is nothing in Quaker theory which would categorically exclude such rites as baptism and communion, provided these were, when experienced, genuine outward expressions of real and holy inward states. But any form which becomes a routine, the details of which are prescribed in advance, inevitably fails to embody what it purports to represent. The inward state is not within man's control. He cannot, therefore, predict the time and form of its outward expression. Any act is sacramental which is a sincere, genuine outward evidence of inward grace. In this sense sacraments are innumerable, as they were in the old religions. In lives of great saintliness every act may become sacramental.

The most sacramental chapter in the New Testament is the sixth chapter of John's Gospel, in which Jesus says, " . . . unless you eat the flesh of the Son of Man and drink his blood, you have no life in you; he who eats my flesh and drinks my blood has eternal life" (John 6:53, 54). These words were uttered when the loaves and fishes had miraculously fed the five thousand. They had no reference to the bread and wine of the sacramental ritual. Perhaps in this way Jesus meant to indicate that every meal may be sacramental. He carefully distinguishes between material bread and "the true bread from heaven," the spirit of the living Christ.

The Society of Friends uses the words "baptism" and "communion" to express the experience of Christ's presence and ministration in worship. As John the Baptist said, "I have baptized you with water, but He will baptize you with the Holy Spirit" (Mark 1:8; John 1:33). Worship reaches its goal when the worshiper feels the baptism of the Spirit. Communion occurs when the worshiper communes with God and with his fellow worshipers. The Last Supper was commemorated by the early Church in the form of a common meal or feast of love together (I. Cor. 11), and this, Barclay says, "we shall not condemn."[7] The early Quaker scholars were aware of the gradual stages by which the Christian priesthood developed so that certain persons were ordained as solely qualified to administer the sacraments. Carrying the Protestant doctrine of the priesthood of all believers to its logical conclusion, the Quakers did away with the outward observance of sacraments.

The form of remembrance of the Last Supper when Jesus discoursed chiefly of love and unity (John 13-17) has, through a strange misfortune, become a point of disunity among Christian societies. In John's Gospel Jesus recommends that his disciples wash one another's feet. If the spirit of this sacrament were carried out, the commemoration of the Supper would unite, not divide.

Rudolf Otto finds in the silence of a Friends meeting a threefold character, the numinous silence of sacrament, the silence of waiting and the silence of union or fellowship.[8] In the silence of sacrament

> . . . what was previously only possessed in insufficiency, only longed for, now comes upon the scene in living actuality, the experience of the transcendent in gracious, intimate presence, the Lord's visitation of his people. . . . Such a silence is therefore a sacramental silence. It was found in the forms of worship of ancient Israel, and is found today in the Roman Mass, in the moment of transubstantiation.

The silence of waiting "passes over naturally into the Sacramental silence."

> When the Quakers assemble for a quiet time together, this is first and foremost a time of waiting and it has in this sense a double value. It means our submergence, i.e., inward concentration and detachment, from manifold outward distractions; but this again has value as a preparation of the soul to become the pencil of the unearthly writer, the bent bow of the heavenly archer, the tuned lyre of the divine musician. This silence is, then, primarily not so much a dumbness in the presence of Deity, as an awaiting His coming in expectation of the Spirit and its message.

Otto points out what he calls the "numinous" quality of silent worship. He speaks of the sense of "creatureliness" before the power and holiness of the Living God, the feeling of awe and wonder when the worshiper is bowed in contrition in the divine Presence. When Woolman writes, "My mind was covered with an awefulness," he here refers to the numinous quality of silent withdrawal from our familiar world lit by its earthly light to that world illumined by the divine Light. Worship brings us to the frontier of thought. Beyond is the dim expanse, infinite and enfolded in mystery. There lies the source and destiny of our being. But awe and wonder will not take us far. As a great devotional writer tells us, only love can pierce the dark cloud of unknowing. When awe and wonder combine with love, the result is reverence, and reverence is the first step to worship.

The Way of Worship

In the vast sum of Quaker literature there is very little which can be used as a guide in silent worship. This is to be expected. The true Guide is the Spirit which, like the wind, bloweth where it listeth. Here Quakerism differs radically from Catholicism. Silent prayer, meditation or contemplation, to use some of the words applied to that form of spiritual exercise which is carried on without words or ritual, is often carefully guided in Catholic practice by a spiritual director. The director assigns exercises which he deems appropriate to the particular stage of progress reached by the soul committed to his care. Different systems are used by different religious orders. One system, the Ignatian, involves first an exercise of memory, then an exercise of understanding, and finally an exercise of will, in which an oblation or offering is made involving sacrifice.

The great Catholic devotional books offer valuable suggestions to persons engaged in the practice of interior prayer and silent worship, provided they are not followed slavishly. Barclay twice quotes with sympathy one of the best of these, the Sancta Sofia or *Holy Wisdom*.[9] He also quotes an epistle of St. Bernard. In referring to books written by Catholic mystics, he says that Quakers are less withdrawn from the world than they. The works of Madame Guyon, Fénelon and Molinos, valuable guides in the life of prayer, could at one time be found in almost every Quaker library.

Common to many of these instructions is a recognition that there are four principal stages in prayer: mental prayer, affective prayer, acquired contemplation and infused contemplation or the mystic union of the human soul with the divine. Elaborate treatises on the subject divide these into substages. For example, in Poulain's treatise on *The Graces of Interior Prayer,* a system much influenced by St. Teresa of Avila, there are four degrees of intensity of the mystic union of the soul with God, ending in Spiritual Marriage which permits life to be lived on the higher and lower levels simultaneously and continuously.

Mental prayer, the first of the four main stages, consists, in its simplest form, of the silent repetition of a prayer which has been memorized—perhaps a short prayer repeated over and over like a refrain. This is possible for anyone, however low his spiritual state. After that he may be able to use his own words, thoughts or imaginations. He may be asked to concentrate on some holy subject, for example the seven virtues as contrasted with the seven sins, the Beatitudes or the Ten Commandments. Or he may be asked to imagine as vividly as he can some event in the life of Christ or carry on an imaginary conversation with some holy person. The value of the exercise will depend to some extent on the director's ability to sense particular needs.

From mental prayer the worshiper may be able to go on to affective prayer, a prayer of the heart without words. Here feeling is more prominent than idea, but some idea, such as love, gratitude, submission, contrition may be made the exclusive center of attention. This is called recollection, the re-collection of the scattered fragments of the soul into one focus of concentration at the point of deepest feeling. The next stage, acquired contemplation, is the prayer of simple regard, utter simplicity. Here truth is no longer sought for, but enjoyed by a single direct glance of the soul. The emotions of the preceding stage are no longer felt, but there is still a need to exercise the will. The boat must be propelled by oars, but not so strongly as before because the harbor is near. The next and final stage, infused contemplation or the mystic union of the soul with God, is not characterized by any feeling of human

effort. It is a pure, undeserved gift of divine grace. Since its essence is love, it cannot be produced by an act of will. Complete
resignation of the surface-will has occurred. There is no consciousness of the self as distinguished from the divine object of its love.
Attention is quiet and effortless. Distractions have vanished. There
is a sense of peace and security for the incomplete life is enfolded
in the complete Life. The human and the divine have flowed into
each other and become one.

It is difficult to summarize what is sometimes called "The
Mystical Theology." The stages outlined above are not foreign to
Quaker experience except for the fact that they are prescribed.
Those most helped by this pattern would agree that to divide the
spiritual ascent of the soul into distinguishable stages is artificial,
though from an intellectual standpoint it may have the same advantage as the analysis of a living organism in parts. The stages
overlap. They may occur in a different order. That the feeling of
oneness with God through love may descend without preparation
as uncontrollably as rain from heaven, is evident from many
spiritual autobiographies. For different temperaments the spiritual
journey proceeds on different paths. What others might call "prayer"
or "meditation" Friends would tend to speak of as "waiting upon
the Lord" or worship. Daniel Wheeler says, "the soul that watches
cannot long be without praying, although but in the language of a
sigh."[10] Most important of all, the negative path, characterized by
simplicity, detachment and inner unity, must lead by the positive
path back to the complex world of strife and disunity in order to
make available what has been found in the silence.

Friends have hesitated to analyze or even to put into words the
ineffable experience of worship. Nevertheless, much which is
helpful in the meeting can be learned from books of devotion.
The worshiper sits down in silence. He seeks to compose his
wandering thoughts. How shall he begin in order that his worship
may not become a dreamy reverie? Perhaps by repeating a prayer,

or a verse of scripture or poetry. As he progresses, he may be able to offer a prayer of his own which merges with thoughts which have to do with the routine problems of his daily life. He must not fear to express selfish desires, for, above all, he must be sincere. He may then find that these desires, when expressed before God, assume a different form, proportion and direction. After a time something may come before his mind, a past event, a future possibility, a saying or occurrence in the Bible or elsewhere on which his attention becomes fixed. This focus of attention is now seen, not in a secular, but in a religious context. It is viewed in its eternal rather than its temporal aspect.

The will and feelings of the worshiper become stirred as the thought before him glows with life and power. He no longer feels that he himself is searching, but that he is being searched through. There is a growing sense of divine Presence. Truth is not thought about, but perceived and enjoyed. It may be that a point is reached at which the worshiper finds that he must communicate to the meeting what has come to him. Or, he may resolve to act at some time in the future in accordance with the Light which he has received. If he waits quietly and expectantly with the windows of his soul open to whatever Light may shine, he may lose all sense of separate existence and find himself aware only of the greater Life on which his own is based. The sense of union with God may come unexpectedly. This occurs more often than is generally supposed, for it is frequently not recognized for what it is. Such complete self-forgetfulness cannot easily be reproduced in memory. There is the lower self-forgetfulness of sleep which cannot be remembered at all, and there is, at the opposite pole, the higher self-forgetfulness in which every faculty of the soul is intensely awake, with the result that consciousness is widened to include that which is beyond thought and memory.

In this realm we must depend on symbols and figures of speech. These are inadequate though probably more intelligible than philosophical abstractions. We can either speak of the spiritual journey upward or of the need to pierce the depths. These metaphors have the same meaning. A common advice to Friends in meeting is to "center down" or "dig deep." There are ideas on the surface of our minds by which we adjust ourselves to our external environment, and there are feelings deep within by which we become attuned to our spiritual environment. In worship we center our attention on that which is deeper than discursive thought; that by which we distinguish between good and evil and know what is for us the will of God. The advice to "dig deep" refers to the parable of Jesus about the two houses, one built on sand, the other on the rock. The rock was reached by digging deep (Luke 6:48) in order to find a truth which cannot be shaken by surface storms.

The experience of the great mystics may help worshipers today. These mystics sometimes spoke of three steps called purgation, illumination and union. In the first, purgation, man seeks to remove all that is self-centered and greedy for power and possessions. In the second, illumination, man becomes aware of the truth imparted by ideas or memories which come before him as he waits in silence. And in the third, which is union, the worshiper loses the sense of separation from God and becomes aware of the Spring of Eternal Life at the basis of all existence. These three may be taken in any order, but are generally taken in the order given. Often the initial stage in worship is purgation through self-examination by which one becomes aware of that which must be removed if he is to attain the goal. As St. Teresa says, self-examination may be carried too far.

> It is a great grace of God to practice self-examination, but too much is as bad as too little, as they say, believe me by God's help, we shall advance more by contemplating His Divinity than by keeping our eyes fixed on ourselves.[11]

George Fox writes:

> Stand still in that which is Pure after ye see yourselves.
> [Ep. 10, 1652]

The first function of the Light is to reveal sin, to show what obstacles cast a dark shadow in the way.

> Wait upon God in that which is pure, in your measure, and stand still in it every one, to see your Saviour, to make you free from that which the light doth discover to you to be evil. [Ep. 16, 1652]

This evil, so discovered, is temptation and trouble.

> When temptations and troubles appear, sink down in that which is pure and all will be hushed and fly away.... Stand still in that Power which brings peace. [Ep. 10, 1652]

When such evils have been removed, the Light will shine more clearly to reveal Truth. This is illumination. It may dawn when a remembered fact or saying glows with new relevance and meaning.

Above illumination is the experience of union. The mystics generally think of this only as union with God, but the Quakers, being more concerned with the world around them than were many of the great mystics, think of it also as union with their fellow men. The sense of union with God and the sense of union with our neighbors are so closely related that one is best realized when felt in conjunction with the other. Fox writes:

> All Friends mind that which is Eternal which gathers your Hearts together up to the Lord and lets you see that ye are written in one another's Heart. [Ep. 24, 1653]

Not only does the Light lead to unity, but unity leads to the Light. He whose soul is irradiated by the Light of Christ is in union with God and his fellows.

This sense of union with our fellow men is not an unusual type of experience. An analogy can be drawn with a player on an athletic team who begins by playing as an individual, self-consciously calculating each move he makes. At some moment a change occurs. He becomes an integral part of the team, moving with it, without thought of self. He is now like a cell in a living organism. He unconsciously wills according to the will of the whole.

In speaking of being at one with God and our fellow men we are touching upon a kind of experience which belongs to our everyday lives. Of all such daily experiences worship is the highest and most inclusive. Progress in worship is progress in simplicity and sincerity. We find ourselves at first in a world of multiplicity and contending forces. Our souls become simplified by attention to a single, absorbing truth, which leads us up to God. The worshiper may arrive at meeting with his mind in a turmoil. Fox's admonition, "Take heed of being hurried with many thoughts, but live in that which goes over them all" (Ep. 95, 1655), is not easy to carry out at once. It takes time for the mind to settle. Fox does not tell us to eliminate the many thoughts, but to live in that which goes over them. The writer of *The Cloud of Unknowing* suggests in regard to intrusive thoughts that we "look over their shoulders." True worship consists not in the absence of the lower, but in the presence of the higher. We must not tear out an important part of our mental structure. "Nothing in the spiritual life can be fruitfully accomplished by violence," says Bede Frost.[12] We may accept the lower, and at the same time concentrate attention on the higher. The lower will not be forced out, but it may recede into the background. At the frontier of consciousness there may then emerge the higher world of the Spirit which will mingle with and uplift the lower.

As we climb a mountain, we come nearer to other climbers and finally we find ourselves together with them at the top. The word "together" does not imply intellectual agreement, but spiritual unity, deep and inward, which sometimes arises unexpectedly in a group. Samuel Fothergill, one of the most eloquent of Quaker ministers, writes of the growth of unity out of meditation when he speaks of the

> . . . cool moments of sedate meditation when the mind is loosened from lower connections . . . reaching onwards to the immutable union and inseparable fellowship of the Lord's family.[13]

Aelfrida Tillyard writes:

> The spark of spiritual apprehension, half dormant in the heart of the isolated believer, is kindled into flame by contact with the gathered fire of many souls together.[14]

And Barclay describes as follows the effect of group meditation:

> As iron sharpeneth iron, the seeing of the faces one of another when both are inwardly gathered into the life, giveth occasion for the life secretly to rise and pass from vessel to vessel. And as many candles lighted and put in one place do greatly augment the light and make it more to shine forth, so when many are gathered together into the same life, there is more of the glory of God and his power appears, to the refreshment of each individual; for that he partakes not only of the light and life raised in himself, but in all the rest.[15]

Worship Outside the Meeting House

Although collective silent worship is a unique and important characteristic of Quakerism, the Quakers have not neglected solitary worship, or, as they sometimes call it, "a period of solemn retirement." William Penn writes in his introduction to Penington's works:

He became the wonder of his kindred and familiars for his awful life and serious and frequent retirements declining all company that might interrupt his meditations.

Penn also writes in his *Advice to His Children:*

. . . as you have intervals from your lawful occasions, delight to step Home, within yourselves, I mean, and commune with your own hearts, and be still; . . . This will bear you up against all temptations, and carry you sweetly and evenly through your day's business, supporting you under disappointments, and moderating your satisfaction in success and prosperity.[16]

A common entry in the *Journal* of Job Scott, a schoolteacher, is "Sat in silence, then to school." He writes:

I do not believe a man can go aside and sit down alone, to make the experiment, merely to see what the consequence of sitting in silence will be, without a real hunger and heart-felt travail; and therein be favored with the flowings of the holy oil.[17]

Of Daniel Wheeler, the Quaker who taught agriculture to the Russians, it was written:

He one day took me to a small field, nearly surrounded by trees on the south side of his house, where he told me he was accustomed to retire alone at an early hour in the morning and late in the evening and often at noon when at home.[18]

But it was not always at home that such retirement took place. It was even more needed as a source of spiritual strength on a religious journey, though sometimes it was more difficult to achieve. Daniel Wheeler writes:

Having no opportunity of sitting down in the cabin, I held my sitting upon deck, and, though I met with many interruptions, yet I was favored with settlement of mind to a good degree.[19]

Two other travelers to Russia found help in this way:

Dear Allen [William Allen] and myself sat down together as usual to wait upon the Lord. This has been our daily practice since we left England, and mostly twice a day.[20]

Dr. John Rutty found daily retirement a necessary antidote to devoting too much thought to his medical studies:

Instituted an hour's retirement every evening as a check to the inordinate study of nature,[21]

To take an example from the *Journal* of a Friend of today we find James Henderson (1855-1942) saying:

Awoke early next morning . . . then took a walk up a hill to a fine grove where I had some private devotion, after which I felt more calm and composed.[22]

Such times were useful in preparing for the meeting. Margaret Lucas writes:

In respect to silent meetings, my spiritual exercises at home had taught me how to improve by them.[23]

Spiritual exercises, whether of daily silent waiting in worship and prayer, or in regular reading of the Bible or other religious literature, help in making the meeting for worship mean what it should mean. If the mind all through the week is occupied with secular affairs, it is not easy, when the meeting for worship begins, to enter into the life of the spirit in the time allotted.

The Quakers have been criticized as inconsistent in appointing a particular time for the public meeting to convene. Why not let the meeting begin when the Spirit directs? The reply to this is that worship does not begin when the meeting begins, but only when the worshiper himself is enabled by the Spirit to begin his worship. But meetings for worship do sometimes begin unpredictably. The Quaker *Journals* contain references to many such occasions; they were called "opportunities." A group would be sitting in the living room of a home or around the dinner table. One member might be discovered to be sitting in silence with a look of solemnity on his face. The whole group would gradually become silent. After a time, the person whose attitude of worship had initiated the meeting would, in all probability, convey a message which he had on his mind. A period of silence would ensue, after which the general conversation would be resumed. Richard Jordan records a number of such "opportunities":

> In the evening . . . after a time of pleasant conversation, being drawn into stillness, I was opened in testimony and it proved a blessed opportunity like the distilling of the precious dew of heaven upon our spirits.[24]

> In the evening, several friends coming to see us after a time we were drawn into silence, and our gracious Master was pleased to favor us, as with a celestial shower, to the comfort and refreshment of our souls.[25]

In his poem "The Pennsylvania Pilgrim," Whittier describes such an "opportunity":

> There sometimes silence (it were hard to tell
> Who owned it first) upon the circle fell,
> Hushed Anna's busy wheel, and laid its spell
> On the black boy who grimaced by the hearth,

To solemnize his shining face of mirth;
Only the old clock ticked amidst the dearth
Of sound; nor eye was raised nor hand was stirred
In that soul-sabbath, till at last some word
Of tender counsel or low prayer was heard.

A regular daily period of family worship, beginning with a reading from the Bible, was, until recently, a practice in almost every Quaker home and is still the subject of a question listed in the Queries by which Friends annually put themselves through a process of self-examination.*

Friends who traveled, sometimes for several years at a stretch, with a concern to visit other meetings than their own, generally visited also the families which made up the meetings. When the visitor or visitors arrived—there were usually two together—the family assembled and a solemn meeting for worship was held. The spoken word was sometimes directed to the particular state of some member of the family. Often, to the astonishment of all, the speaker seemed aware of secret thoughts and actions of the individual. That silent worship cultivates a high degree of sensitivity to the condition of other persons is well illustrated by many instances recorded in the Quaker *Journals*.[26]

The Friends have throughout their history been aware that there is a form of prayer "which can be exercised at all times," "a lamp continually lighted before the throne of God." These two phrases are taken from the latest edition of *A Guide to True Peace*, a compilation[27] made from the writings of Fénelon, Guyon and Molinos widely used by Friends during the nineteenth century.

As a young girl, Mary Proud, later the wife of Isaac Penington, took the first of a series of steps which led her to the Quaker position by reflecting on the text, "Pray without ceasing." This,

*See Appendix I, Query 10.

she realized, could not refer to formal prayers out of a book, the only kind she then knew. That a person can live continually in a state of prayer, although not generally conscious of it, was pointed out by Robert Barclay. This he calls "inward prayer" to distinguish it from a more deliberate, conscious effort.

> Inward prayer is that secret turning of the mind towards God, whereby, being secretly touched and awakened by the light of Christ in the conscience, and so bowed down under the sense of its iniquities, unworthiness and misery, it looks up to God, and joining with the secret shinings of the seed of God, it breathes towards Him and is constantly breathing forth some secret desires and aspirations towards him. It is in this sense that we are so frequently in scripture commanded to pray continually.[28]

Such a state of continuous prayer is the goal, but seldom the attainment, of the Christian life.

Notes

1. Robert Barclay, *Apology,* p. 518.

2. William Penn, *A Tender Visitation. Works,* 1771, p. 441.

3. Hicks, Elias, *The Quaker,* I, 1827, p. 47.

4. Evelyn Underhill, *Worship,* 1937, p. 313.

5. John Woolman, "Considerations on the Keeping of Negroes," *Works,* 1774, p. 325.

6. Woolman, "Considerations," p. 326.

7. Barclay, *Apology,* p. 475.

8. Otto Rudolf, *The Idea of the Holy*, pp. 216-20.

9. Barclay, *Apology*, p. 380.

10. Daniel Wheeler, *Memoirs*, London, 1842, p. 158.

11. St. Teresa, *Interior Castle*, revised and annotated by Rev. Prior Simmerman, O.C.D., 1921, I, 2.

12. Bede Frost, *The Art of Mental Prayer*, p. 140.

13. Samuel Fothergill, *Memoirs and Letters*, p. 387.

14. Aelfrida Tillyard, *Spiritual Exercises*, p. 160.

15. Barclay, *Apology*, p. 383.

16. William Penn, *Works*, 1771, p. 850.

17. Job Scott, *Journal*, p. 93.

18. David Wheeler, *Memoirs*, London, 1842, p. 47.

19. Wheeler, *Memoirs*, p. 64.

20. Stephen Grellet, *Journal*, I, 388.

21. John Rutty, extracts from *The Spiritual Diary*, 1840, p. 13.

22. James Henderson, *Journal*, 1944, p. 126.

23. Margaret Lucas, *Journal*, p. 80.

24. Richard Jordan, *Journal*, 1829, p. 32.

25. Jordan, *Journal*, p. 35.

26. See, for example, Elizabeth Ellison Newport, *Memoirs*, compiled by Ann A. Townsend, 1878, pp. 39, 43, 47, 49, 62. She exhibited remarkable powers of intuition in her ministry.

27. Fénelon, Guyon, and Molinas, *A Guide to True Peace*, 1948.

28. Barclay, *Apology*, p. 892.

CHAPTER V

Vocal Ministry

VOCAL MINISTRY IS AN IMPORTANT, but not an essential element in Quaker worship. Both theoretically and actually a meeting which worships in complete silence may be as valuable as one in which speaking occurs. "It was a heart tendering time, though there was not a word spoken amongst us," writes Richard Jordan in his *Journal.* Many such comments could be cited. A silent meeting is generally preferred to one in which speaking does not arise from an inspired source. But experience shows that meetings in which there is little or no vocal ministry for a length of time decline in membership and power. There are usually some members of a meeting who require no vocal aid or guidance in their worship, but there are others who are greatly in need of this help. Because the search for Truth and Life is a group search as well as an individual search, even those furthest along the way derive strength and encouragement from others in the meeting.

The author has participated in periods of meditation among the Zen sect of Buddhists in Japan. These gatherings, which included many persons arranged in orderly rows in a meditation hall, were held in complete silence. They seemed much like Friends meetings, but an important difference was felt. There was no communication. Each individual was engaged in a solitary search for truth and reality. But the meditator might sometimes leave the hall and seek a brief interview with his *roshi* or teacher, who would offer special guidance. The meditator would then return to his meditation. This teacher supplied, in a way very different from the Quaker way, the need for ministry.

In still another manner the spiritual director in the Catholic Church offers help and guidance to the solitary seeker silently engaged in interior spiritual exercise.

The minister among Friends differs from the Zen instructor and the Catholic director. He speaks as the immediate mouthpiece of the group of worshipers whose insight into Truth has been brought to utterance by the Holy Spirit, the Presence in the midst. It is as if the general spiritual potential of the meeting increased until at some particular point it crossed the boundary from silence to speech, as a spark passes from one pole to another when the electric potential is sufficiently high. The first person singular pronoun is seldom heard in Quaker ministry, nor does the speaker declare his own experience except as his experience may illustrate a more general truth. As Charles Lamb said of one whom he heard ministering in a Quaker meeting, "He seemed not to speak but to be spoken from."

The theory of the Quaker ministry is simple. As the worshipers sit together in silence to wait upon the Lord, anyone among them may find arising in his consciousness a message which he feels is intended for more than himself alone. It is then his obligation to deliver that message and to cease speaking when he has delivered it. He must learn to recognize the unique sense of urgency which is evidence of a divine requirement. If a thought comes to him with peculiar life and power, he may be justified in assuming that this is a sign from God to speak. He may sometimes be mistaken. There is no sure test of divine guidance in this or any other undertaking. If, however, through prayer and humble waiting he has become sensitive to the "still, small voice," he will be increasingly enabled to recognize a call when it comes. He will learn to recognize and reject the wish to speak which comes from a different source, however disguised, such as an inclination to exhibit his own powers or knowledge or simply a lack of inhibition. Usually he knows quite well whether what is on his mind will help the meeting or not. Often a suggestion is provided from the true Source which is intended, not for the meeting as a whole, but to be kept by the recipient, as Isaac Penington cautions, "for bread at home."

In the Quaker *Journals* we frequently read of the sense of burden and uneasiness which often precedes speaking. He who ministers does not wish to break the solemn silence. It may seem to him an evidence of pride that, by his own decision, he should take such a responsibility upon himself. But when he becomes aware that the responsibility is not solely his, but that of the divine Master who has called him, if he is faithful, he will yield to the requirement. Quaker *Journals* frequently mention the sense of complete peace which follows obedience to the call. But there is not always peace. Sometimes the most revered of Friends sit down with a sense of uneasiness and a feeling of having "outrun the guide." This was John Woolman's experience the first time that he spoke in a meeting for worship. It was a long time before he felt able to speak again. Not infrequently, mention is made of a sense of dryness and consequent pain felt by well-known Friends when they found themselves unable to speak to a large company assembled with the expectation of hearing them. "Sat in suffering silence" is an occasional entry in the *Journal* of Job Scott. Sometimes this lack of ability to speak seems justified. Richard Jordan records,

> I sat through it [the meeting] in silence, I believe to the great disappointment of many, but I was thankful in being preserved from gratifying the itching ears.[1]

The purpose of vocal ministry in a Quaker meeting is different from the purpose of preaching from a pulpit. The primary function of pulpit ministry is to teach by expounding the Scriptures and explaining the way of salvation for men. This the preacher exhorts his hearers to accept by an act of faith. The old-fashioned plan of salvation which concerns a future life is often replaced today by a plan of social salvation for this life.

A teaching ministry is not entirely absent from meetings of the Society of Friends, but in general, it is exercised upon occasions especially appointed for the purpose. When exercised by a speaker of genuine prophetic power, teaching may find an appropriate place in the solemn waiting upon the Lord. A more thorough-going instruction in religious history, theory and practice is needed in the Society of Friends, as it is elsewhere, but it fits the lecture platform better than the meeting for worship.

George Fox says that the object of Quaker ministry is "to bring people . . . to the end of all preaching."[2] Isaac Penington says, "The great work of the minister of Christ is to keep the conscience open to Christ."[3] Ministry may supply a subject for meditation which will focus wandering thoughts, but he who ministers must carefully avoid making his hearers dependent upon him.

In Catholic books giving instruction to spiritual directors there is frequent admonition that the director must not take too much on himself or give too explicit guidance. Rather he should seek to reach the Spirit of God within the person under his care. St. John of the Cross says:

> Let spiritual directors . . . remember that the Holy Ghost is the principal agent here, and the real guide of souls; that He never ceases to take care of them and never neglects any means by which they may profit and draw near to God as quickly as possible and in the best way. Let them remember that they are not the agents, but instruments only, to guide souls by the rule of faith and the law of God... Their aim should be, then, not to guide souls by a way of their own suitable to themselves, but to ascertain if they can, the way by which God Himself is guiding them.[4]

Such advice is equally applicable to speakers in a Quaker meeting. The minister is an instrument of that Spirit which is in his hearers as well as in himself. If he keeps close to the one Center, he can reach any person along a particular radius.

No rules can be laid down for Quaker ministry. The Spirit leads where it will. In general, the spoken word should be a simple affirmation of truth rather than an argumentative defense of it. The method of Jesus was to state a truth which the hearer could recognize as such without debate. Just as the artist offers his picture or the poet his poem to be accepted for what it is without reasons, so the speaker should offer his message, trusting that the Light in him will answer the Light in others. The life which flows from one person to another moves the will, but if the will is coerced by arguments, it moves, if it moves at all, without full consent.

An analytic ministry which dissects religious experience may be as destructive of life as is the dissection of a plant or an animal. As we know the life in our bodies by direct intuition without analysis, so we recognize the life of God in the soul. Analysis has its peculiar scientific value, but the Spirit which passes from one person to another as a flame leaps from one coal to another grasps truth in its wholeness as a living thing united within itself. Such an experience is like that which might occur in a society of ornithologists discussing the different kinds of birds if a real and unusual bird flew into the room.

Ministry in a Friends meeting should be spontaneous in the sense that no one comes to meeting either expecting to speak or expecting not to speak. To use a figure of Jeremiah, our religion should arise from a spring, not be drawn from a reservoir. The spoken message should well up freshly and genuinely from the life of the meeting. To change the figure, a seed may have been sown earlier to await the right conditions for germination. A concern which develops finally into a spoken message may arise in the mind at any time during routine engagements of daily life or during a time of private retirement for prayer and worship. It must then be allowed to mature and be reserved until there is a clear sense that the time has arrived to give it utterance.

A Friend of the eighteenth century named Mary England dreamed that when she dipped her pitcher into the spring and drew it out at once to carry it away, the water ran out, but when she held the pitcher in the spring long enough the water did not run out. By this she took warning not to act too quickly upon an urge to speak in meeting.

Since the vocal message is followed by silence, opportunity is given for the hearers to carry it further for themselves. The spoken word in a Friends meeting ought to be suggestive of more that might have been said, rather than being in itself exhaustive. It may even be to some extent shadowy. Spiritual truth cannot be sharply defined like scientific truth. It exists on the dim edge of the unexplored region beyond the horizon of self-conscious thought. The language of the Spirit is symbolic and its suggestions are not so much facts as signs which point beyond themselves to the unseen ground of all existence. So inarticulate sometimes is the voice of the Spirit that it can be expressed only by a sigh, or even by complete silence.

Speaking in a Quaker meeting may concern any subject, provided it be in a distinctly religious frame of reference. In mathematics what is a circle in one frame of reference may be an ellipse in another. Similarly, what appears one way in a secular setting may assume a very different form in a religious frame of reference. The difference between the religious and the secular, like the difference between beauty and ugliness or good and evil, is, perhaps, impossible to define, but most persons have the capacity to recognize it. The important question from a religious standpoint is not "what shall we do" but "what is the will of God for us."

For religious utterance moral platitudes are not as effective as a simple call to dwell in the Spirit of the Living Christ. He who lives in that Spirit will follow naturally the teachings of the Christ of history. If we sincerely experience the Presence of Christ in the Midst, every word will be in harmony with his spirit. Similarly, if we are in conversation with some person honored for his character and achievement, all that is said is in keeping with his nature. As someone has remarked, "We may beat about the bush but we do not beat about the Burning Bush."

That type of sermon which inspires fear because of the consequences of sin is not typical of Quaker preaching. It is the appreciation of good rather than the dread of evil which leads the soul in the way of perfection. Yet it was said of Stephen Grellet by William J. Allinson that his ministry was "solemn, close and alarming" as well as "persuasive, prophetic and encouraging."[5] The first function of the Light is to reveal sin and evil. None should hesitate to point out the dark shadow cast by obstructions to the Light.

A realization of the terrible reality of wickedness and the consequent feeling of humility and dependence is the first step toward regeneration. Without it there can be no beginning of the spiritual journey. But the soul must not remain in the abyss. The object of the meeting for worship is not exposure to darkness, but exposure to the Light which overcomes the darkness. Worshipers should accordingly be directed to the goal and to the Life of God in man's soul which alone will give power to reach it. It was such a ministry that George Fox exercised when he wrote to Cromwell's daughter, Lady Claypole, who was "sick and much troubled in mind":

> Whatever temptations, distractions, confusions the light doth make manifest and discover, do not look at these temptations, confusions, corruptions; but look at the Light which discovers them. . . . For looking down at sin and corruption and distraction ye are swallowed up in it but looking at the Light which discovers them, ye will see over them.
> [*Journal* 1, 488]

The highest vocal exercise in a meeting for worship is spoken prayer. The worshiper may discover that the spirit of prayer in a meeting is coming to utterance through him. He then becomes the mouthpiece of the group in prayer to God. Not "I" but "we" is the language of his supplication. Prayers for oneself are generally best offered in silence. To some persons prayer seems so private and intimate that audible petition is impossible. Others shrink from it for fear of insincerity or formalism. Yet nothing so effectively lays a covering over the meeting as the humble utterance of sincere prayer. Many are grateful for words which they themselves feel unable to utter.

To educated and uneducated, old and young, men and women, the call may come to yield to the requirement to speak in a meeting for worship. Three hundred years of Quaker history has made it clear that the gift of the ministry is not confined to any particular kind of person. There is no ordination other than evidence that a divine gift has been bestowed. George Fox's earliest "opening" taught him that it was not necessary to be trained at Oxford or Cambridge in order to be a minister. Some of the early Quaker preachers were highly educated, most of them were not. The same was true of the apostles and prophets of Biblical times. By no group were the first Friends more harshly treated than by university scholars at Oxford, Cambridge, Edinburgh and Aberdeen, who were angered by the low value that Friends placed on learning as a prerequisite for the ministry. When Friends were taunted that they could not read the Scriptures in the original languages they replied, as did Fox,

> . . . that the Word of God is the Original . . . and the Word is it which makes a Divine . . . and this is the Word that makes both men and women divine and brings them into the divine nature. [Ep. 249, 1667]

That Friends valued education as fitting men and women for the activities of life is shown by the schools which they set up and maintained. Though education might be a help in the spiritual life, it might also prove a hindrance and it is not an essential requirement for vocal ministry.

From the very beginning Quaker women shared the vocal ministry with men. To show that women could receive as genuine a call to this service as men, Friends had only to point to results. Barclay writes:

> God hath effectually in this day converted many souls by the ministry of women and by them also frequently comforted the souls of his children, which manifest experience puts the thing beyond all controversy.[6]

Paul's instruction that women should keep silent in the church (I Cor. 14:34) was read in the light of his instruction in the same epistle regarding the headdress of women when prophesying (I Cor. 11:5, 13). A text often used by Friends to defend their position on the ministry of women was taken from Peter's quotation of the prophet Joel delivered at Pentecost, "I will pour out my spirit upon all flesh and your sons and your daughters shall prophesy" (Acts 2:17).

> The inequality of men and women, Fox says, was a result of the Fall but "in the restoration by Christ . . . they are helps meet . . . as they were before the Fall" (Ep. 291).

The method of laying the responsibility for ministry on the congregation as a whole rather than on a person or persons specially prepared and delegated for it obviously involves serious difficulties. The ministry in Quaker meetings has always been, and will continue to be, a problem. Persons unqualified because of shallowness of experience or failure to attain the highest motivation take advantage of the liberty. George Fox warns against preaching in a "brittle, peevish, hasty, fretful mind" (Ep. 131). Some even fail to understand the religious character of the meeting and introduce subjects more appropriate to a forum or lecture platform than to a group that is gathered to wait upon the Lord. Some, who have undoubtedly received a gift in the past, may have outlived it and not be aware of their loss. Too much ministry may lead to overdependence on the spoken word. Joshua Evans remarks in his *Journal:*

> At our meeting lately we had the company of four Friends who were ministers. It occurred to my mind that in a season of drought we looked to the clouds for rain. Sometimes many clouds produce but little rain, so when divers preachers are in the gallery and the minds of the people turned towards them and not to the Bishop of souls, disappointment often happens.'

In the parable of the sower, some seed did not grow because it fell on hard ground. The ground may have become hard because so many were tramping up and down to sow seed.

The attender at a Friends meeting must accustom himself to hearing much that he feels is unprofitable, at least to himself. His forbearance in respect to speakers who are struggling, perhaps blindly, toward the Light and missing the way is in itself a valuable exercise. If the meeting is failing because of the wrong kind of ministry, each member must realize that the quality of the meeting depends partly on him and his faithfulness. He must also realize that in a Friends meeting, as in a democracy, a price is paid for freedom as contrasted with regimentation. A Friends meeting can rise higher or sink lower than a church service which is so regulated as to be conducted on a well-defined level.

As a free, unprogrammed, spontaneous vocal ministry gives rise to certain problems, a professional, programmed ministry gives rise to other problems, perhaps equally serious. The division between clergy and laity does not conduce to congregational unity. Lack of responsibility on the part of the laity does not conduce to spiritual growth. Regular preparation of a sermon in advance may result in what Barclay calls "conned and gathered stuff" (Apology 852) or what Fox calls "brain-beaten, heady stuff" (Ep. 275, 1669). Friends sometimes called this "grinding with the water that is passed." The spoken word is more alive if it springs freshly out of the life and searchings of the worshipers. In a Quaker meeting a single sentence uttered in response to a flash of insight may have more effect than a long sermon.

The professional minister is no longer challenged by Friends for receiving pay; indeed, it is recognized that he is meagerly rewarded. Nevertheless, the fact that he is paid may quite unfairly detract from the effectiveness of his message as a sincere expression of his feelings. He is also faced with another handicap. Too often there is no silence in which the message can sink into the hearts of his hearers.

The difficulties inherent in an unprogrammed meeting were partly met throughout most of Quaker history by the appointment of elders, whose primary duty was to counsel those who spoke in meeting. Problems raised by the freedom of a Friends meeting were more difficult in the early days of the Society than later because the movement was still fluid and unorganized. Many came into connection with it who were only partially aware of what it stood for. Even before there was a system of enrolled membership, Friends had to issue public statements of disownment.

From the beginning of the Society of Friends until recent times, the Friends who were accustomed to speak in meeting met together at regular intervals to advise and help one another. Monthly, Quarterly and Yearly meetings of these Friends who had a special concern for the vocal ministry did much to strengthen the spiritual life of the meeting. These were genuine "schools of the prophets." In the course of time Friends came to feel that those who were often engaged in the work of the ministry needed criticism from their hearers as well as from themselves. The following minute of Philadelphia Yearly Meeting, dated 1714, marks the beginning in America of an important change in these gatherings:

> This meeting agrees that each Monthly Meeting where meetings of ministers are or may be held, shall appoint two or more Friends to sit with the ministers in their meetings; taking care that the Friends chosen be prudent, solid Friends.

These came to be called "elders." The meeting of ministers was then called the "meeting for ministers and elders." Ministers were admitted to this meeting when they were "approved," "recommended," or "recorded," which meant that the meeting had expressly stated unity with their ministry. When such ministers wished to visit other Friends meetings, their meeting, if it approved of the journey, granted them a "minute" expressing unity with them. This served as a kind of credential and letter of introduction. Generally, an elder accompanied a minister in his travels as guide, helper and critic.

"Eldering" is an essential element in a meeting based on the principle of freedom. Its aim is to lay as much limitation on the freedom of the individual as will enlarge the freedom of the group as a whole. Among the many kinds of equilibrium required in a Friends meeting, there must be a delicate adjustment between the freedom of each and the freedom of all. If the individual is too much dominated by the group, the group may never have the benefit of new and perhaps unpleasant truth which the individual is qualified to impart. Nor must the group be at the mercy of the caprices of individuals, or it may find that the main purpose in meeting together is thwarted. Only as both the group and the individual submit humbly to the divine Light of Truth will they fulfill their proper functions and live in unity.

"Eldering" came to be a synonym for adverse criticism but encouragement was often required. Since speaking in a Friends meeting is a self-assumed responsibility, humble or timid persons tend to hold back. This is especially true of the young. In 1723 Philadelphia Yearly Meeting records in its minutes:

> It is to be observed that the God and fountain of all our mercies has opened and is opening in divers of our young people a divine spring of living ministry. Therefore, our earnest desire is that both ministers and elders may be as nursing fathers and mothers to those that are young in the ministry.

In 1765 we find:

> It is earnestly and affectionately recommended that ministers and elders watch over one another for good; to help those who are young in the ministry in the right line; discouraging forward spirits that run into words without life and power; advising against affectation of tones and gestures and everything that would hurt their service; yet encouraging the humble, careful traveller, speaking a word in season to them that are weary.

A good example of constructive eldership was given by William Penn and recorded by the recipient. At a large meeting when it might have been expected that the main burden of the ministry would be assumed by certain leading Friends, a young, unknown man, John Richardson, spoke at length. Penn said to him afterwards:

> The main part of the service of this day's work went on thy side and we saw it and were willing and easy to give way to the truth, though it was through thee, who appears but like a shrub, and it is but reasonable the Lord should make use of whom he pleases.[8]

John Rutty, a physician and writer of medical books, was an elder of Dublin Meeting. He includes in his *Spiritual Diary* many brief prayers, among them (in 1796) the following:

> Lord, if I be not a knife among the utensils of the spiritual house, make me a whetstone.[9]

An elder must be able to improve the instruments which God uses to convey his truth. Fox advises:

> Friends, be careful how ye set your feet among the tender plants that are springing up out of God's earth, lest ye tread upon them, hurt, bruise, or crush them in God's vineyard.[10]

William Dewsbury writes:

> What gift soever thou receivest, . . . whether praises, prophesy or exhortation, I am commanded of the God of heaven to lay it upon thee that thou quench not His Spirit but bring thy gift unto God's altar and in the strength of His life in the Light, sacrifice unto Him. So shall thy talent be increased and the babes shall be refreshed. And dear people of God, be tender over the least breathings of God's Spirit in one another and all wait to be clothed with a healing Spirit."[11]

The essence of all proper advice to ministers is that given by John Williams:

> Begin with, keep with and quit with the Life.[12]

Ministry in the Society of Friends is sometimes classified as prophetic utterance, though no Friends would style themselves prophets. Their ministry is prophetic only in the sense that it is given without human prearrangement under what is believed to be the direct leading of the Spirit. Such utterance may sometimes give evidence of prophetic unction. Of Samuel Fothergill it was said:

His ministry at times went forth as a flame, often piercing into the inmost recesses of darkness and obduracy; yet descended like dew upon the tender plants of our Heavenly Father's planting; with these he travailed in deep sympathy of spirit.[13]

Of Josiah Coale, who first visited America in 1658, Sewel, the historian, writes:

When he spoke to an ungodly world, an awful gravity appeared in his countenance, and his words were like a hammer and a sharp sword. But though he was as a son of thunder, yet his agreeable speech flowed from his mouth like a pleasant stream, to the consolation and comfort of pious souls.[14]

The presence of prophets in the New Testament Church was considered an all-important precedent by the Quakers. Paul in listing the gifts of the spirit in the order of their importance puts, ". . . first apostles, second prophets, third teachers then workers of miracles, then healers, helpers, administrators, speakers in various kinds of tongues," and adds, ". . . desire the spiritual gifts, especially that you may prophesy" (I Cor. 12:28; 14:1). But the prophetic function which was ranked so high during the first century of Christian history became subordinated to the priestly office and, during the second century, it was eliminated altogether. Attempts to revive prophetism, such as the Montanist movement in the second century, were violently suppressed. In Christianity the ancient struggle between priest and prophet, which is responsible for so many dramatic events recorded in the Old Testament, was won very early by the priest for two reasons, the necessity of maintaining sound doctrine and the importance of a specially qualified person to administer the sacraments. "Ye are subject to the bishop as to Jesus Christ," writes Ignatius, perhaps no more than sixty years after Paul had written, "The spirits of prophets are subject to prophets" (I Cor. 14:32).

The presbyter, that is, the elder, or, as he eventually became, the priest, was thought necessary to control prophets whose utterances were unpredictable, upsetting, sometimes revolutionary. We know very little about developments during the last third of the first Christian century, but it is probable that the Christian prophets opposed the trend toward sacerdotalism in the same way that the Hebrew prophets opposed the priestly emphasis six centuries earlier. The love feast in memory of the Last Supper, a meal eaten together as recorded in the 11th Chapter of I Corinthians, was becoming a ritual to be presided over by a person especially ordained for this service.

The two contributing causes of the decline of prophecy in the early Christian Church, the growth of a sacramental religion and of an orthodox creed, were both absent in Quakerism. The sacraments were interpreted by the Society of Friends as inward experiences directly accessible to all persons without priestly offices. No fixed authoritarian creed was ever adopted as a basis for membership, although Friends did not hesitate to state what they believed when occasion required. More important was the maintenance of a form of worship which encouraged a free, spontaneous, prophetic ministry untrammeled by outward authority. As a result, the prophetic type of ministry lasted much longer in the Society of Friends than it did in Christianity.

It was inevitable that in the Society of Friends, as in every religious group, the priestly type of mind should appear. As in early Christianity, so in the Society of Friends the elder assumed some of the priestly functions, though to a less degree and in a different way than in early Christianity. During the eighteenth century the influence of the elders gradually increased. Theirs was an important and necessary function. Quakerism at this time developed a distinctive cultural pattern, a clear-cut way of life. The Quaker was distinguishable by the way he talked, dressed and behaved. The elders became guardians of tradition* and, like all persons of priestly inclination, were more interested in the conservation of old truth than in the discovery of new. It was inevitable and necessary that Quakerism should pass through this period of inward intensification which brought the Quaker religion from the meeting house and market place into the home and into every aspect of life. The elders eventually went too far and tended too strongly to repress the untraditional springing up of new life. It was not, however, until the Philadelphia elders in the first quarter of the nineteenth century attempted to regulate theological doctrine that there was a concerted resistance to their authority. In England the transition to a freer mode of discipline took place without such schism. In America the Society of Friends became divided into branches.

The decline of a prophetic type of ministry in the twentieth century in that part of the Society of Friends which attempted to preserve a free, unprogrammed ministry cannot be attributed to the elders. They took extreme precautions to guard the living spring from all contamination. Its decline is due primarily to the high degree of intellectualism and secularism which appeared in all religious groups. Higher education, particularly college education, became more general. A self-conscious, rationalistic point of view frequently approaching humanism has resulted. The vocal ministry has increased in intellectual content. For the most part, this has been a gain. There has, however, too often been a corresponding decrease in spiritual content. There is no real reason why the intellectual and the spiritual should not develop together

*The enforcement of discipline as far as moral behavior was concerned was in charge of officials called overseers, first appointed in America about 1704. They are not mentioned here because they were not concerned with the ministry.

and reinforce each other. Human reason and the Spirit, which is more than human, are both essential, but the balance is not easy to maintain.

Within a single generation the older type of prophetic ministry, characterized by complete abandon to inner leadings however unconventional and unreasonable they might be, has largely disappeared from the more conservative forms of Quakerism. Elsewhere it disappeared earlier. The Quaker prophets were persons of unique individuality who spoke as they felt. Each of these men and women could be described in words that William Penn used regarding George Fox: "He was an original, being no man's copy." They could remind their hearers of unpleasant truths in such a spirit of love and genuineness that no anger resulted. Their faces shone with the peace of God because inner strains had been removed by obedience to the divine will. They were not troubled about their weaknesses because they were confident that God would not require of them what was "beyond their measure."

The mass-mindedness of the present epoch does not often produce such unique characters. Colleges, as well as factories, pass their product through a uniform mold. The surface world of tools, whether mental or industrial, has become so highly developed that the deeper world of ultimate meanings concerned with the final destiny of man has faded from sight. But the Spirit is still present like an underground stream waiting to be tapped and brought to the surface. The ministry which is devoted to the solution of social problems must not be abandoned, but it must be deepened and strengthened by that ministry which reaches solutions by bringing men into union with God and with one another.

Whittier's sonnet entitled "Utterance" states the problem which faces him who is called to speak in a meeting for worship:

> But what avail inadequate words to reach
> The innermost of Truth? Who shall essay

Blinded and weak, to point and lead the way,
Or solve its mystery in familiar speech?
Yet if it be that something not thy own,
Some shadow of the Thought to which our schemes,
Creeds, cult, and ritual are at best but dreams,
Is even to thy unworthiness made known, Thou mayest not
hide what yet thou shouldst not dare
To utter lightly, lest on lips of thine
The real seem false, the beauty undivine.
So weighing duty in the scale of prayer,
Give what seems given thee. It may prove a seed
Of goodness dropped in fallow grounds of need.

Notes

1. Richard Jordan, *Journal*, 1829, p. 80.
2. See Chap. 2, note 11.
3. Isaac Penington, *Works*, p. 239.
4. St. John of the Cross, *The Living Flame of Love*, Stanza III.
5. William Wistar Comfort, *Stephen Grellet*, p. 191.
6. Robert Barclay, *Apology*, p. 328.
7. Joshua Evans, *Journal*, 1837, p. 111.
8. Richardson, *Journal*, in *Friends Library*, IV, 87.
9. John Rutty, extracts from *The Spiritual Diary*, 1840, p. 242.
10. George Fox, *Journal*, I, 391.
11. William Dewsbury, *Works*, p. 179.
12. John Williams as quoted by Samuel M. Janney, *Memoirs*, 1881, p. 41.
13. Samuel Fothergill, *Memoirs and Letters*, p. 526.
14. William Sewel, *History of the people called Quakers*, 1725, p. 463.

CHAPTER VI

Reaching Decisions

THE QUAKER MOVEMENT began as a group held together by no visible bond but united by its own sense of fellowship, a kinship of spirit kept vital by concerned Friends who were continually traveling from one meeting to another. But it was soon found necessary to have some sort of organization dealing with practical matters. For example, there was immediate need of systematic help for persons suffering loss of property through distraint of goods to meet fines. Arrangements had to be made for the validity of marriages without the usual service of an officiating clergyman. The poor were cared for, burials arranged, records kept of births, marriages, sufferings and deaths. There were children to be educated and traveling Friends, if their own resources were insufficient, needed financial help. Friends often desired to petition King or Parliament. Disorderly persons were sometimes to be dealt with in order "that Truth might be cleared" of misunderstanding by the scandalized public. But the very need for organization gave rise to a serious theoretical problem—how can a free fellowship based on divine guidance from within set up any form of church government providing direction from without?

As early as 1652, William Dewsbury urged Friends to set up general meetings, to be attended by Friends in a limited area to meet immediate needs. His instructions were given forth as "the word of the living God to his Church." Other leaders spoke in

similar terms and with the same prophetic authority. But care was
taken not to produce an authoritarian code. In 1656 at a meeting
of Friends in Balby, Yorkshire, a letter was composed "From the
Spirit of Truth to the children of light," giving advice rather than
formulating rules on twenty points of behavior. This letter concluded with the well-known sentence:

> Dearly beloved Friends, these things we do not lay upon
> you as a rule or form to walk by; but that all, with a mea-
> sure of the light, which is pure and holy, may be guided:
> and so in the light walking and abiding, these things may
> be fulfilled in the Spirit, not in the letter; for the letter
> killeth but the Spirit giveth life.[1]

Additional advices were issued from time to time by various
meetings with a similar caution regarding the priority of the Spirit.
In 1659 the General Meeting at Skipton for Friends in the North
issued a document for guidance in conduct. Here again Friends
are urged to stand fast in their liberty,

> that no footsteps may be left for those that shall come
> after, or to walk by example, but that all may be directed
> and left to the truth, in it to live and walk and by it to be
> guided, that none may look back at us, nor have an eye
> behind them, but that all may look forward waiting in the
> Spirit for the revelation of those glorious things which are
> to be made manifest to them.[2]

This letter epitomizes the underlying principle of Quaker church
government:

> That the power of the God-head may be known in the body,
> in that perfect freedom which every member hath in Christ
> Jesus; that none may exercise lordship or dominion over
> another, nor the person of any be set apart, but as they

continue in the power of truth that truth itself in the body may reign, not persons nor forms: and that all such may be honored as stand in the life of the truth wherein is the power not over, but in the body.[3]

In other words, the meeting is to act as a whole and be governed by Truth, not by persons appointed to rule. If individuals are chosen for some particular service to the meeting, they should be continued in such service only so long as they are guided by the Truth. Thus the basis of Quaker church government was early expressed in a way that eliminated the possibility of individual authority. Only the authority of the group acting by the dictates of Truth was valid. The supremacy of a majority over a minority was completely dispensed with. There was no voting.

General meetings drawing Friends together in limited areas at periodic intervals developed in the decade from 1650 to 1660. Some of these occasions were simply meetings for worship, others also included sessions for the transaction of corporate affairs. By 1658 general meetings were held yearly with public Friends in attendance from all over England. The support of Friends traveling in the ministry to distant places often claimed attention.

When George Fox was released from his three years' imprisonment at Lancaster and Scarborough in 1666, he found the Quakers suffering severely because of the Conventicle Act which forbade attendance at any assembly for worship other than those of the Established Church. There were also a number of other serious difficulties. Nearly all the leading Friends were in prison. Fanatics, such as the hysterical women whose adulation of James Naylor earlier led to public scandal, were bringing the movement into disrepute. The followers of John Perrot were teaching that the essence of religion required no outward frame of reference. This party held that even fixed times for public worship were man-made devices. To counteract such tendencies toward religious anarchism a group of leading Friends issued a letter asserting the authority of a meeting to exclude from its fellowship persons who persisted in rejecting its judgment. This was shortly before George Fox's release.[4] This letter, by definitely subordinating individual guidance to the sense of the meeting as a whole, marked an important step in Quaker development.

Bruised and weakened by his experience in jail and scarcely able to mount his horse, Fox at this critical juncture went about England and Ireland for four years bringing order out of confusion by setting up Monthly Meetings as executive units of the Society of Friends. His visit to America in 1671-73 was largely for the same purpose. While there had been some Monthly Meetings before this time, they now became standard procedure and have continued to be basic throughout Quaker history.

A Monthly Meeting is made up of all the Friends in a given district. It sometimes includes more than one meeting for worship. The constituent parts of a Monthly Meeting came to be called Preparative Meetings, their function being to prepare for the Monthly Meeting which made the important decisions. Combinations of neighboring Monthly Meetings are organized into Quarterly Meetings and the Quarterly Meetings in turn are united in a Yearly Meeting. This system developed gradually. At first the Yearly Meeting in London consisted exclusively of Friends engaged in the ministry. By 1672, and regularly after 1678, it included representatives sent from all the Quarterly Meetings in England. By 1760, the Yearly Meeting was open to all Friends. The evolution of this system in America followed similar lines, except that, owing to the geographical situation, six Yearly Meetings emerged in the colonies.

The first Quaker meetings for business (or church government) were made up of men only, but by 1656 women's meetings began to appear. In 1671 Fox wrote a circular letter urging that they be set up everywhere. Eventually there were Monthly, Quarterly and

Yearly Meetings for women. For some years the business before the women's meetings differed from the business before the men's meetings though there was no sense of inferiority. It consisted of matters which were felt to be of peculiar interest to women, such as care of the poor, the sick and the imprisoned. The important Six Weeks Meeting, begun in 1671, which supervised the affairs of London Quakers was a joint body of men and women. Today all Quaker business meetings except in two or three conservative areas in America are made up of men and women. The assignment of important executive responsibilities to women was a bold step in the seventeenth century. The training which Quaker women received in these meetings as well as in meetings for worship qualified them to become leaders of their sex.

The system of Monthly, Quarterly and Yearly Meetings as it finally developed in England and America suggests the organic principle of the affiliation of cells or small units in a large organism. The Monthly Meeting is the primary cell in the Society of Friends. Only there does membership exist. Individual Friends have the same responsibilities in the larger group as in the smaller. There is no delegated authority. As Fox writes in a long epistle on church government, "The least member in the Church hath an office and is serviceable and every member hath need one of another" (Ep. 264, 1669).

The larger group does not exist to exert authority over its smaller parts, nor do the smaller parts dominate the larger. Each is both means and end. The larger exists to widen the range of acquaintance and judgment and to carry out undertakings too big for the smaller group. The larger group asks its constituent parts to contribute money to support its enterprises; gives credentials and financial aid when necessary to ministers and others traveling long distances; supports the larger schools; appoints committees to deal with a variety of issues and concerns beyond the range of the smaller meetings, such as peace, temperance, race relations, publications, the social order, national legislation and the relief of suffering at home and abroad.

A concern, that is, a strong inward sense that some action should be taken to meet a certain situation, may arise in the mind of any individual. It often develops in the silence in a meeting for worship. The member brings it before the Monthly Meeting which may or may not sympathize with it. If circumstances require a wider concurrence, the Monthly Meeting may forward the matter to the Quarterly Meeting. The Quarterly Meeting may then act upon it or may send it on to the Yearly Meeting. In this way a concern secures the support of a group large enough and wise enough to carry it out. The power of the individual to accomplish what he feels has been laid upon him is many times multiplied if his concern is taken up by all three, the Monthly Meeting, the Quarterly Meeting and, finally, the Yearly Meeting. In some instances an individual may first present his concern to a Quarterly or Yearly Meeting or to a specialized committee. In this case the reverse process may occur, the concern being referred to the Monthly Meeting for action.

The Yearly Meeting issues advices for the guidance of Monthly and Quarterly Meetings and of individual members. It also addresses Queries to constituent meetings in order to ascertain their condition and discover if help is needed. Advices and Queries are not orders issued by a superior to an inferior. The Monthly Meetings are the real executive units of the Society.

Early in the eighteenth century selections from the minutes of the Yearly Meetings were gathered in book form under captions alphabetically listed. This compilation came to be called the *Book of Discipline*. The manuscript book issued in 1762 by Philadelphia Yearly Meeting is entitled *A Collection of Christian and Brotherly Advices Given Forth from Time to Time by the Yearly Meetings of Friends for New Jersey and Pennsylvania*. As need arose additions were inserted, each with its appropriate date. This book, abbreviated to contain only active regulations, was printed in 1797. Later the alphabetical system was replaced by a topical arrangement. The *Discipline* has been reissued and revised from time to time up to the present. It is both a moral guide and a manual of church government. Additions and revisions show the evolution of moral consciousness as it became increasingly sensitive to slavery, war, intemperance, racial and class discrimination and other evils.

As an example of this growth of moral sensitivity, we find under the heading "Negroes or Slaves" twenty-four manuscript pages of entries, dated 1688 to 1790, recording each step of the process by which the Society of Friends in America freed itself from holding slaves.* Under "Queries" there are three sets of questions dated 1743, 1755, 1765 respectively. Those dealing with slavery are:

> 1743. Do Friends observe the former advice of our Yearly Meeting not to encourage the importation of Negroes, nor to buy them after imported?

> 1755. Are Friends clear of importing or buying Negroes and do they use those well which they are possessed of by inheritance or otherwise, endeavoring to train them up in the principles of the Christian Religion?

> 1765. The same query as in 1755.

---

*1696 advice against the importation of Negroes; 1730 advice against buying imported Negroes; 1754 advice against buying any Negroes; 1758 appointment of a committee of five to visit all Friends who hold slaves and persuade them to set their slaves at liberty; 1762 substantial success is reported and the committee asks to be released. Quarterly and Monthly Meetings are instructed to deal with Friends who still hold slaves; 1778 the Yearly Meeting declares that Quaker slaveholders who "continue to reject the advice of their brethren" should be disowned by their meetings.

In 1776 the Query was amended as follows:

> Are Friends clear of importing, purchasing, disposing of
> or holding mankind as slaves? And do they use those well
> who are set free and are necessarily under their care and
> not in circumstances through nonage or incapacity to min-
> ister to their own necessities? And are they careful to edu-
> cate and encourage them in a religious and virtuous life?

Here are three steps showing increasing sensitiveness to a clearly
defined evil. First, Friends were not to buy imported Negroes; next,
they were not to buy any, though it was assumed that they might
inherit them; finally, they were not to hold them in servitude at
all. The evolution of the *Book of Discipline* is a testimony to the
power of the Quaker method in educating and sensitizing conscience.

In the same year that the Declaration of Independence stated
"that all men are created equal, that they are endowed by their
Creator with certain unalienable Rights, that among these are Life,
Liberty and the pursuit of Happiness," the Quakers made their
own declaration which took these great words at their full value.
They did not support their own revolution by violence, but none-
theless they carried it through in a thoroughgoing way.

The perennial problem of the relative rights and responsibilities of the individual and the group was never so clearly solved
that it did not give rise to difficulties. The Wilkinson-Story party
separated from the main body in England in 1678, principally because it was opposed to any authority exercised by the group over
the individual. The separation in Philadelphia which took place
in 1827 was to a large extent the outcome of differences between
the more individualistic and the more authoritarian trends in the
Society of Friends.

Yet in a large measure the Quaker form of church government
succeeded in securing a reasonable balance between freedom and

order. Without some authority over the individual the movement would certainly have disintegrated as did the various groups of religious anarchists. Without considerable liberty the Society of Friends would have crystallized into a formal system. The adjustment depended upon group authority over the individual tempered by individual initiative in affecting the judgment of the group.

Among Friends the meeting for the transaction of church business is as distinctly a religious exercise as is the meeting for worship, but it has a different objective. The meeting for worship is focused upon the divine-human relationship and the meeting for business is mainly concerned with interhuman co-operation, the two being interdependent. From another point of view, the meeting for worship concerns *being* while the meeting for business concerns *doing*. What is implicit in worship becomes explicit in action. The meeting for business should, therefore, be preceded by a period of worship in which the hard shell of egocentricity is dissolved and the group united into a living whole. It is also well to conclude the business meeting with a period of silent devotion. George Fox writes to Friends:

> Friends, keep your meetings in the power of God, and in his wisdom (by which all things were made) and in the love of God, that by that ye may order all to his glory. And when Friends have finished their business, sit down and continue awhile quietly and wait upon the Lord to feel him. And go not beyond the Power, but keep in the Power by which God Almighty may be felt among you. [Ep. 162, 1658]

Since there is but one Light and one Truth, if the Light of Truth be faithfully followed, unity will result. "The Light itself," says Thomas Story, "is not divided, but one and the same entire, undivided Being continually."[5] The nearer the members of a group come to this one Light, the nearer they will be to one another, just as the spokes of a wheel approach one another as they near the center. The spirit of worship is essential to that type of business meeting in which the group endeavors to act as a unit. True worship overcomes excessive individuality by producing a superindividual consciousness. If serious differences of opinion appear, it may come about that by recourse to a period of silence a basis for unity can be discovered. If a high degree of unity is not reached, action is postponed, provided an immediate decision is not necessary. For such a meeting the only essential official is a clerk whose business it is to ascertain and record or be responsible for recording the sense of the meeting.

The business before the meeting, presented by the clerk, a committee or an individual, is "spoken to" by those who have opinions or judgment regarding it. When the consideration reaches a stage which indicates that a reasonable degree of unity has been attained, the clerk announces what he believes to be the sense of the meeting. If the meeting agrees with his wording as given or revised, this becomes the judgment of the meeting and is so preserved in the minutes. The degree of unity necessary for a decision depends on the importance of the question and the character and depth of feeling of those who oppose the general trend of opinion. On many items of routine business little or no expression is necessary. Even silence may give consent. But on important matters care is taken to secure the vocal participation of all who feel able and willing to express themselves. Some problems have been postponed for more than a century awaiting unity. An example was the toleration of slavery within the Society of Friends. Had a vote been taken as early as 1700 slavery would probably have been voted out, but a substantial minority would not have concurred. The subject was brought up again and again, progress was made slowly until in 1776 the Society was united in refusing membership to persons who held slaves.

An opposing minority, however small, is not disregarded, especially if it contains members whose judgment is highly respected. The *weight* of a member in determining the decision of the meeting depends on the confidence which the meeting has in the validity of his judgment. On certain subjects some Friends are more reliable than others. On a financial problem the opinion of a single financier might determine the sense of the meeting, although his opinion might carry less weight on some other subjects. If an individual lays a concern before the meeting, much depends on the degree to which the concern has gripped him. If he feels it deeply and perhaps brings it up again and again in spite of opposition, the meeting may finally acquiesce even though some hesitation is still felt by some.

If a serious difference of opinion exists on a subject which cannot be postponed, decision may be left to a small committee. Not infrequently the minority withdraw their opposition in order that the meeting may come to a decision. It is, however, surprising how often real unity is reached, even though the discussion in its initial stages shows a wide variety of opinions, or a pronounced cleavage arising from strongly held convictions. As the consideration proceeds, unity gradually emerges and is finally reached. The decision may be along lines not even thought of at the beginning. This procedure takes more time and patience than the voting method, but the results are generally more satisfactory to all concerned.

The clerk is theoretically a recording officer, but in practice he must frequently assume the duties of a presiding officer. He must be sensitive to all trends of opinion, including those not well expressed. When two or more persons rise at once, he must recognize one as having the floor. He must determine the appropriate amount of time to be devoted to each item on the agenda in view of the total business before the meeting. He must decide on how much expression he can safely base his minute. He is responsible for keeping one subject at a time before the meeting. He may request talkative members to limit their remarks and silent members to express themselves. All this appears to lay a heavy burden upon the clerk, but in any contingency he may derive help from any member. Theoretically, it is the meeting as a whole, rather than the clerk, that exercises authority, but the clerk may occasionally find himself in a position in which some exercise of authority is unavoidable.

If this Quaker method of arriving at unity does not succeed, the difficulty is generally due to some members who have not achieved the right attitude of mind and heart. Dogmatic persons who speak with an air of finality, or assume the tone of a debater determined to win, may be a serious hindrance. Eloquence which appeals to emotion is out of place. Those who come to the meeting not so much to discover Truth as to win acceptance of their opinions may find that their views carry little weight. Opinions should always be expressed humbly and tentatively in the realization that no one person sees the whole truth and that the whole meeting can see more of Truth than can any part of it. When B speaks following A, he takes into consideration A's opinion. C follows with a statement which would probably have been different had A and B not spoken. Every speaker credits every other sincere speaker with at least some insight. Finally, a statement is made which receives the approval of all. A number of persons say "I approve," "I agree" or some equivalent.

This method is similar to some other consensus methods; for instance, those suggested by M. P. Follett in *The New State* or Frank Walser in *The Art of Conference*. It differs radically in being religious. George Fox Writes, "Friends are not to meet like a company of people about town or parish business, neither in their men's or women's meetings, but to wait upon the Lord" (Ep. 313, 1674). Quakers have used this method with a large degree of success for three centuries because it has met the religious test, being based on the Light Within producing unity. As the Light is God in His capacity as Creator, Unity in Him creates Unity in the group. When the method has not succeeded, as in the divisions during the nineteenth century, spiritual life was low and Friends too impatient to wait for unity to develop.

At its best, the Quaker method does not result in a compromise. A compromise is not likely to satisfy anyone completely. The objective of the Quaker method is to discover Truth which will satisfy everyone more fully than did any position previously held. Each and all can then say, "That is what I really wanted, but I did not realize it." To discover what we really want as compared to what at first we think we want, we must go below the surface of self-centered desires to the deeper level where the real Self resides. The deepest Self of all is that Self which we share with all others. This is the one Vine of which we all are branches, the Life of God on which our own individual lives are based. To will what God wills is, therefore, to will what we ourselves really want.

The voting method is a mechanical process whereby the larger force is pitted against the smaller one over which it prevails, possibly without even an attempt to adjust to it. The Quaker method produces synthesis in which each part makes some adjustment to the whole. In general, voting creates nothing new, one party is simply more numerous than the other. The organic method may actually produce by a process of cross-fertilization something which was not there at the beginning. As in all life, the whole is more than the sum of its parts. A new creation emerges through the life or soul of the whole which was not completely present in any of the parts. As the meeting becomes a unit, it learns to think as a unit. This is an achievement. Every partial, fragmentary view contributes to the total view.

The voting method is usually quicker. Organic growth is a slow process, but that which has life is adaptable, while mechanisms tend to be rigid. In the voting method when the vote is taken, each individual has one or a fixed number of votes, irrespective of his interest or knowledge, while in the Quaker method, each individual possesses or should possess weight proportional to his interest and his knowledge of the particular subject before the meeting.

It might appear that, because the Quaker meeting must wait for unity, this method would tend toward conservatism. This is sometimes the case, but, in general, Quaker pioneering in social reforms shows that conservatism has not generally prevailed. The first response of many people to a new proposition is negative; hence the voting method which is the quickest may itself produce a negative response. Minorities tend to be more radical than majorities. If decision is postponed in the effort to secure unity, time is given for an advanced minority to convince the majority. In the end a more novel decision may result.

A minor consideration is that of size. The Quaker method works better in small than in large groups. This is true both of the meeting for worship and of the meeting for business. It is easier to achieve unity in an intimate group the members of which are well acquainted with one another than in a large group where there is bound to be more diversity. But experience shows that even in large groups, especially if they contain some able, "well seasoned Friends," this method can be employed successfully. Biologists believe that evolution can take place best in groups of a moderate size. If the group is too small, there are not enough variations to insure progress. If the group is too large, variations are swamped by the impact of the mass.

Therefore, if a Monthly Meeting becomes overgrown, it should divide. Such cell-division is the organic method of growth which has been characteristic in the Society of Friends from the beginning. Division may also be occasioned by the scattering due to economic reasons. Members, especially young people, may move to localities where there is no Friends meeting. Perhaps they will start meetings in their homes. Such a meeting may begin in a very small way, but as like-minded persons find out about it and isolated Friends realize that such a project has been undertaken, the meeting will probably grow. This simple method of growth gives Friends a strategic advantage. Religious sects which require professional pastors and special apparatus cannot afford to begin so informally. But Friends can start a meeting anywhere and under the simplest conditions with as few as two members. In colonial days, Friends spread rapidly in many pioneer communities because a Friends meeting could so readily be held in a home.

The Quaker method is likely to be successful in proportion as the members are acquainted with one another; better still if real affection exists among them. When differences and factions arose in the Corinthian Church its members wrote to ask Paul's advice. After making several concrete suggestions, he goes on to say in the famous 18th Chapter of his letter that love is really the only solution. In a similar situation John speaks in his first letter of love as essential. "We know that we have passed out of death into life because we love the brethren" (I John 3:14).

For "love" Paul and John use the Greek word *agape* instead of the more usual Greek word *eros*. *Agape* means unselfish love which seeks to be possessed rather than to possess. Paul said, "*agape* does not insist on its own way" (I Cor. 13:5). This is the highest binding force within a religious group. It signifies the Spirit which draws men together and to God without at the same time resulting in the domination of one will by another. It is love that brings into harmony the apparently contradictory concepts of unity and freedom.

Agape is closely akin to friendship, a uniting force which at the same time respects individuality and freedom. In the Gospel of John Christ identifies love of this type with friendship when he says, "Greater love has no man than this, that a man lay down his life for his friends" (John 15:13). Since the word "love" has so many different meanings, it was more appropriate that the Quakers should call themselves a Society of Friends than, as one contemporary group did, a Family of Love. It may be that the appellation "Friends," which has become so familiar that its origin is seldom inquired into, came from the saying of Jesus, "No longer do I call you servants, for the servant does not know what his master is doing; but I have called you friends" (John 15:13). In the early minutes of the meetings in Pennsylvania the Quakers call themselves "The Friends of God."

The Society of Friends in choosing their name gave expression to the feeling that their religion was based on friendship in distinction from a code of duty appropriate to servants whose obligation is to yield obedience. Here the early Friends made a religious emphasis different from the Protestants of their time. The Puritans held that man's hope of salvation depended on obedience to commands set down for all time in the sacred book. These commands were thought of as instructions which a servant receives "who knows not what his lord does" and must needs obey, whether he understands or not. But if God's will is revealed not so much by a law from without as by the Light of Truth which produces action inspired from within, the relation is one of friendship and freedom based on understanding. There is no external domination. Hence arises the difference between the Puritan concept of duty with its inner tension and compulsion and the Quaker concept of conscience with its sense of freedom and peace. A servant may serve because of a sense of duty, but a friend helps his friend for a reason other than duty.. Those who render God service from a sense of duty may hear the divine voice saying, "So you also, when you have done all that is commanded you, say We are unworthy servants; we have only done what was our duty'" (Luke 17:10).

In addition to the religion of friendship and the religion of obedience, there is another type of religion which extols the kind of love which unifies through possession. Such love is described by many of the great Christian mystics. It is the Spiritual Marriage, the very top of the mystical ladder, the allegorical interpretation of the Song of Songs. In emotional content it is akin to the marriage of husband and wife. Unity with God results in so complete a submergence of the individual that individuality is lost, just as a drop of water falls into the ocean and is lost. In emphasizing this experience, many devotional writings of the saints strike a note foreign alike to Quaker and Protestant. Unity through obedience, unity through emotion and unity through friendship, all are deep aspects of human experience. The Quaker emphasis allows greater significance to individuality and freedom.

The Society of Friends endeavors to maintain an organization which does not destroy freedom. Freedom appears in an act of concurrence performed not from any sense of inner or outer compulsion but in following Truth for the love of it. The Light Within being both Truth and Love, draws people together from within. It exerts no outside pressure. It respects the unique personality of each individual. The Ranters, Antinomians and others with anarchistic leanings, some of whom early left the Society of Friends because they felt that any form of organization would limit their freedom to follow the Light of Truth wherever it might lead, did not realize that the Light was Love as well as Truth. To love the truth is to follow that which draws humanity together into a unity of friendship or nonpossessive love, the highest condition in the universe, the very Presence of God Himself. William Penn wrote in his *Maxims*, "Nor can spirits ever be divided that love and live in the same Divine Principle, the Root and Record of their Friendship."

This problem of freedom within an organized group was faced by the early Christians. After Paul had founded the Galatian Church, certain persons came there who told the Galatian Christians that in order to be Christians they must carry out in full the law of Moses. When Paul heard of this he wrote with more fervor than in any of his other letters that have come down to us, showing that Christianity is not the old law, neither is it a new law. It is freedom from law. At first this may appear to be pure anarchy. But Paul was not speaking of unlimited liberty for self-indulgence (Gal. 5:18). With the external restraint of law, he contrasts internal guidance based on the love of God. This is pure freedom because, through union with God, man wills what God wills and God is free. Man, therefore, may share in God's freedom. Paul speaks in terms of the Christ Within. "It is no longer I who live, but Christ who lives in me" (Gal. 2:20). This is true also of the Galatian converts, "As many of you as were baptized into Christ have put on Christ" (Gal 3:27). And so he exclaims with joy and wonder, "Christ has set us free; stand fast, therefore, and do not submit again to the yoke of slavery."The law is for children and slaves but "because you are sons, God has sent the Spirit of his Son into our hearts" (Gal 4:6).

This is not an easy doctrine. It is not surprising that the Christian Church has been slow to understand Paul or has not striven to understand him. The Church was eventually presided over by an ecclesiastical hierarchy which left little opportunity for liberty of the Spirit. Paul admits the need of regulations to govern the immature who have not yet won their freedom in Christ (Gal. 4:1-3). But the Church eventually allowed little freedom except at the top. Early Protestantism with its doctrine of depravity required an external rule and the power of external grace in place of an internal governing Spirit. The Scripture furnished a code interpreted by creeds that was as binding as the law of Moses. The Quakers stand alone in having attempted a form of church government which, however it may have developed in practice, allowed in theory for the liberty of those who are led by the Spirit. Like Paul they recognized the need of precepts for the spiritually immature such as children in school, but even the Quaker schools were so devised that compulsion was minimized.

The attainment of unity within the meeting is not the same as the attainment of uniformity. Unity is spiritual, uniformity mechanical. Friends have never required of their members assent to a religious or social creed, though not infrequently a body of Friends has issued a statement expressing their religious or social views at a particular time. There is, however, always the reservation that the Spirit of Truth may lead to further insight. Differences within the group on the particular application of general principles are tolerated, provided they are being actively explored in a spirit of friendship and in a continued search for truth. Such differences are often of great value in helping new aspects of truth to emerge.

The discovery of truth through differences of opinion is well illustrated in the history of science. "A clash of doctrines is not a disaster—it is an opportunity," says Whitehead.[6] As an illustration he shows how disagreement in the results of experiments on the atomic weight of some elements led to the discovery that the same element may assume two or more distinct forms or isotopes. Of two different opinions we can say as Christ said in the parable, "Let both grow together until the harvest." The harvest is the fuller discovery of truth which includes both. Thus, as Whitehead shows, Galileo said that the earth moves and the sun is fixed. The Inquisition maintained that the earth is fixed and the sun moves. The modern theory of relativity includes both of these earlier theories. For this harvest it is sometimes necessary to wait a long time.

But differences cease to have value when fundamental principles are ignored. In science a difference between one theory which is based on the scientific method and another theory based on a different method such as magic or astrology would not be productive of new scientific truth. In similar fashion a difference between two points of view, one arrived at by free search and another arrived at by blind agreement with an authoritarian pronouncement, would not be productive of new truth. To be creative the authoritative edict must be subjected to a discriminating inquiry which might alter it. If viewed as fixed it is dead and unproductive.

In Quakerism as in science the new can only arise out of the old. In science a creativity which did not take past discoveries into consideration would generally be unproductive of new truth. Similarly, the Quaker method will not progress without acknowledgment of all the great truths which have been discovered in the past. The meeting should hesitate to accept any suggestion which runs counter to the accumulated wisdom of the saints and prophets who have gone before. When it seeks to arrive at a decision which is an expression of truth, it must consider as part of itself the invisible company of all those who discovered truth. Their insight must be given due weight in arriving at a decision. In religion as in science we do not start from nothing. The doctrine of the Light Within does not mean that an individual must depend only on his own measure of Light. As in science we do not expect everyone to be a Newton or a Darwin, so in religion we do not expect everyone to be a Paul or a Fox. The religious genius, like the scientific genius, must be allowed to give to those who are not geniuses the full measure of guidance.

It must be borne in mind that a synthesis of opinion achieved within a group is not good simply because it is a synthesis. Unity may occur on a high level or a low level. A group of bandits may achieve consensus in carrying out their schemes. A nation may be at one in deciding to wage aggressive war. A mob may achieve a united opinion at a lower level than the code of conduct of the individuals who compose it. The clue to this problem is the concept of the Light as that which leads *up* to God. If the proper method is followed, the Light which unifies the group will be found to be an elevating Principle. As Truth is sought through prayer, worship and an earnest effort to purge all that is self-centered and concerned with possessive desires, the group will rise through deliberation to a higher level than that on which it started. This

occurs when there is real interdependence between the meeting
for worship and the meeting for business. "Agreeing Upward" is a
chapter heading in the works of the Chinese philosopher, Motze.
It is toward this agreeing upward that a meeting should aspire.

The organic method of arriving at decisions by consensus appears at the primitive preindividual level as well as at the advanced
postindividual level. In the first case self-centeredness has not yet
developed; in the second case it has been overcome. Of the
Solomon Islanders, W. H. R. Rivers writes that "in the councils of
such peoples there is no voting or other means of taking the opinion of the body."[7] Quakers traveling in America in colonial times
sometimes visited the Indian councils and remarked that their
method of coming to decisions was like that of a Quaker business
meeting. John Richardson while visiting William Penn observed
that the Indians "did not speak two at a time nor interfere in the
least with one another." He says, "My spirit was very easy with them,"
and continues, "I did not feel that power of darkness to oppress
me as I had done in many places among the people called Christians."[8] It was also observed that in these councils the women participated as well as the men. Thomas Chalkley writes that in
traveling beyond the Susquehanna in 1706 he asked permission
of the Indians to hold a religious meeting,

> upon which they called a council in which they were very
> grave and spoke one after another without any heat or jar-
> ring and some of the most esteemed of their women do
> sometimes speak in their councils.
>
> . . . Our interpreter told me that they had not done any-
> thing for many years without the counsel of an ancient,
> grave woman, who, I observed, spoke much in their
> council.[9]

Of a similar council Catherine Phillips notes:

> Several of their women sat in this conference who for fixed
> solidity appeared to me like Roman matrons.[10]

Such councils where sex equality is maintained and voting unknown indicate that the organic method is in accord with human
nature as it evolved out of primitive, matriarchal conditions. The
more mechanical method of voting becomes natural in a later stage
of development when society has become more individualistic. But
there is a still further stage when self-conscious individualization
is surpassed but not eliminated, in a divine-human community so
inspired by the one Spirit that it can act as a unit. The third stage
resembles the first but it is higher because those who are in it have
passed through the intermediary condition and become individuals. In the first stage there is unity; in the second, individuality; in
the third, the synthesis of unity and individuality which makes
possible participation in group life with freedom.

Notes

1. *Letters Etc. of Early Friends,* edited by Abram Rawlinson Barclay,
   1841, p. 282.
2. *Letters,* p. 288.
3. *Letters,* p. 289.
4. *Letters,* p. 319.
5. Thomas Story, *Sermons,* 1785, p. 61.
6. Alfred North Whitehead, *Science and the Modern World,* 1925, p. 266.
7. William Halse, Rivers, *Instinct and the Unconscious,* 1924, p. 95.
8. John Richardson, *Journal,* 1856, p. 135.
9. Thomas Chalkley, *Journal,* 1754, p. 49.
10. Catherine Phillips, *Journal,* 1798, p. 144.

CHAPTER VII

The Meeting Community

THE QUAKER MEETING with its double function of worship and business constitutes a community. If it carries out its functions successfully, it becomes a well-integrated group in which the individual is united to the whole as a cell is united to an organism. "Organism" is a figure of speech used to suggest the kind of unity which exists in a group of free self-conscious personalities. Obviously, this is different from the coherence which exists within a biological organism where individuality and freedom of the parts is nonexistent. A unity based not only on a single free choice at the beginning, but on a continued series of free choices, is an achievement which can take place most easily in a comparatively small group. Having been achieved there, it can then be carried over more readily by the same individuals into a larger group. The habits of behavior formed in the small group inevitably spread to wider associations.

The family, for example, is a small group which can be a valuable training ground for right behavior in a larger community. The members of a normal family co-operate with one another and share equally the family resources, the weak being entitled to receive what they require on the same terms as the strong. The food placed on the table is distributed according to need, not power to seize it. This kind of behavior differs from that of the competitive world. For example, in an area where oil is discovered, everyone seizes as much as he can regardless of other persons. Yet the difference between the code of behavior in the family and the code of behavior outside it is mitigated by the fact that the habits of co-operation and sharing found within the family frequently continue to be exercised when its members go out into the world. In similar fashion, a religious group may so conduct its affairs that the habit of behavior formed within it as a direct result of its doctrines and habits may find expression beyond its borders. The early Christian Church did not condemn slavery. But when Paul wrote to Philemon asking him to take back his escaped slave who had become a Christian, he said that master and slave were equal within the Church. This equality within the Church led Christianity eventually to condemn all slavery.

Participation in the activities of a group is the oldest and most effective form of education. It' is older than the human race. Beginning at birth, it can continue to the end. Such an education of the whole person in body, mind and spirit becomes deeply ingrained in character. By participation in group activities the members learn by living rather than by formal instruction, though instruction may prove to be an important part of life itself. Participation in life as a whole reaches down below the level of ideas to the deeper feelings which move the will. Ideas in themselves, received in the school-room or from books, have little motive power unless they are linked to this deeper process. They require reinforcement through activity. If the bridge between thought and action is crossed often enough, thought and action become integrated and the result is training in its most profound and enduring form.

The Origin of Social Concerns

The meaning of the group in Quaker practice can be suggested by a diagram. Light from God streams down into the waiting group. This Light, if the way is open for it, produces three results: unity,

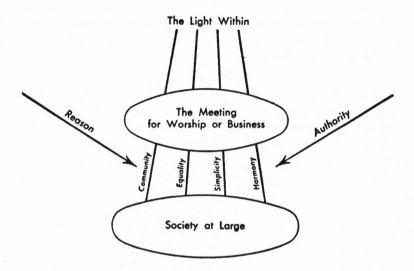

Concerns originating in the Quaker Community as a result of the impact of the Light Within become directed toward Society at Large. Concerns may result from the impact of Authority or Reason though this is not typical of the Quaker Method.

knowledge and power. As a result we have the kind of behavior which exists as an ideal in a meeting for worship and a meeting for business. Because of the characteristics of the Light of Christ, the resulting behavior can be described in a general way by the four words Community, Harmony, Equality and Simplicity, though these are not to be taken as all-inclusive. These four types of behavior which are closely interrelated, being first generated in the intimate circle, become applied more widely as its members go out beyond its limits to the larger world. The members acquire habits in the meeting which are inevitably retained, at least to some degree, in whatever business they may engage. But because these habits can be acted upon with less opposition in the small, congenial, comparatively homogeneous group than in society at large where conditions are less favorable, there will probably be a certain adjustment and compromise. Some members, more devoted than others, will attempt to avoid compromise.

In a vital and dynamic meeting a concern may arise first in a meeting for worship or for business which is at the outset thought of as applicable only to the membership. It may, however, eventually emerge as an activity to be performed outside the little group in the field of society at large. Thus a sense of responsibility for extending economic aid to fellow members who need it should become a concern to extend economic aid to all who are in need. A habit of dealing with members of the meeting in a peaceable manner should similarly become a habit of dealing with others in a peaceable manner.

A requirement may originate, not as a result of the Light Within operating upon the soul of an individual, but through the compelling power of some authority or as a result of a logical process of reasoning. This would be a process different from the usual Quaker method. Authority and reason are indispensable supplements to inward guidance. Their absence would indicate a state of ineptitude. But by themselves they are not enough. To take a specific example, if someone should refuse to be drafted into the army, this refusal might arise out of obedience to the Sermon on the Mount, or it might arise out of a philosophic or scientific theory, or a knowledge of instances of the futility of war. It might also arise out of the guidance of conscience illumined by the divine Light while waiting upon God.

The Quaker stresses the guidance of the enlightened conscience. He relies upon illumined reason and authority as checks. His position may appear, even to himself, to be contrary to reason and to respected authorities. But if the Light in his conscience gives him a clear leading, he must follow it as the primary organ for ascertaining religious and moral truth. Conscience is cognitive in its field as thought is in its field. The psychologist Jung, in describing the principal mental functions which he calls Thought, Feeling, Intuition and Sensation, lists thought and feeling as cognitive. Feeling gives us our knowledge of values. This agrees with the Quaker point of view. In a Quaker meeting for worship or for business a speaker seldom remarks "I think" but generally "I feel." If he agrees with another speaker, he will probably say, "That is in accord with my feelings," or, "I would feel most comfortable [or perhaps 'most easy'] if that were done." A sense of inward tension and discomfort is frequently interpreted as a sign that something needs to be done. A feeling of inward peace is a sign that the right thing has been done. Authority and reason are transferable tests. Because of this they are essential in convincing other persons. Feelings arising out of conscientious scruples cannot be transferred from one person to another any more than aesthetic judgments can be transferred. But the conscience of another person can be appealed to on the theory that the same Light is within all men to illumine and bring all consciences into agreement. In this way the Light in one person will "answer" the Light in another, to use George Fox's figure of speech. This kind of "answering" can take place under any conditions but most effectively in a small worshiping group.

In addition to authority and reason there is also the pragmatic test. An action is judged to be good if its results are good. This test has some affinity to that of reason because the results of a proposed action must be viewed in the light of similar past actions. Reason makes the comparison and concludes that if the results were good or bad in the past, they will be good or bad in the future if the conditions are the same. The pragmatic test also has its roots in feeling, for it is by feeling that we judge whether results are really good or bad. If we used only the pragmatic test, we might fail in decision because immediate results would have to be judged in terms of their results, and these results in terms of further re-

sults, and so on without end. Since no one can foresee a final result, some test not wholly pragmatic is essential.

That Friends do not, as a rule, judge the merits of a proposed
action in terms of apparent consequences may be illustrated by
two examples. William Allen, highly successful both as a scientist
and businessman, writes in his diary:

> I think I have been instructed not to look for great things
> in religious matters but to go on in the simplicity, to labor
> more and more to get rid of all reasonings and the appre-
> hension of consequences.[1]

John Woolman writes in his *Journal:*

> Travelling up and down of late I have renewed evidences
> that to keep pace with duty and to be content with the
> allotments of Divine Providence, is a most necessary and
> useful lesson for me to be learning; looking less at the
> effects of my labor than at the pure motion and reality of
> the concern, as it arises from heavenly love.[2]

In seeking guidance regarding a proposed course of action, we
find ourselves using four main tests: authority, reason, results and
intuitive feeling. If the four agree, we have a secure basis for action. In using authority we appeal to the insights of persons past
and present whose judgment we respect. As most of our knowledge is based, not on our own experience, but on the experience
of others, this test is probably the criterion most often used. A
scientist, for example, can test very little of his scientific knowledge by his own experiments. He must accept as fact what he has
learned from the experiments of others. In the same way the Christian will depend on the insights of the writers of Scripture, the
Church Fathers, the outstanding persons of his own religious
group, and others whom he respects as being of saintly character.
Important also is the test of reason which, as has been pointed

out, is the test of consistency. The pragmatic test is also helpful. "By their fruits ye shall know them."

But it can be shown that ultimately in the field of religion and morality the test of feeling must be trusted. By feeling in this field is meant our intuitive apprehension of the Light of Truth. By feeling we accept some authorities and reject others. By feeling we accept certain premises as a basis for our reasoning and reject others. By feeling we accept certain results as good and reject others as bad. When early Friends placed the Light above Scriptures, Church, Reason and short-range experience of results, they assumed a tenable position.

The position of the Quakers would have been more difficult in practice if they had based the test of feeling on a purely individual apprehension of truth. In appealing to the group to confirm each one's inward leading, a useful check is provided. Nevertheless, if the individual feels clearly and strongly that the group is wrong, he may be obliged to ignore its judgment.

Instances of appeals to the group, followed by disregard of all other tests but that of feeling, not infrequently appear in the Quaker *Journals*. An event in the life of Thomas Shillitoe will serve as an example. Traveling in the ministry in Europe, he came to the German city of Hamburg in 1821 and found the Sabbath observed as a time of merry-making with scant attention to religion. He had no friends in the city and did not know the language, but he resolved after a time of inward retirement to attempt to remedy the situation. He prepared an address to the people of the city and forwarded it to London for the approval or disapproval of Friends there. Finally, his address came back, translated into German, with the approval of London Friends. He himself aided in distributing the appeal throughout the city. His arrest brought about some desirable publicity for his concern and an opportunity to speak with public officials. His main objective was constantly present to his mind—that "I should be clear in the sight of my

Maker was all I was to aim at." When he was put in prison, he said, "My heart leaped for joy to feel myself once more so much of a free man." This freedom resulted from the sense that he was no longer carrying the burden of an unfulfilled requirement. Thomas Shillitoe left Hamburg with a feeling of inward peace in spite of the fact that his work apparently had no result. He had followed feeling when his reason might have told him that his mission was hopeless. He had secured the approval of his meeting and his conscience. The results could be left to God.

One more instance may suffice. In 1762 John Woolman felt "a motion of love" to visit Indians two hundred miles from Philadelphia because "some of them were measurably acquainted with that Divine Power which subjects the rough and froward will of the creature."[3] He laid the matter before his Monthly, Quarterly and General Spring Meeting and secured approval. Before starting, he learned that the Indians were on the warpath. He writes:

> My heart was turned to the Lord for his Heavenly instruction. . . . In this conflict of Spirit there were great searchings of heart and strong cries to the Lord that no motion might be in the least degree attended to but that of the pure Spirit of Truth.[4]

Proceeding on the journey he saw many signs of war with the English. Though in danger of being captured and tortured, he writes that "the Lord in great mercy gave me a resigned heart in which I found quietness." A satisfying meeting was held with the Indians. John Woolman returned home safely. It would be difficult to say just what was accomplished by such a journey, but John Woolman never for a moment doubted his leading. The evidence of right guidance was the constant inward sense of peace and resignation, not the results in more visible terms.

When John Woolman was a member of a committee to persuade Friends who held slaves to give them their freedom, his appeal had little to do with the evil results of slavery, though mention of these was not wholly omitted. The appeal was to the feelings of the slaveholder. Did he feel comfortable in holding these men and women in bondage? The slaveholder often had to admit that he did not feel comfortable about it. He could reason that he needed slaves in order to compete successfully with others who held slaves, and he could quote authorities, even scriptural authorities, in support of slaveholding, but his feelings, if he admitted the truth, did not give him inward peace.

The Quaker methods for guiding conduct were implemented by two devices: committees to visit those who fell short of the standard, and the Queries. In the early years of the eighteenth century the visiting committees were gradually replaced by overseers appointed to exercise pastoral care, especially in matters involving morals. The overseers (or special committees appointed for the purpose) usually visited every family in the meeting at least once a year. Moral offenders were lovingly and sympathetically labored with and, if brought to repentance, were asked to make an acknowledgment of their error in writing and to bring it in person to the monthly meeting. If the offender refused to make an acknowledgment, the committee continued its labors for at least a year. If no signs of change or repentance were observed and the offense was sufficiently serious, the offender was then dropped from membership by the meeting.

The overseers were guided by the Queries, which were questions answered by the lower meetings to the higher meetings at first vocally by appointed representatives and later, after 1755, in writing. Answers to the Queries were expected to reveal shortcomings in the membership. Thus the Quarterly Meeting could learn the state of the Monthly Meetings, and the Yearly Meeting could learn the state of the Quarterly Meetings and extend advice and help as might be required. The Queries were a kind of group confessional by which every individual and every meeting was able at regular intervals of a year or less to check actual conduct against an ideal standard of behavior. The Queries covered all that was expected of the consistent Friend. They were frequently revised as new moral insights prevailed or old testimonies become obsolete.*

The following entry in the minutes of Sadsbury Monthly Meeting in 1780 will indicate the procedure:

> The committee appointed in that weighty service of reformation with respect to due and wakeful attendance at our religious meetings, plainness of speech, behavior, apparel and household furniture, with other deficiencies complained of in the Queries, report they attended to the service and find that there appears a willingness in most to endeavor to remedy deficiencies; and many things that appeared superfluous have been removed.

To be successful such committees must proceed in the right spirit. Philadelphia Yearly Meeting in 1719 declared:

> It is the advice of this meeting that in speaking to or dealing with any, it be done in a Christian spirit of love and tenderness, laboring in meekness, by laying the evil before them, to bring such persons to a sense of it in themselves, that they may be restored if possible. And although such as transgress or lose their hold on Truth are apt to be testy, while they are in that condition, yet we ought patiently and meekly to instruct and advise them, that so we may not only have a testimony of peace within ourselves, but that it may likewise so affect the spirit of the Friend spoken to, that he may be sensible we have performed a truly Christian duty and an office of brotherly love toward him.

---

* A modern set of Queries appears in Appendix II.

Community

The Quaker meeting used to be, and to some extent still is, both a religious and an economic unit. The members sometimes found themselves dependent on one another for material support. This was especially important in the early days when the Quakers lost much of their property through fines and imprisonment. Some were dismissed by their employers because they became Quakers. Others found themselves engaged in businesses which had to be abandoned because of their principles: for example, employment which had to do with luxuries or equipment for war. This economic interdependence still exists to some extent in Quaker meetings and continues to be the subject of an annual Query.

In 1737 a list of persons entitled to support was drawn up by each meeting. This list constituted the first list of members and introduced the concept of a definite membership. Since the children of members would also be in need of help, their names appeared on the list. This occasioned the provision for birthright membership. Birthright membership results from the assumption that a meeting is like a large family whose members are dependent on one another, not only for material necessities, but for intellectual and spiritual well-being. Children are born into the meeting in a sense similar to that in which they are born into a family. As in the case of the family, they are free to detach themselves at the age of maturity. Since they are children of the meeting as well as children of their parents, their education is a meeting responsibility. If the parents cannot pay for the education of the children, the meeting is expected to do so, or at least to assume the responsibility. That the children are considered members of the meeting community from the start is an important factor in their education. As has already been pointed out, participation in community activities is the most potent form of education. Birth, marriage, death, all the important events and crises of life, are concerns of the meeting and call for its care.

As membership in the meeting is membership in a community, the test of membership is compatibility with the meeting community. Members are either born into the meeting or join it because they desire to fit into the pattern of behavior peculiar to the meeting and find themselves able to do so. The test of membership is not a particular kind of religious experience, nor acceptance of any particular religious, social or economic creed. Sincere religious experience and right religious belief are both important, but they develop in the course of participation in the activities of the meeting. Anyone who can become so integrated with a meeting that he helps the whole and the whole helps him is qualified to become a member.

The following selections from early minutes are typical of many that indicate the character of the economic interdependence developed in the meeting community:

> Ordered Caleb Pusey and Walter Fawcett take care to hire a cow for the Widow Rudiman and the Quarterly Meeting is obliged to answer them 30s. [Chester, 1689]

> Information being given this meeting that W.P. is very poor and in necessity, the meeting orders A.B. to get a good pair of leather britches and a good warm coat and waist coat, one pair of stockings and shoes and make a report of the charge to the next meeting. [Falls, 1701]

> The condition of J.C. (a Friend of Bucks County) being laid before the meeting, having lost by fire to the value of 162 pounds, this meeting orders that a collection be settled in each particular First Day's meeting and two appointed to receive them. [Chester, 1691]

> The friends appointed to make Inspection concerning
> Mary Moot report she hath a right to our meeting and also
> is in real need of relief, we therefore recommend her to
> the Friends appointed for the care of the poor of this meet-
> ing as a proper object thereof. [Concord, 1763]

The following minute indicates the care which Friends took of
those not in membership with them who suffered from the blockade of the New England coast during the Revolutionary war:

> The Friends appointed to take in subscriptions for the
> relief of the poor and destitute in New England reported
> they have taken in subscriptions in the amount of £33 14s.
> [Darby, 1775]

Because of its responsibilities in taking care of the poor, the
meeting was alert to prevent poverty. It watched over its members
to see that they were not taking undue risks in business and not
spending more than they earned. "Are Friends careful to live within
the bounds of their circumstances and to keep to moderation in
their trade or business?" was long an annual Query. The following
minute of a Yearly Meeting was issued in 1710:

> It is the advice of this meeting to the several Quarterly
> Meetings, that care may be taken that substantial Friends
> be appointed to visit every family among us where they think
> there is occasion to suspect they are going backward in
> their worldly estate.

That the meeting exercised oversight over the members as all
parts of one family may be indicated by the following acknowledgments of error:

> William Williams, son of Robert, and Joan, daughter of
> James Pugh declared their intentions of marriage with each

other before this meeting and he acknowledged his mis-
step in proposing his mind to the young woman before he
had her father's consent, but is allowed to proceed.
[Goshen, 1723]

Whereas I was forward and hasty in making suit to a young
woman after the death of my wife, having made some pro-
ceedings in that way in less than four months, which I am
now sensible was wrong. [New Garden, 1740]

In the early eighteenth century business meetings were attended
only by those who because of the excellence of their judgment
were invited to attend so that aid to the poor, personal delinquen-
cies and quarrels between members which ought not to be made
public could be discussed within closed doors. Today, as the business meetings are open to all members and to the public as well,
personal matters are considered more privately in special committees. For this reason examples of meeting action in such matters
can only be found in the older minutes.

The meeting community is probably more needed today as a
stabilizing element in society than ever before. The family is small
and often unable to withstand the storms which sweep over it in
our unstable economic system. This was less true in the days of the
large, patriarchal family, which often included grandparents, aunts
and uncles as well as a number of children. For the unmarried
woman the Society of Friends has always had significant work
of an educational, social or religious nature to claim her full
attention.

Today the state is assuming the function of providing a degree
of economic security. But the state is so large that its functioning
is impersonal. It may provide economic maintenance, but it is not
in a position to offer the psychological support which is equally
necessary. The family being too small a unit and the state too large,
the religious group, the meeting or church, in which all the mem-

bers have a strong interest in one another's welfare, may be able to fulfill the need. Within such a group the required aid can be extended with the same warmth and understanding as within a family. More groups of this size and kind, having a certain degree of economic interdependence, are urgently needed at present to offset the increasing atomization and disintegration of our social structure. Due to the disappearance of the village form of life and of the even older types of multiple family life, modern society finds itself to be an incoherent mass of lonely individuals.

Harmony

The means of obtaining harmony within the meeting have already been discussed in connection with the Quaker method of reaching decisions in the meeting for business. By harmony is meant a pacifist technique by which unity of action is reached without the use of any form of coercion, such as the exercise of personal authority or the prevailing of a majority over a minority. The appeal to the Light Within as the source of unity does not imply the victory of a person or a party over another person or party, but the victory of Truth which is often on the side of the weak.

The Query which has been longest in continuous use by the Society of Friends is this: "Are love and unity maintained amongst you?" It dates from 1682. Any quarrels or disagreements within the group become an object of concern to the meeting and the old Query, "Where differences arise are endeavors made speedily to end them?" could usually be answered in the affirmative. It was contrary to the Discipline for any Quaker to settle his difference with another Quaker by a lawsuit. He must appeal to the meeting. A few examples will illustrate the action of the meeting in settling differences.

Considered and agreed upon by the hearing of differences
between Joseph Richards and Charles Ascham about the
admeasure of land—that the said Joseph shall pay Charles
for the same without any further disturbance. The same is
ended between them and the money is paid in the presence of the meeting. [Concord, 1684]

The difference between Joseph Richards and William
Woodmansey offered to the meeting in order to a compo-
sure of the same. William Woodmansey acknowledges he
spoke foolishly in comparing him to a London pickpocket
and the like and that he was grieved and sorry for the same,
which Joseph Richards did accept of, desiring and intend-
ing hereby that there be n end of strife from the beginning to this day. [Chester, 1686]

Friends, whereas I contended with my neighbor William
Shipley for what I apprehended to be my right, by endeav-
oring to turn a certain stream of water into its natural
course, till it arose to a personal difference, in which dis-
pute I gave way to warmth of temper so as to put my friend
William into the pond, for which action of mine, being
contrary to the good order of Friends, I am sorry and
desire through Divine Assistance to live in unity with him
for the future. From your friend Joshua Way. [Wilmington,
1751]

Sometimes the meeting did not believe the claim of Friends
who had quarreled that they had composed their differences.

It is our opinion that Concord Friends have been put by
their proper business in the case of John Larkin and Robert Pyle by giving way to their outward appearance of love
and friendship being restored between them, when their

hearts have been evilly affected toward each other. And, as we fear the testimony of Truth has suffered by too much delay, we think that unless something more of love appears between them than has hitherto done, Friends should testify against them.

This report was signed by a committee of twelve of Concord Monthly Meeting in 1769 after laboring with the offenders for two years. Both were in consequence disowned from membership.

Equality

Equality was the earliest Quaker social testimony. Even before the Quakers became pacifists Quaker soldiers were dismissed from the army because they refused to treat their officers as superiors. This testimony may have been in part an inheritance from the Levellers and Diggers, pre-Quaker groups with strong equalitarian leanings. Lilburne, the leader of the Levellers, became a Quaker, but Winstanley, leader of the Diggers, did not. Except for his communism, Winstanley's opinions coincided with those of George Fox.

The Quaker doctrine of equality does not mean equality of ability, economic resources or social status. It means equality of respect and the resulting absence of all words and behavior based on class, racial or social distinctions. It did not, for example, place on an economic equality employer and employee or master and servant. The Quakers agreed with the Puritans that each person must follow his vocation, a religious word indicating God's call to a particular kind of occupation appropriate to one's ability and interest. The doctrine of equality tended to eliminate the sense of superiority or inferiority attaching to different callings.

Advices concerning the treatment of servants appear as early as 1656 in statements on church discipline. Dewsbury writes in a letter that "now mistress and maid are to be hail fellows well met."

Some of the greatest of the early Quaker women ministers were maidservants. One such was Mary Fisher who addressed the Sultan of Turkey and his Court, and Dorothy Waugh who was jailed by Peter Stuyvesant for preaching in the streets of New York. Servant and master addressed each other by their given names and servants often ate at the family table.

Within the meeting equality appears in the equal opportunity for all to take part, regardless of age, sex or ability. No persons enjoy special privilege, though some, because of unusual gifts, have more weight than others in the meeting's deliberations.

Outside the meeting this doctrine brought the Quakers of an earlier time into serious disrepute, many of the prevailing customs having as their base the highly stratified condition of English society. Friends were compelled to disregard these modes of behavior and in consequence they often appeared rude or ill-mannered.

Friends refused the use of titles of honor and salutations which implied that one person was superior to another. There were three reasons for this. First, the Quakers wished to remove all recognition of social distinctions based on class or race. Secondly, they were opposed to any form of flattery which tended to puff up self-esteem. And, thirdly, most titles were out of harmony with the truth. Addressing a superior by the plural "you" instead of "thou"* which was customary practice in the seventeenth century was given up for these reasons. Barclay writes of the prevailing custom of saying "you" to one person:

> This way of speaking proceeds from a high and proud mind . . . because that men commonly use the singular to beggars and to their servants; yea and in their prayers to

* In America "thou" has become "thee." It is not unusual in the development of language for the accusative to replace the nominative, as, for example, "you" an accusative has replaced "ye" a nominative.

God—so hath the pride of men placed God and the beggar in the same category.[5]

Friends might have avoided this distinction by using "you" to everyone, but that would, with the then current norms of speech, have been considered as flattery. Also "you," being a plural, would have been considered untruthful. For similar reasons "Mister" and "Mistress" were avoided as no one used these titles to persons rated as inferior. Titles such as "Your Grace," "Your Highness," "Sir," "Your Honor," "Your Humble Servant," "The Reverend," "Your Majesty," "Your Obedient Servant," were ruled out not only as flattery, but because they were false descriptions of the person addressed. The prefix "Saint" was omitted even in place names.

> Who are they that are honorable indeed? Is it not the righteous man? Is it not the holy man? Is it not the humble hearted man, the meek spirited man? . . . Now of these may there not be poor men, laborers, silly fishermen?[6]

The "plain language" included also the designation of the names of the months, and the days of the week by numerals rather than by their usual names which were derived in most cases from heathen deities (Ex. 23:13). At one time the adoption of the "plain language" like the adoption of the "plain dress" followed a spiritual crisis and was a symbol of the new way of life and the "taking up of the cross." Today the plain language, including the use of the accusative "thee" as a nominative, in America has become a sign of family intimacy and religious fellowship rather than a testimony.

The Quakers were often hailed into court for one reason or another. On such occasions their refusal to doff their hats as a mark of respect to the judge aroused anger and resulted in harsh treatment. Though they never removed their hats to any human being, in worship the head was uncovered during vocal prayer in reverence to God. Young converts appearing before their parents wearing their hats suffered stern rebuke and sometimes violence. This happened to young Thomas Ellwood who lost three hats in rapid succession. Sometimes the hat was quietly and deftly removed by a servant or official deputed for this act, as was the case when Stephen Grellet had an audience with the Pope. Advices issued by Yearly Meetings condemn all "bowings and scrapings" and every form of subservience whatsoever.

Before the Friends freed their slaves they treated them with respect. Slaves were taken to meeting, which was against the law in the West Indies, and often their children were sent to Quaker schools along with the white children. It took Friends some time to realize that slavery was not a "calling," like that of a servant.

In general, except for a few notable exceptions, such as John Bellers who in 1695 proposed a communistic form of community life, and William Allen who was associated with Robert Owen in the ownership of the colony in New Lanark,[7] Friends were not interested in radically altering the social order. "Any form is good if administered by good men," writes William Penn. Perhaps Friends came the nearest to being social radicals when, like John Woolman in his "Word of Remembrance to the Rich," they found the seeds of war in the love of possessions.

A recent Query is a sign of modern interest in the reform of the social order.* There are a number of examples of Quaker businessmen who have introduced a considerable degree of labor participation in the management of their factories, but this has not been sufficiently extensive to merit particular attention.[8] Quaker relief workers frequently try to put themselves on an equality with those among whom they labor. This is particularly true of the work camps of the American Friends Service Committee. Racial equality is being slowly realized in Friends schools today, but not in all.

* See Appendix I, Query 7.

Many Quakers have an active concern against all forms of racial discrimination. They maintain committees to seek solutions to this pressing problem. There is a growing endeavor to eliminate what Joseph John Gurney called "the aristocracy of the skin."[9]

Simplicity

Simplicity, the fourth aspect of the Quaker code of behavior, finds primary expression within the meeting for worship in the simple manner of waiting upon the Lord in surroundings unadorned in respect of furnishings and architecture. In the eighteenth century simplicity was insisted upon. The meeting houses of that period exhibit not only plainness but fitness, beauty and proportion. In the nineteenth century this good norm was departed from, but recent structures show a return to functional simplicity. While the concern for simplicity was fresh and living, its expression showed good taste, but when it became largely traditional, Quaker meeting houses as well as Quaker homes and furniture degenerated in form and style.

Friends have had no testimony against excellence of quality. Their testimony was against superfluity in "dress, speech and behavior."

In general, Friends are not ascetics who find virtue in a mortification of the flesh. They condemned pleasure when it existed as a superfluity, interfering with more serious undertakings. The following passage from Clarkson's *Portraiture of Quakerism* illustrates this attitude:

> Music, if it were encouraged by the Society, would be considered as depriving those of maturer years of hours of comfort which they now frequently enjoy in the service of religion. Retirement is considered by the Quakers as a Christian duty. The members, therefore, of this Society are

expected to wait in silence, not only in their places of worship, but occasionally in their families, or in their private chambers, in the intervals of their daily occupations, that, in stillness of heart, and in freedom from the active contrivance of their own wills, they may acquire both directions and strength for the performance of the duties of life. The Quakers, therefore, are of the opinion that, if instrumental music were admitted as a gratification in leisure hours, it would take the place of many of these serious retirements and become very injurious to their interests and their character as Christians.[10]

The same used to be true of the arts in general. Simplicity meant the absence of all that was unnecessary, such as ornamentation in dress, speech, manners, architecture, house furnishings. Dispensing with that which was qualitatively and functionally good was not advocated.

There was also an economic reason for simplicity. William Penn says that "the very trimming of the vain world would clothe all the naked one."[11] John Woolman writes:

As He is the perfection of power, of wisdom and of goodness, so I believe He hath provided that so much labor shall be necessary for men's support in this world as would, being rightly divided, be a suitable employment of their tune; and that we cannot go into superfluities nor grasp after wealth in a way contrary to His wisdom, with out having connection with some degree of oppression and with that spirit which leads to self-exaltation and strife, and which frequently brings calamities on countries by parties contending about their claims.[12]

Luxuries and superfluities cause an increase in the amount of labor required of men. They therefore, contribute to oppression in exacting this labor, and oppression leads to self-exaltation and war. John Woolman would have had small sympathy with the modern argument that in buying luxuries people aid the poor by providing employment. He firmly believed that luxuries are a source of vanity, oppression and ultimately war. If men would remain humble and confine their desires to real needs, overwork, oppression and strife would disappear and there would be enough of the necessities of life to go around.

In his *Conversations on the True Harmony of Mankind,* John Woolman expresses the intimate connection between his religion and simplicity:

> If I put forth my strength in any employ which I know is to support pride, I feel that it has a tendency to weaken those bands which . . . I have felt at times to bind and unite my soul in a holy fellowship with the Father, and with his Son, Jesus Christ.

From the Quaker dress all the ornamentation, so characteristic of the age of the Stuart kings, was removed. Sober-minded Puritans bore a similar testimony. Later the Quakers continued to dress in the fashion of an earlier time. Eventually this became standardized and was adhered to on the theory that submission to changes in fashion which compelled people to buy new clothes when they did not need them was a useless concession to worldly ways. There is nothing in Quaker theory to support the avoidance of bright colors except, perhaps, their tendency to increase self-esteem. Margaret Fox condemned what she saw to be a growing insistence on drab in the early eighteenth century.

The uniform costume which became habitual was a quick and effective way of telling the world where one stood, and some Quakers claimed that it kept them out of places where they should not go. Once having assumed the Quaker dress they felt compelled to live up to it. Eventually many came to recognize it as an empty form, modern dress being for the most part plain and functional.

Simplicity in speech was also a distinguishing mark of the consistent Friend. Ornamental and superfluous words were omitted in speaking and writing. This gave the Quakers a reputation for bluntness. In speaking in meeting or elsewhere oratorical flourishes were discouraged. Attempts at fine writing are seldom found in Quaker books. Reverent restraint is always shown in speaking of the deepest religious experiences. William Penn in listing twelve characteristics of Friends gives as number eight, "They recommend silence by their example, having very few words upon all occasions."

The doctrine of simplicity or absence of superfluity is applicable to all aspects of life. Committees are appointed to see to it that plainness is observed at weddings and funerals. For more than a century tombstones were testified against as superfluous. When they came to be used as markers, they were small and inconspicuous. In the testimony for simplicity in house furnishings the most modern usage has now come around for aesthetic reasons to the early Quaker point of view. Friends objected to the arts not only because they seemed useless but also because they were representations of life, which tended to take the place of life itself. The actor in a theater, for example, expresses feelings which he does not genuinely feel, and the writer of a novel gives an account of events which never took place. Music arouses feelings which find no outlet in action and hence may be harmful. For similar reasons St. Augustine calls singing "this contentment of the flesh, to which the soul must not be given over to be enervated."[13] The arts were thought to cultivate an untrue and misleading picture of reality inclining those who follow them to live in an imaginary, unreal world. The modern motion picture is an example of an art which may have the effect of causing its viewers to live in a realm of dreams.

The early Quakers were certainly mistaken regarding the true nature of the world of imagination. Art has a reality of its own and a language of its own which can convey meanings beyond the reach of ordinary action or speech. Modern Friends do not hesitate to give to the arts their appropriate place, though long disinclination to appreciate some forms of beauty has left the Society of Friends somewhat dormant aesthetically.

Since Friends condemned superfluities, Quaker businessmen could not sell them and this often limited their business severely. Tailors, hatters, booksellers, funeral directors, printers, silversmiths and merchants were affected by this tenet. John Hall (1637-1719), a Quaker tailor, "was willing to lose all rather than his peace with the Lord."

But business itself could become a waste of time and a superfluity if overindulged in. When its claims became too absorbing the Friend found that he could no longer attend to his religious duties. If religion was his primary interest, he reduced his business. That was most frequently true in the case of traveling ministers. Almost all the Quaker *Journals* contain examples of curtailment of business when it had become so engrossing as to require time that properly belonged to religion.

A few examples taken from the *Journals* will indicate the reasons for this limitation of business. Daniel Wheeler found his business as a seed merchant so prosperous that it interfered with his career as a Friend:

> As I have from time to time endeavoured to dwell near and abide in and under the calming influence of His power, I have been led to believe that something sooner or later would be required as a sacrifice on my part. . . . I therefore fully believe that it will be most conducive to my present peace, as well as future well being, entirely to give up the trade I am at present engaged in, and retire with my family into a small compass."

William Evans (1787-1867), when offered a partnership in a large
dry goods business, refused it:

> My present business, being small and one that I understood,
> was managed with ease. It required little capital and in-
> volved me in no engagements that I did not hold the means
> to meet; so that I was free from anxiety on that account,
> and at liberty to attend, unincumbered, appointments of
> the Society or any impression of duty to go to a meeting
> that I might have. . . . It seemed that if I pursued the pros-
> pect of adopting the proposed change of business, that I
> should be lost to religious society and to the work of reli-
> gion in my own heart. . . . I looked forward with renewed
> peace and satisfaction at the path and the business before
> me, though small, remembering that the earth is the Lord's
> and the cattle on a thousand hills.[15]

Thomas Shillitoe (1756-1836) speaks of an

> apprehension which at times presented to my mind that
> the time was fast approaching when I must be willing to
> relinquish a good business and set myself more at liberty
> to attend to my religious duties from home. The language
> which my Divine Master renewedly proclaimed in the ear
> of my soul, was "Gather up thy wares into thy house for I
> have need of the residue of thy days."[16]

Thomas Shillitoe had five children to settle in life, but he left
that "to the same Almighty Power who had so abundantly cared
for us." Nevertheless he writes, "The prospect of relinquishing a
good business was at times a close trial to my soul."

Martha Routh whose school was too large for its quarters describes how she went out to look at a larger house:

> As I passed from room to room I was attended by a secret
> but clear intimation that I was not to entangle myself with

a greater number of scholars than the house we already had would accommodate, so I entirely gave up the thought and found peace.[17]

Sometimes Quaker scholars found it necessary to reduce their studies in order to give more time to religion. William Allen, a notable scientist, writes in his *Journal:*

> Rather comforted this morning, it seemed to open on my view with respect to my great attraction to natural science that when I felt it strong and likely to get the ascendency, it would be my duty to indulge less in it, abridge the time devoted to it and fast from it.[18]

John Rutty, Irish physician and author of important medical books, prays:

> Lord deliver from living to eat, drink, sleep, smoke and study.[19]

Simplicity not only meant absence of superfluity in speech. It also meant genuineness and sincerity. Quakers leaned over backwards and sometimes made themselves objects of ridicule in their efforts to tell the exact truth. Fearing overstatement they resorted to understatement. Phrases like "As far as we know," "Nothing appears," were used in answering the Queries. A Friend would not say, "I object," but more probably, "I cannot see my way clear to unite."

One by-product of truth-telling was the initiation of the one price system in business. It was the custom in the seventeenth century for merchants to ask more than they expected to receive and for the customer to offer less than he expected to give. By a process of bargaining a price was agreed on. The Quaker stated at the outset the price which he was prepared to accept. As a result Quaker business flourished. A child could be sent to make a purchase from a Quaker merchant.

The search for an understanding of the creation and insight into its beauty, sincerity and genuineness led many Quakers to scientific pursuits, particularly botany and ornithology. Some became professional scientists. Science seemed closer to reality than did art. With the exclusion of many forms of amusement, it also afforded delight. Superfluities in education were eliminated as completely as other nonessentials. Jonathan Dymond, the Quaker moralist, writes in 1825:

> Science is preferable to literature, the knowledge of things to the knowledge of words.[20]

Verbalism and formalism were opposed in education as they were in religion. Knowledge of nature as God's creation was thought to bring man nearer to the divine than a knowledge of man's works. To quote Dymond again:

> It is of less consequence to man to know what Horace wrote or to be able to criticise the Greek anthology than to know by what laws the Deity regulates the operations of nature and to know by what means those operations are made subservient to the purposes of life.[21]

As a consequence of this scientific interest, which was a direct result of the effort to come closer to sincerity and reality, the list of Quaker scientists is a long one. A. Ruth Fry observes in *Quaker Ways* that between 1851 and 1900 in England a Quaker "had forty-six times more chance of election as a Fellow of the Royal Society than his fellow countrymen."

No testimony resulted in more suffering than the Quaker stand against judicial oaths. Many Friends spent long years in foul prisons and some died there in support of this testimony. The Quaker refused to swear for at least two reasons: (1) swearing was contrary to the command of Christ—"Swear not at all." (Matt. 5:34)—and of James—"But above all things, my brethren, swear not" (James

5:12); (2) it also set up a double standard of truth, one in the courtroom and one outside it, with the implication that untruth would be uttered in the absence of an oath. When Quakers were brought to trial and the evidence against them was faulty or lacking, they could be tendered the oath of allegiance and imprisoned for refusing to take it. By refusing to take an oath, Friends were also disqualified from conforming to customs regulations, from suing for debts, from giving evidence in court, from defending titles to property, and from holding office. Penn's epigram, "People swear to the end they may speak truth; Christ would have them speak truth to the end they might not swear"[22] summed up the Quaker case. Penn points out how futile oaths had been in the past hundred years in England when each ruler required an oath for the support of a particular form of religion which was quickly renounced by many of the clergy when an oath to support another form of religion was required by the next ruler. Finally, after a long struggle, an act was passed by Parliament in 1696 permitting affirmation. But a minority of Friends felt that they could not use the new formula because it contained the word "solemnly," a religious word. For twenty-five years London Yearly Meeting struggled to agree on a form of words which would satisfy everybody. This was an example of the extremely patient efforts made by a majority to satisfy a minority. Finally, in 1722 a formula was agreed upon and its enactment into law was secured.

In Pennsylvania, Penn's Charter allowed affirmation, but it was not until 1725 that a special act of the Colonial Assembly was ratified by the King in Council permitting a form of affirmation which satisfied all Friends. Quaker magistrates who administered oaths were disowned in the early period.

> Joseph Thornton so far condemns his having administered an oath, as to declare himself determined not to accept of any office for the future which may subject him to the ne-

cessity of doing it, and that he now sees the practice inconsistent, both with the rules of the Society and the convictions of his own mind, which this Meeting agrees to accept
of as satisfaction for what is past. [Middletown Monthly
Meeting, 1762]

After the Revolutionary War laws were enacted imposing a test
oath or affirmation abjuring the King and declaring allegiance to
the new government. Many Friends suffered for refusing to take
this oath, with the result that enforcement of the law was soon
given up. Although affirmation was permitted, the Yearly Meeting
declared, "We cannot be instrumental in setting up or pulling down
any government."

In America the meeting community, acting according to a well-
defined code of behavior, reached its highest development in colonial times when the number of competing interests was small
and when the meetings were surrounded by a population largely
Quaker. The minutes of this period contain many references to
the care taken for implementing the testimony for simplicity. A
few typical examples follow:

> Our Women's Meeting enters a complaint against
> Elizabeth Bennell for much deviating from plainness in
> dress and address and frequenting places of musick and
> dancing. John Milhouse and Liba Ferriss are appointed to
> joyn women Friends in treating with her and report her
> disposition at next meeting. [Wilmington, 1778]

> N. H. hath given in a paper condemning himself for
> his playing at cards, which paper the meeting receives,
> and orders him to read the said paper in the place where
> he was playing, in the presence of Benjamin Fredd
> and William Halliday and he is desired to forebear coming
> to meetings of business until Friends are better satisfied

> with him as to conversation and sincerity to Truth. [New
> Garden, 1725]

> A Concern having taken hould of this Meeting to suppress
> pride and it seems to appeare somewhat in women in wear-
> ing of hoopes pettecouts which is a grate truble to many
> friends minds and it is the unanimous sense of this Meet-
> ing that none amongst us be in the practis thereof that all
> our Overseers and other solled friends do inspect into their
> members and where any appeare to be guilty do deal with
> them and discharg them either in that of hoops or other
> indecent dresses. [Concord, 1739]

On two occasions, 1695 and 1723, Philadelphia Yearly Meeting
issued warnings to its members to keep clear of all astrologers,
sorcerers or anyone professing to practice the black arts. Acknowledgments of error were required of all who had recourse to such
persons. Joseph Walter offered an acknowledgment "for going
to a man to be informed concerning my horse. I can truly say I
had no desire he should make use of any bad art in that affair"
(Concord, 1738).

From the earliest days the Quaker meetings were swift to deal
with members who used intoxicating beverages to excess or who
were engaged in manufacturing or selling them. The following
Query was answered beginning in 1755:

> Are Friends careful to avoid the excessive use of spirituous
> liquors, the unnecessary frequenting of taverns and places
> of diversion and to keep to true moderation and temper-
> ance on account of births, marriages, burials and other
> occasions?

This Query was gradually modified in the direction of greater
strictness. "Spirituous liquors" was changed to *all* liquors. The
inclusion of *all* liquors in the Query was brought about in Phila-

delphia by a revolt in 1874 of the young men against the older men on the facing benches of the meeting. Joshua L. Baily, writing of this, says: "It was like the House of Commons against the House of Lords and the Commons prevailed."[23] Finally, but not until near the beginning of the twentieth century, was the Query applied to total abstinence.

The ancient doctrine of simplicity might be applied today to diminish the superfluous activities which prevent leisure and relaxation. The multiplication of time-saving gadgets seems, paradoxically, to increase the general busyness and complexity of life. The baton of some invisible conductor seems to be gradually increasing the tempo of life. The solution, as the sages and seers of all the great religions have pointed out, is not to increase our attainments but to decrease our desires; in other words, to follow the path of simplicity.

Notes

1. William Allen, *Life*, London, 1846, I, 41.

2. John Woolman, *Journal*, edited by Janet Whitney, 1950, p. 61.

3. Woolman, *Journal*, p. 118.

4. Woolman, *Journal*, p. 120.

5. Robert Barclay, *Apology*, p. 528.

6. Barclay, *Apology*, p. 523.

7. See William Allen, *Colonies at Home*, 1832.

8. Thomas Carlyle considers the Quaker an ideal type of employer in his *Past and Present*, 1918.

9. John Joseph Gurney, *Chalmeriana*, or Colloquies with Dr. Chalmers, 1853, p. 64.

10. Thomas Clarkson, *Portraiture of Quakerism*, 1808, I, 34.

11. William Penn, *Reflections and Maxims*, 1850, No. 73.

12. Woolman, *Journal*, p. 114.

13. Augustine, *Confessions*, Chap. X, sec. xxxiii.

14. Daniel Wheeler, *Memoirs*, London, 1842, p. 44.

15. William Evans, *Journal*, 1870, pp. 30-31.

16. Thomas Shillitoe, *Journal*, in *Friends Library*, III, 93.

17. Martha Routh, *Journal*, in *Friends Library*, XII, 419.

18. William Allen, *Life*, London, 1846, I, 32.

19. John Rutty, extracts from *The Spiritual Diary*, 1840, p. 9.

20. Jonathan Dymond, *Essays on the Principles of Morality*, 1830, Essay II, Chap. XI.

21. Rutty, *Spiritual Diary*, p. 9.

22. William Penn, *A Treatise on Oaths*, sec. ix.

23. Joshua L. Baily, *The Friend*, Jan. 7, 1915.

CHAPTER VIII

The Meeting and the World

IT WAS INEVITABLE AND ESSENTIAL that the type of behavior developed within the Meeting Community should spread to the world outside. Community, equality, harmony and simplicity create attitudes of mind and heart which cannot be confined to any one place or group. Because life within the Meeting Community is different but not too different from life outside it, this radiation is possible. The code of behavior developed in a monastery, for example, is so different from that of the world around it that it is more difficult for the monastic way to be universalized. The Quaker code of behavior can be universalized and has been widely extended, with the possible exception of the doctrine of pacifism. This doctrine, therefore, will receive particular attention here. "There is no better test," writes William E. Hocking, "of any rule of life than its way of settling accounts with pugnacity."[1]

Quaker efforts toward social and political reform have been largely carried on in the fields of religious liberty, education, the abolition of slavery, help for Negroes and Indians, improvement of mental hospitals, relief work during and after wars, prison reform, and endeavors toward removal of the causes of war. As these efforts have received wide attention and as they involve no principles different from those already discussed, a brief outline will be sufficient.* The

* Quaker work for temperance and in foreign missions is omitted for the sake of brevity. This work has involved no unique principles.

176

Society of Friends is a small group and the amount which it has accomplished may appear quantitatively insignificant. Quaker work has, however, sometimes proved important because of its pioneering quality. Friends have not hesitated to support new and unpopular undertakings. In many cases, after their endeavors have received the support of larger groups, they have withdrawn and expended their energies elsewhere in behalf of less popular causes. The names of persons who are prominently associated with certain causes, such as William Wilberforce and William Lloyd Garrison in the cause of slavery, John Howard in prison reform, and Dorothea Lynde Dix in the reform of mental hospitals, are not Quaker names. However, the initial steps in the reforms they effected had been taken by Quakers and these leaders received much of their backing from members of the Society of Friends. In all of their major efforts at social betterment the Quakers have been assisted by many like-minded persons outside their membership.

The pioneering quality of Quaker social work is largely due to the character of the meeting for worship. Silent waiting worship permits a fresh and direct facing of facts under conditions in which the conscience becomes sensitized. There is no screen of words and abstract concepts between the soul and reality. Music, sermons, prayers, responses, all such spiritual exercises may be received passively or with a resistance of which the recipient is often quite unaware, but that which arises from within is closer to the springs of the will. The worshiper finds a certain condition in the outside world presented to his mind at the very time at which he is seeking God's guidance for his actions. The horizontal human relationship becomes correlated with the vertical divine-human relationship in such a way that certain actions appear to be required independently of any human opinion or demand. A concern develops and with it a sense of uneasiness over a situation about which something needs to be done. This uneasiness persists until the required action is undertaken either successfully or unsuccessfully. If unsuccessful, the Friend who had experienced the concern can at least feel that he has lived up to the measure of light and power given him. Needless to say, all meetings for worship are not sources of inspiration; many are unfruitful due to drowsiness or inertness. Also it must be remembered that the spirit of creative worship may be fruitful at unexpected times and places outside the united gathering.

Work among Negroes and Indians

"Let your Light shine among the Indians, the Blacks and the Whites that ye may answer the truth in them," writes George Fox in 1690.

From earliest times until the present the disabilities suffered by Negroes and Indians in a culture dominated by the "whites" have been an object of Quaker concern. William Penn's policy of buying land from the Indians and of making treaties with them began a lasting friendship which resulted in safety for the Friends on the colonial frontier. No peaceful Quakers suffered injury during the French and Indian War. An interesting sidelight appears in the early Disciplines which strongly condemned the sale of rum to the Indians.

In 1795 the Yearly Meetings began to appoint committees on Indian affairs. These were the earliest standing committees. They still continue their labors. Quaker delegations often went to Washington to plead for the aborigines. The Associated Executive Committee of Friends on Indian Affairs and the Indian Rights Association have been active in these efforts. When General Grant was elected President he met with a Quaker committee sent to plead for a peaceful Indian policy. He told them that, if they would send him the names of Quakers fit to be Indian agents, he would appoint them. This was done. The Quaker Indian agents succeeded in pacifying tribes then at war with one another. They distributed supplies, taught the Indians agriculture, and set up schools on the pattern of the Quaker Boarding Schools. To this work the Yearly Meetings made regular contributions. During the succeeding administrations most of the Quaker Indian agents were dismissed.

Quaker Indian schools first appeared in western New York in 1796, in Ohio in 1822, in Kansas in 1837, in Maine about 1850, and in North Carolina in 1888. In 1898 there were two boarding schools and seven day schools in Oklahoma. These schools have gradually been merged with the public school system. The Tunessasa school in New York has recently become a community center.

When George Fox visited Barbadoes in 1671, he advised Friends to let their slaves go free after a certain length of time, but not empty-handed. The first protest in America against slavery was made by German Quakers in Germantown, Pennsylvania, in 1688. In 1711 the Quaker Assembly of Pennsylvania forbade by law the importation of Negroes, but this enactment was vetoed by the Royal Council in England. The gradual steps by which the Society of Friends freed its own slaves, so that by 1776 there were no Quaker slaveholders, have already been noted. From the beginning until long after the Civil War, the Disciplines and minutes of all the American Yearly Meetings, North and South, contain instructions regarding the care and "spiritual and temporal" education of Negroes and the obligation of Friends "to advise them in respect to their engagements in worldly concerns" (1778). Many Friends abstained from the use of anything produced by slaves, such as sugar. They were mainly instrumental in developing "The Free Produce Association," a group which refused to buy the products of slave labor.

Friends in the South had a difficult time freeing their slaves, for the freed slaves were captured and sold to harsher masters. Laws were passed forbidding anyone to free his slaves. Largely as a result of these difficulties, most of the Southern Quakers migrated in covered wagons to Ohio and other states of the Old Northwest, where slavery was forbidden. This was near the beginning of the nineteenth century. In some cases the members of a meeting migrated together and maintained the continuity of their meeting organization.

Many Quaker homes were stations of the Underground Railroad by which slaves were handed on from one hiding place to another in their escape to the North. Thomas Garrett and Levi Coffin were each instrumental in effecting the escape of some three thousand.

After the Quakers had freed their own ranks of slaveholding, they set to work to abolish slavery altogether. Books by John Woolman and Anthony Benezet exerted a wide influence. In 1780 the Assembly of Pennsylvania passed the first law abolishing slavery. Abolition societies multiplied during the early years of the nineteenth century, both in England and in America. Several Quaker periodicals devoted to the cause of emancipation were published. One of these, edited by Benjamin Lundy, converted William Lloyd Garrison. Lucretia Mott, Thomas Shipley, Levi Coffin, Isaac T. Hopper, Elizabeth Comstock, John G. Whittier, were active leaders in the abolition movement, though they did not go along with those who advocated violence. In England the Friends and others engaged in the abolition movement were more successful than were those in America in bringing about nonviolent emancipation. In the British colonies from 700,000 to 800,000 slaves were freed by purchase about 1838. As a result of this nonviolent emancipation there is today a less serious race problem in the West Indies than in the United States, where the war and its aftermath produced tensions and hatreds which still continue.

During and after the Civil War about three million Negroes were set free without education or resources for making a living. All the Yearly Meetings formed committees and associations to help them. Food and clothing were distributed in areas where the destitute

Negroes were gathered in concentration camps. Implements for farming were furnished. When state and federal agencies took over this work, the Quakers turned their attention to education which included industrial and agricultural training. Every American Yearly Meeting set up Negro schools. The Philadelphia Freedman's Association at one time maintained forty-seven schools. Gradually after 1875 these schools became merged with the public school system.

Quaker schools for Negroes had existed long before the Civil War. In 1770 and 1786 Negro schools were set up in Philadelphia. Many Monthly Meetings appointed special committees to look after Negro education. After 1760 the records of Virginia and Baltimore Yearly Meetings regularly contain instructions regarding the education of Negroes. This was never a popular task in the South. In the North in 1832 one Quaker who admitted Negroes to her Boarding School had her school practically destroyed by a mob.

Today the concern for fair treatment of Negroes and Indians finds its main outlet in the work of standing committees against all forms of discrimination based on race. The American Friends Service Committee, east and west, sponsors local groups furthering this interest. The acute conditions in South Africa are stirring the few Friends in that area to examine their own responsibility for the present serious situation.

Education

The story of Quaker education is long and will not be rehearsed here.[2] Only those aspects which exhibit a pioneering spirit will be cited. The Quakers have on the whole followed conventional educational methods, but their schools have demonstrated a few innovations.

Quaker schools, either privately owned or under the care of committees of meetings, existed in considerable numbers during

the first century of Quaker history. Toward the end of the eighteenth century in America special efforts were made by the Yearly
Meetings to see to it that every Monthly Meeting supported, or
aided in supporting, an elementary school. A number of these
still survive, either as elementary schools or secondary day schools.
The first half of the nineteenth century witnessed the founding of
eight American Yearly Meeting Boarding Schools; the second half,
the founding of ten American Quaker colleges. In the twentieth
century adult education was undertaken in summer schools, conferences, institutes, and in two special institutions founded for the
purpose, Woodbrooke in England and Pendle Hill in the United
States.

The Quaker schools were pioneers in at least three fields: the
equal education of boys and girls, the use of nonviolent methods,
and the introduction of scientific and practical subjects into the
curriculum. Other Quaker educational policies, such as the development in the students of the sense of belonging to a religious
community, the creation of a religious atmosphere in the school,
and "simplicity and moderation in dress, speech and deportment,"
are distinctive only in the degree to which they were carried out.
The Quaker schools did not attempt to teach the truths of religion directly. Friends have maintained that only the divine Spirit
within can accomplish this end. Verbal instruction, which results
in "head knowledge," cannot be relied upon to effect knowledge
which is of the heart. The school community, through its meetings for worship often attended by visiting Friends, its daily read-
ings from the Bible followed by periods of silence, and by the
influence of religiously-minded and dedicated teachers created a
setting in which religious feelings developed. The Quaker pattern
of behavior was reproduced as far as possible in the school. The
older schools were distinguished by their efforts to guard the students against every influence from the outside which would tend
to weaken or change this way of life.

The equal education of boys and girls was a natural outcome of the equality of the sexes in the Quaker meeting and ministry. The co-educational Quaker Boarding School was a unique institution carried on like a large family. The heads of such a school were, as in the case of a family, a man and wife, who divided executive responsibilities. Since Quaker women received an education equal to that of men, which was a better education than other women received, they became leaders of their sex, particularly in the struggle for women's rights in the nineteenth century.

Since the Light of Christ in the conscience exists in children as well as in adults, it is appealed to or "answered" in cases of misdemeanor. The Puritan doctrine of total depravity had a different educational result. According to this doctrine, goodness can be imposed by instruction, often enforced by fear. Although the Quaker schools were by no means free from attempts to coerce in maintaining discipline, they tended on the whole to depend more than did other schools on an appeal to the inward sense of right and wrong.

The doctrine of simplicity, in so far as it meant absence of superfluity, was the source of most of the Quaker educational innovations. In the days when the curriculum was largely based upon the classics, mathematics and other subjects designed primarily to polish and adorn, the Quaker schools emphasized practical subjects. George Fox set up the first Quaker schools in 1668 to teach "whatsoever things are civil and useful in creation." Quaker schools were among the earliest, if not actually the first, to introduce science into the curriculum. In the days when trades were learned by apprenticeship to a master craftsman, the Quaker schools gave instruction in applied sciences. It was natural that a religious body which believed in a religion based on experience should relate education to that which can be experienced.

By far the most important recent innovation in this field is the type of education afforded since 1934 in the work camp movement. While these work camps have other than educational objectives, such as giving help to those who need it and the removal of tensions in conflict areas, the effect of the work camps on the campers themselves, both young men and young women, is often highly educational, sometimes revolutionary. In these camps where the campers work along with persons who need help or who are engaged in the practice of their regular daily tasks, education through action and experience is carried as far as possible. Such education to be most effective must be supplemented by intellectual efforts characteristic of more conventional education.

The Method of Nonviolence

(A) PRISONS

The Quaker peace principles can be best understood when viewed in a context considerably wider than the refusal to take part in war. Prison reform, renunciation of violence in the case of the mentally ill, contributions toward a democratic constitution for the United States, and the struggle for religious liberty are also evidences of the same fundamental doctrine that the best way to deal with men is "to answer that of God" in them. Violence when applied to human beings reduces them and the user of violence to the level of the physical world where only force operates, but men who are open to the divine Light are most effectually moved by spiritual influences from within. By force men are degraded to a subhuman level; by friendship they are uplifted to the divine.

Thousands of Quakers who were imprisoned and treated like common criminals during the forty years of persecution learned by experience of the horrible condition of seventeenth-century prisons, dungeons and underground rooms, unventilated, overcrowded, covered with filth and alive with vermin. There was no separation of the healthy and the diseased, of hardened criminals

and the young or even innocent, the sane and the insane. Some
times there was no separation of male and female prisoners. Those
unable to pay the jailer for their food and bedding suffered severely from hunger and cold. The Quakers refused to pay bribes
to the jailers. In consequence, they often suffered as severely as
the poorest. Prisoners awaiting trial were treated in the same way
as those who had been sentenced. There was no work for anyone.
It would be difficult to imagine conditions more completely de-
moralizing and degrading.

In England the Quakers could at first do nothing except issue
memorials to Parliament and to various officials, such as Fox's
address *To the Protector and Parliament of England* in 1658, but in
Pennsylvania there was full opportunity for radically changing the
whole system. The Pennsylvania prisons became models, highly
praised by foreign visitors as the best in the world. No convict paid
for his board and lodging. Work was compulsory, there was classi-
fication of inmates and religious instruction was provided. Later
in establishing the Eastern Penitentiary in Pennsylvania the Quakers carried this principle of isolation too far. They are credited
with initiating the system of solitary confinement. Fiske writes in
his history of *The Dutch and Quaker Colonies* that Pennsylvania was
distinguished throughout the world for the administration of its
prisons and the humanity of its discipline. Unfortunately, Penn's
law to abolish imprisonment for debt was canceled at an early date.
He did, however, succeed in reducing the number of crimes which
could be punished by death from two hundred to two; namely,
treason and murder.

Many Friends who traveled in the ministry insisted on inspect-
ing the prisons in the cities which they visited and on ministering
to the spiritual needs of the prisoners. This was particularly true of
Stephen Grellet, William Allen, Thomas Shillitoe and William
Forster. After a visit to a prison they reported what they had
seen to the chief authorities. Conditions were often so bad that

even the most hardened officials admitted that something ought to be done.

The first systematic attempt to reform the prisons through an organization was initiated by Elizabeth Fry in 1813. In visiting the women's section of Newgate Prison in London, she found conditions as bad as those described by the early Quaker prisoners. The reforms which she, and the *Association* she founded, brought about transformed this "hell on earth" inhabited by idle, savage, drunken, unruly women whom visitors feared to approach, to a peaceable, industrious group. Children, naked and uncared for, were clothed and taught. Eventually her work led to better conditions in prisons throughout England and on the Continent as well.

Friends continued to make efforts to improve prisons and to prepare discharged prisoners to re-enter society. The events in this story are not so important for our present purpose as the underlying motives which brought about this humanitarian work. The Friends believe that prisoners have certain rights which belong to all human beings regardless of their character or crimes. The revenge of society on those who offend it is inconsistent with the gospel of Christ and the doctrine of the nature of man as a child of God. It is also ineffective. In the undeclared war between society and those who violate its rules, peace can be based only on love, understanding and good will, not on violence, hatred and vengeance. To those who hold a low opinion of man as naturally inclined to evil this doctrine may appear fantastic, but the few hesitating steps already made to treat a defect in character as we treat a defect in the body have been richly rewarded. To go beyond punishment to measures obviating the need for it is the ideal today.

By those who believe that the object of punishment is reformation, capital punishment is obviously condemned. That a human being should suddenly be deprived of the possibility of reformation or of making amends for his misdeeds is not only futile but morally wrong. If the taking of life is a crime for an individual, it is also a crime for the state. In America Friends are now slowly reawakening to their historic interest in this important subject.

(B) MENTAL HOSPITALS

If the Quaker method as applied to criminals seems to many unworkable, it may seem even less practicable when applied to the mentally ill. Nevertheless, the use of this method has produced important and unexpected results.

In the eighteenth century and earlier the treatment of the insane was more inhuman than the treatment of criminals. They were imprisoned, chained, beaten, deprived of the ordinary necessities of life, and made objects of ridicule by visitors who were free to torment them.

As early as 1709 Philadelphia Monthly Meeting proposed the erection of a general hospital for the sick and insane, but the plan did not materialize. The first general hospital in America, the Pennsylvania Hospital in Philadelphia, was founded in 1756 largely by Friends who appealed to Benjamin Franklin to lead the effort. "It was the first institution where cure rather than custody and repression was the underlying principle in the treatment of the insane."[3]

"It was also the first where a humane approach to the problem of insanity was attempted."[4] Friends are given credit for introducing occupational therapy in this hospital as a means of cure.[5] But there was nevertheless at this hospital much harshness and crudity in the methods of treatment which showed little insight into the nature of mental illness.

The first institution expressly founded to carry out nonviolent ideas in the treatment of the insane was established by Quakers in York, England, in 1796. This institution was called *The Retreat* to avoid the stigma attached to the words "asylum" or "madhouse." Here a "family environment" was created and institutional characteristics were avoided. Patients were treated as guests, though employment was required. Chains were forbidden and also all resort to terrorism. There was little medical therapy. Mechanical restraint was sometimes used, but it was reduced to a minimum.

The influence of Samuel Tukes' *Description of the Retreat near York* was soon manifest in the establishment of two similar institutions in America: the Friends Asylum in Frankford, Pennsylvania, opened in 1817; and the Bloomingdale Asylum in New York, opened in 1821. The constitution of the Friends Asylum expressly stated that it "is intended to furnish, besides the requisite medical aid, such tender sympathetic attention and religious oversight as may sooth agitated minds." The system of treatment instituted at the York Retreat was followed. No chains were used. The Bloomingdale Asylum, developed as part of the New York Hospital, was founded by its president, Thomas Eddy, a Quaker who established the methods of "moral management" used at the York Retreat. Eddy was helped in this effort by correspondence with his friend, Lindley Murray, the Quaker grammarian and author of School Readers, who was then residing in York.

Another aspect of this same subject appears in the wide difference between the Puritans and Quakers in their attitude toward witchcraft. The Salem witchcraft mania of 1691-92, and the trials and executions for witchcraft elsewhere, were undoubtedly evidences of serious mental disorder in both accusers and accused. Nothing like this occurred in the Quaker colonies. The Quakers believed in divine possession but not in demoniacal possession. In Pennsylvania there was one trial for witchcraft. The jury found the culprit guilty only of "having the fame of being a witch." The early meeting minutes record several cases of action by the meeting in requiring acknowledgments of error from persons who took seriously witchcraft, necromancy or any "black art."

In recent times a new phase of the concern for the mentally ill has appeared. During World War II many Quaker conscientious objectors were assigned to mental hospitals as assistants. They and other pacifists were much less dependent on violent methods than were other attendants. Sympathy and kindness proved to be more effective than force, though force applied in a sympathetic manner was sometimes necessary. These conscientious objectors, both during and after their service, succeeded in bringing about changes for the better in several hospitals, and helped in establishing an organization to improve administration, facilities and care.

(c) The State

The extreme form of democracy prevailing in the Quaker meeting for worship and the meeting for the transaction of the church business was a pacifist technique for creating co-operation without compulsion. It was inevitable that, when the Quakers had the power to determine the form of government in a state, they should make it as democratic as possible. In five of the American colonies—Rhode Island, Pennsylvania, New Jersey, Delaware and North Carolina—the Quakers took the lead politically for a long or short period of time, but only in Pennsylvania and New Jersey did they have the opportunity to make the constitutions. When William Penn was writing the *Concessions and Agreements* for West Jersey in 1676, he said,

> There we lay a foundation for after ages to understand their liberty as men and Christians, that they may not be brought into bondage but by their own consent; for we put the power in the people."

New Jersey lost some of its earlier freedom when it became a crown colony in 1702, but the *Frame of Government* given by Penn to Pennsylvania lasted until the American Revolution and carried on the same democratic philosophy. There was complete religious liberty. Anyone who believed in God could hold office. The *Frame of Government* provided ways for its amendment and was changed three times in the first ten years. The Assembly met and adjourned by laws passed by itself. Affirmation was permitted as a substitute for a legal oath. All these provisions were unique and far ahead of current practice. Two provisions, one for universal education at the expense of the state and the other for the abolition of imprisonment for debt, turned out to be too advanced for the Pennsylvania colonists.

There can be no doubt that the Constitution of the United States, written in Philadelphia, owed much to Penn's "Holy Experiment." Penn's theories, because they had been carried out in practice and not just written in books, had a powerful influence. John Locke's *Second Treatise of Government* (1688) also influenced the members of the Constitutional Convention in Philadelphia, and there is evidence that Locke himself was influenced by Penn.[6] The Charter written earlier by Locke for Carolina was based on aristocratic feudalism and authority based on fear. Later Locke became acquainted with Penn and assisted him in writing the *Frame of Government* for Pennsylvania. This, apparently, caused a radical change in Locke's political philosophy. The *Frame* exists today in Penn's handwriting interlined with notes and comments by Locke and Sidney. Later the doctrines that government is based on the consent of the governed, that Church and State should be separated completely, and that the legislative and executive branches should be separate, as embodied in Penn's Frame, became the basis of Locke's political theory in the *Second Treatise*. Penn's influence on the American Constitution was exerted also through his suggestion for a political union of the colonies. This plan was presented to a Royal Commission in 1697. It contained some provisions and even words and phrases later embodied in the American Constitution; such as, for example, an annual "congress" (our modern senate), made up of two representatives from each province, to arrange for the interprovincial administration of justice, to regulate interprovincial commerce, and to consider ways and means to support and protect the union.

Penn was the only political theorist of first rank produced by the Society of Friends. Yet the long and bitter struggle on the part of many persons for religious liberty both in England and America laid the basis for that type of political thought which later became fundamental in American life. One important result of this struggle is the exemption from military service of religious conscientious objectors. It was not the theocracy of New England nor the aristocracy of the South, but the liberal democracy of the middle colonies which determined the future form of the American state.

The historian George Bancroft writes:

> The rise of the people called Quakers is one of the memorable events in the history of man. It marks the moment when intellectual freedom was claimed unconditionally by the people as an inalienable birthright.[7]

(D) Religious Liberty

The nonresistant method of creating changes for the better by refusal to obey a law is illustrated in the bitter struggle for religious liberty. About 21,000 Friends suffered fines and imprisonment in England, many of them more than once. About 450 died in prison. At one time there were as many as 4,200 in prison. 230 were banished, of whom, however, only a score were actually transported.

There were many factors which brought about the passage of the Toleration Act in 1689, but it is certain that the stubborn resistance of the Quakers to the Quaker Act of 1662 which was explicitly directed against attendance at Friends meetings, and to the Conventicle Acts of 1664 and 1670 directed against all non-conformist religious services, had much to do with the advent of religious liberty in England. That Friends bore the brunt of the persecution is indicated in the records which show that many more Quakers were convicted under the act than nonconformists.[8] This was because the Quakers met openly while others met secretly. This fact was admitted by some nonconformist writers. Baxter says:

> . . . here the fanatics called Quakers did greatly relieve the sober people for a time; for they were so resolute, and gloried in their constancy and sufferings that they assembled openly—and were dragged away daily to the Common Gaol, and yet desisted not, but the rest came the next day nevertheless, so that the Gaol at Newgate was filled with them. Abundance of them died in prison and yet they continued their assemblies still—yea, many turned Quakers because the Quakers kept their meetings openly and went to prison for it cheerfully.[9]

Efforts to stop the Quakers from meeting together by destroying their meeting houses failed. They then met on the rubbish. When every adult member was taken to prison, the children kept up the meeting. No human power could reach them. Much credit for the final victory is due to the persistent work of the Meeting for Sufferings, the central executive committee in London led by William Penn, the foremost champion of religious liberty in England. The care and leadership of this body unified the Society, so that the fires of persecution could not consume it. For a century after the Act of Toleration Friends continued to suffer heavy losses through fines, and occasional imprisonment for refusal to pay tithes to the Church of England.

In part of America the struggle for religious liberty was carried on as bitterly as in England. The Independents (Congregationalists) had largely accepted religious liberty in England under the

Commonwealth but they themselves denied it to others in New England. Only the Baptists of Rhode Island tolerated the Quakers. Historians who say that religious liberty is a special gift of Protestantism are partly right, but they tend to forget the persecution of Quakers by non-Quakers and the complete absence of persecution of non-Quakers by Quakers. Only the colonies of Pennsylvania, Delaware and Rhode Island, where the Quakers were strongest, did not at some time have a state church. Brooks Adams writes:

> *Freedom of thought* is the greatest triumph over tyranny that brave men have ever won. . . . we owe to their heroic devotion the most priceless of our treasures, our perfect liberty of thought and speech, and all who love our country's freedom may well reverence the memory of those martyred Quakers by whose death and agony the battle of New England has been won.[10]

(E) International Peace

If nonviolent methods, based on good will and an appeal to the inward sense of rightness in every man, are frequently successful in dealing with abnormal persons, they are more frequently successful in dealing with normal persons. No pacifist claims that his method is always successful. Every method fails sometimes, including the method based on violence. If two persons or two nations resort to fighting, one is bound to lose, so the method of fighting cannot at the most be more than 50 per cent successful. The nonviolent method may, however, operate in such a way that both sides win. Together they may arrive at a decision which is better than that which either one of the parties desired in the first place. This pacifist technique was fully discussed in the chapter "Reaching Decisions."

The Quakers who traveled abroad on missionary journeys assumed that their hearers already knew something of the Truth
which they wished to communicate. George Fox, for example, appealed to the Koran in writing to the Bey of Algiers. When Mary
Fisher had addressed the Sultan of Turkey and his Court she was
asked what she thought of Mahomet. She replied "that she knew
him not, but Christ enlightened every man who came into the
world. Him she knew. . . . And concerning Mahomet," she said,
"they might judge him false or true according to the words and
prophecies he spoke." The Turk confessed this to be true. With
this reply we can contrast the reply of Thomas of Tolento in
Malabar, India, in 1307 to the same question:

> I tell you Mahomet is the son of perdition and hath his
> place in hell, and not only he but all such as follow and
> keep his law, false and persistent and accursed as it is and
> hostile to God and the salvation of souls.

The difference between the two answers illustrates the nature
and source of Quaker pacifism. When John Woolman visited the
Indians in order to hold a Friends meeting with them, he gave as
one of his reasons, "that I might learn something from them."
The method of nonviolence is not a method for pushing one's
own ideas. It is a method for arriving at the truth on whichever
side it may be.

The refusal to take any part in war or preparation for war was
not universal among Friends at the start. Some Quakers in
Cromwell's army were dismissed because of their equalitarian principles. Others became pacifists long before the Quaker movement
began.[11] Not until 1661 was there a public announcement from
the leaders that a Quaker would not fight. This was written in protest against the arrest of Quakers who were thought to have participated in the insurrection of the Fifth Monarchy Men who tried
to seize London by force in preparation for the Second Coming of

Christ. No regularly constituted body of the Society of Friends has ever made a declaration contrary to the strict pacifist position, but in every war some members have, as individuals, supported the war or taken part in it.

Friends arrived at their pacifist position in the same two ways by which they reached their other social testimonies: they followed the Light of Christ in their consciences and they followed the words of Christ in the New Testament. The Quaker scholars, such as Barclay, Penn, Penington, Claridge and Fisher, were familiar with the writings of the early Church Fathers and quoted them in defense of their position. Barclay, in the *Apology,* gives about forty quotations or references to show that, for the first three centuries, the Christian leaders opposed participation in war. He quotes, for example, the answer of Martin to Julian called the Apostate, "I am a soldier of Christ, therefore I cannot fight."

The Friends were not disturbed because fighting can be defended by the Old Testament. If the Old Testament is to be taken literally, then it would be necessary, as Barclay points out, for Christians to follow all the precepts of the Mosaic law. Christianity, they believed, is a new dispensation which has replaced the old. In using the New Testament in their controversies with the Protestants who accepted the Bible as authoritative, they met their opponents on their own ground. Such texts were used as "Love your enemies," "Blessed are the peacemakers," "Resist not evil," "All they that take up the sword shall perish by the sword," "If my kingdom were of this world then would my servants fight," "We wrestle not against flesh and blood," "The weapons of our warfare are not carnal," "Render to no man evil for evil," "Wars and fightings come of your lusts." But it was not so much particular texts as it was the example of Christ being led to the cross without resistance and the whole spirit of New Testament religion, commanding its followers to take up the cross in the same way, that formed the principal basis for this position. Two sayings of Jesus, "I came not to bring peace but a sword" and "He that hath no sword let him sell his cloak and buy one," were interpreted in the light of their context which gives them a figurative turn. Ambrose and Origen, Barclay shows, gave these texts the same symbolic interpretation.

Friends believed that their pacifism followed so naturally and inevitably from their other more fundamental principles that little is said about it in early Quaker writings. It was taken for granted that a consistent Friend would not fight. As we have seen, the whole procedure of the meeting for worship and the meeting for business was based on a technique which did not admit the over-coming of some persons by other persons. Rather it tended to create an integration of various points of view into a new one on a level higher than any individual opinion. The Light, as has been shown in every application of Quaker doctrine to social problems, is a source of unity. It is not one force among other forces. The Light is in all men, and the closer they come to it, the closer they come to one another. Force can produce a superficial unity like that which exists in a machine or in a social mechanism such as an army. It cannot produce organic unity any more than a human body with a soul can be manufactured in a machine shop. To appeal to the Light of Truth in another man is to influence him from within. In appealing to this Light in him, we also appeal to the same Light in ourselves and as a result we may find that he is right while we are wrong. We cannot honestly set out to change other men without being willing to be changed ourselves.

All the world admits that a peaceful solution to a controversy is better than a violent solution, but some hold that, men being what they are, peaceful methods are impractical. The realistic pacifist, they say, will wait until others are also pacifists. But Friends have believed that the only way to bring about a peaceful world is to begin here and now, regardless of the risk involved. When Joseph Hoag in 1812 was publicly pleading for his peace principles, a man in the audience said, "Well, stranger, if all the world was of your mind I would turn and follow after." Joseph Hoag replied, "So then thou hast a mind to be the last man to be good. I have a mind to be one of the first and set the rest an example."[12] Isaac Penington writes of the peaceable kingdom foretold by prophecy:

> When so ever such a thing shall be brought forth in the world it must have a beginning before it can grow and be perfected. And where should it begin but in some particulars, (individuals) in a nation and so spread by degrees. . . . Therefore, whoever desires to see this lovely state brought forth in the general . . . must cherish it in the particular.[13]

Joseph Sturge correctly states the manner in which all causes for human betterment originate:

> It seems to be the will of Him who is infinite in wisdom that light upon great subjects should first arise and be gradually spread through the faithfulness of individuals in acting up to their own convictions.[14]

The common argument that the pacifist can apply his principles only in an ideal society is untrue. We are not commanded to love our enemies only when there are no enemies, nor to overcome evil with good only when there is no evil.

The object of the Christian religion is to bring about the Kingdom of God on earth, not by the power of men, but by the power of God working through men. This can be done only by methods which are compatible with the code of behavior described by Christ as characteristic of God's Kingdom. The Kingdom begins to exist when Christ's way of life begins to be lived. The Kingdom, the ideal society which men work for and pray for when they utter the Lord's Prayer, cannot be brought about by means inconsistent with itself. If fighting is inconsistent with an ideal society, then fighting will not bring the ideal society. A spiritual result is produced by spiritual means and a material result by material means. If war is evil, as almost everyone today admits, then it cannot be the right way to produce a good result. The children of Mars are not angels of peace. As William Penn says, "A good end cannot sanctify evil means, nor must we ever do evil that good may come of it."[15]

Barclay and Penington point out that the state, not having accepted the gospel of Christ as its standard of behavior, may be expected to engage in war as consistent with its own principles. It is under the old dispensation which existed before the coming of Christ. It acts accordingly. But this behavior of the state is no excuse for those individuals who have themselves accepted the higher standard of Christianity. They have received a greater measure of Light and must be faithful to it. This is not to be interpreted as vocational pacifism, as if God had called some to fight because fighting is necessary and others to be peaceful so as to show by their lives the nature of the Christian goal. All men and nations are called to be peaceful but every man must live up to his measure of light, however dim. We cannot censure the insensitive for not going beyond what they have. As their measure increases they will come closer to that peaceable Kingdom in which swords are beaten into plowshares and spears into pruning hooks. For seventy-five years it was demonstrated in Pennsylvania that even a state can be devoted to the ways of peace.

Friends have generally favored the use of police power if that power impartially protects the rights of the criminal and the rights of society. Such power must be reduced to a minimum and used with sympathetic understanding. The exercise of police power differs from international war in which the innocent often suffer more than the guilty and where the object is the taking of life. Under present international conditions a so-called international police force wages war. This police action is not directed toward guilty individuals as is the case with the police action of the federal government of the United States. Friends have never been anarchists. They hold that the state is important. They support it as long as its requirements do not oppose the leadings of the Light.

Friends are often asked what they would do if attacked by a person intent on murder. Many would protect themselves by force if that force did not involve serious injury or the taking of life. Some would reply to this question as Thomas Chalkley did:

> I being innocent if I was killed in my body, my soul might be happy; but if I killed him, he dying in his wickedness would consequently be unhappy; and if I was killed he might live to repent; but If I killed him, he would have no time to repent."[16]

In the case of being called upon to protect another person, the decision would be more difficult, but the same general line of reasoning might apply. Death is not itself an evil, but the taking of life is an evil. The soldier who is killed suffers a material injury; the soldier who kills suffers a spiritual injury.

There are many instances in Quaker history of bandits who were persuaded to desist from attack. The famous Quaker doctor Lettsom on encountering a highwayman "converted him into a useful member of society."[17] Catharine Shipley said to a man who was attempting to snatch her purse on a dark street, "Let us kneel down on the pavement and ask Heavenly Father whether He means thee to have it." The man fled.

In defending their pacifism the Quakers have seldom given as their reason the destruction of life and property caused by war. Loss of life and property is not in itself an evil. The loss of life might lead to a happier condition hereafter, and the loss of property is sometimes an actual benefit for a person who is too closely tied to his possessions. The evil results of war—hatred, brutality, callousness to suffering and deceit—are spiritual and moral rather than material.

It is now possible to defend pacifism by an appeal to biology which was formerly thought to align itself with militarism. The theory that higher species evolved in the course of evolution through a process of savage competition by which the strong overcame and eliminated the weak has been superseded by the view that co-operation plays a greater part than competition. Those species which are most sensitive to the needs of others and are most adaptable to changes in environment because of greater sensitivity to a wider range of existence are most likely to survive. The heavy fighters, equipped with strong claws, disappear in the course of evolution; the small, tender, sensitive, adaptable species survive. According to Whitehead, "Any physical object which by its influence deteriorates its environment, commits suicide."[18] This is true among nations as among animal organisms. The militaristic empires such as Assyria and Rome, where the soldier was most admired, have had comparatively short careers; the somewhat more pacific cultures, such as those of China and India, where the scholar or the holy man was most admired, have continued since the dawn of civilization. The two recent world wars have shown that those nations which are least militaristic have the greatest power of survival.

There is a story told of the Chinese sage Lao-tse, the founder of Taoism, which illustrates this point. When he lay dying he asked his disciple to look into his mouth. "What do you see?" the old man asked. "I see nothing," replied the disciple. "No teeth?" "No, no teeth, but I see a tongue." By this Lao-tse taught him this lesson: that which is hard, sharp and brittle disappears, while that which is soft and yielding survives.

Pacifism is not a doctrine which can be practiced with absolute consistency by one who is an integral part of society. The Quakers have not generally retreated from society in order to be consistent pacifists. They believe that God does not require more than is possible for human beings living a normal life. Inward peace and the sense of freedom from guilt is not the result of complete success in an undertaking. It comes rather from living up to what appears to be the divine requirement, however small or large the requirement is. The primary virtue is obedience to the Inward Light which may not, at the particular stage of religious growth attained by an individual, require absolute consistency. Inconsistency is not the worst evil. It is better to be inconsistently good than consistently bad. The pacifist finds strength to be good in a particular area of life. If he succeeds, more may be required later. If his inconsistencies result in humility, they are not without value.

The doctrine of some Protestant theologians that man is doomed to perpetual inner tension and a constant sense of guilt because of original sin or because he cannot avoid sinning finds no support in the Quaker *Journals*. Once the journalist, after a period of conflict, has learned how to submit himself to divine Guidance, he finds peace. There is no sense of guilt until he again disobeys. The main evidence of obedience to the Light is inner peace, and many Quaker lives have demonstrated that life can be lived in a state of almost continuous inner peace, even in this evil world. John Pemberton writes to Susanna Fothergil in the midst of the French and Indian War: "There are such as can in humility and thankfulness say they are favored with a quiet habitation." When Christ said, "My peace I give unto you," he was not making a promise which could not be fulfilled. His followers learn that, even if they, like him, take upon themselves the burden of the world's suffering, it is still possible to feel within a sense of his peace. William Penn writes of those who accepted the message of the early Quakers: What "people had been vainly seeking without, with much pains and cost, they by this ministry found within the right way to peace with God."[19]

Pacifists who have no inner sense of peace are not well fitted to work for peace. Their own inner conflict will infect what they do.

Inner conflict, as modern psychologists have often pointed out, produces outer conflict, especially when that inner conflict is not recognized by him in whom it exists. The person beset with inner conflict seeks relief by projecting it on the situation around him. A whole nation may be so afflicted with an inner conflict that it seeks relief by projecting it on other nations or races and war results. The peacemakers are called blessed because they are children of God, and God, as Paul truly says, "is not a God of confusion, but of peace" (I Cor. 14:33). God does not appear in the world as one force among other forces, but as the source of unity among conflicting forces. "God is Love."

The assault on the pacifist position by the older Protestantism has been renewed today in somewhat different form by the Neo-Calvinists. Pacifists are chided for perfectionism and utopianism. The Neo-Calvinists hold that perfectionism is a mistaken theory because man as man is bound to sin, not only because of original sin, but also because he is an integral part of a sinful society. We have no choice between evil and good, but only between one evil and another. War and tyranny are both evils. When we are forced to choose one or the other, we choose war as the lesser evil. Therefore, war is justified in spite of the fact that it is contrary to the teaching of Christ and the Will of God. Christ's teachings cannot be followed literally in an evil world. They exist for the purpose of creating a perpetual tension between the ideal and the real so that the real may seek the ideal, even though this ideal is forever beyond its reach.

Utopianism is held to be wrong for the same reasons. The Kingdom of God is not in history, that is, it does not exist as a real possibility here on this earth. It exists only in a timeless eternity where it has already come to pass. Christ's work is finished. Man's task is to accept it through faith.

All this seems to be so much at variance with the teachings of the New Testament and the religious experience of the great

Christians that it is difficult to see how it can be held sincerely. In the first place, it seems to deny the central Christian doctrine of the Incarnation. If Christ lived a perfect life in a sinful world, then such a life is clearly possible; either that, or the Incarnation was not real, but only an appearance. The Incarnation means that Christ was a revelation of God in genuinely human terms and, if genuinely human, then he expressed, by his life and teachings, a real example for men to follow. If Jesus was himself a pacifist, as even the Neo-Orthodox admit, then we must be pacifists also if we obey his command to follow him.

That the New Testament code of behavior is applicable only in some timeless heavenly realm is inconsistent with the whole spirit of the gospel which tells us how to behave here and now. Christ's commands are not expressed in a future tense but in the present. To hold that the Christian religion cannot be lived here on this earth is an acceptance of defeatism which finds no support in New Testament Christianity which was triumphantly optimistic, even though the early Christians were opposed by a great totalitarian state. In the early Church each Christian community thought of itself as an island of the Kingdom of Heaven, confident that, as the number of islands increased, they would eventually unite to form the great continent of the new perfected social order where the Spirit of the Living Christ would rule. Pentecost was not a revival meeting. When Peter stood up to explain what had happened, he did not proclaim Christ as a personal savior but as one who would introduce a new order in the world. Christ had said that the Kingdom was already germinating. It was a grain of mustard seed which would grow into a great tree, a creative leaven operating in the world to transform the world unto itself. This conception does not necessarily conflict with the belief that the Kingdom has already come in a timeless eternity nor with the apocalyptic belief held by many Christians that the Kingdom would come suddenly. The sun may burst suddenly above the horizon, but its coming is predicted by the twilight before the dawn. Did not the early Christians feel that they tasted "the powers of the age to come" (Heb. 6:5)?

That our choice is always between one evil and another, between war and tyranny, for example, is not true. There is a third choice which has often been taken in Christian history, though it may lead to martyrdom. If we refuse war, and, as a result, are subjected to tyranny, we can refuse tyranny also and go to prison or to death. The prisoner may be free spiritually, however confined in body, but he who submits to tyranny or war is free neither spiritually nor physically. In *On the Duty of Civil Disobedience* Thoreau says of a prison that it is

> the only house in a slave state in which a free man can abide with honor. . . . As they could not reach me, they had resolved to punish my body, just as boys, if they cannot come at some person against whom they have a spite, will abuse his dog.

At the Assembly of the World Council of Churches in Amsterdam in 1948 it was agreed that the will of God is against war and that the will of God takes precedence over the will of the state. That the moral law takes precedence over the will of the state was the basis of the condemnation of the Nazis at the Nuremberg trials. The pacifist who disobeys the law and goes to prison engages in civil disobedience for the sake of principle. He is as willing to sacrifice himself for his cause as the soldier to sacrifice himself for his cause. He uses a spiritual weapon in a spiritual warfare. The present conflict between East and West is a spiritual conflict, a conflict of ideas and moral principles. As such it will never be settled by material weapons with which ideas and moral principles have nothing in common. As Barclay says peace comes not by

> knocks and blows and such like things, which may well
> destroy the body but never can inform the soul, which is a
> free agent, and must either accept or reject matters of opin-
> ion as they are borne in upon it by something proportioned
> to its own nature.[20]

So far the Quaker principle of pacifism has been treated in the
negative way, as refusal to take part in war. The positive side, which
is equally important, includes the efforts to remove causes of
war and repair damage done by war, particularly damage in terms
of hatred and prejudice. International agreements by which
differences between nations can be settled by arbitration have
been a concern of Friends from the beginning. William Penn's
Essay towards the Present and Future Peace of Europe (1693) and John
Bellers' *Some Reasons for a European State proposed to the Powers
of Europe* (1710) offered plans for an organization not unlike the
present United Nations. On a number of occasions Friends have
endeavored to promote the settlement of differences by arbitration. Such instances include Barclay's letter in 1678 to the pleni-
potentiaries who were negotiating the terms of peace at Nimeguen;
Joseph Sturge's attempted mediation between Denmark and
Schleswig-Holstein in 1850; the peace deputation to the Czar of
Russia in 1854 headed by Joseph Sturge, which, had there been
less hysteria in England, might have prevented the Crimean War;
John Bright's successful efforts to secure arbitration between
England and the Northern States in 1861; the attempt of the
Quaker government of Rhode Island to avert by arbitration King
Philip's War in 1675; the efforts of John Fothergill and David
Barclay in frequent conference with Benjamin Franklin to avert
the American War of Revolution and the successful efforts of
George Logan, grandson of Penn's secretary James Logan, to
prevent war between the United States and France in 1798 after
the American Commissioners had failed to secure the release of

American sailors in French prisons. In addition to these and other efforts of individuals, Quaker bodies frequently address governments through epistles and visiting committees on the subject of the peaceful settlement of differences. Peace Societies, beginning in England in 1814 and in America in 1815, worked continuously for arbitration.

The suffering incurred by Quakers and other pacifists in every war in the Western World during the past three centuries because of their refusal to fight is too long a story to rehearse here, even in outline. The adventures of ship captains who did not carry guns as a defense against pirates and privateers and attacks by mobs on Quakers who refused to put lights in their windows in celebration of military victories are among the less known events in this story. That a peaceful attitude inspired by good will and complete absence of fear is often a greater source of safety than weapons has been demonstrated by many instances. In the Indian wars on the frontier in colonial times and in the Irish wars of 1690 and 1798, Quakers were seldom harmed.

(f) RELIEF WORK

Relief work undertaken to repair damages caused by war or conflict is a natural corollary of the peace principle. Although this work has not been large in material terms, the results have been disproportionately great in terms of bridging gaps created by hatred and misunderstanding.

Relief work inside the Society of Friends was essential from the beginning, owing to the general loss of property by fines for civil disobedience. Relief work outside the Society seems to have first occurred during the Irish war in 1690 when Quakers supplied prisoners of war with food and clothing. In 1755 the Acadians, banished from Canada, were aided by Friends of Philadelphia, largely through the efforts of Anthony Benezet. In 1775-76 Friends in the Philadelphia area collected a large sum of money for the relief of sufferers from the siege of Boston and the blockade of the New England coast by the British fleet. Towns through which the Quakers had once been whipped recorded their thanks. During the Napoleonic wars soup kitchens were set up to relieve distress in London. During the nineteenth century the Balkan countries were in almost continuous revolt against the Turks and there were many refugees in European cities. In 1822 English Friends sent a large sum to the Greek refugees. In 1876 relief supplies were distributed in Macedonia and Bulgaria and again in 1912. In the Crimean War in 1854 the English fleet had ravaged the coast of Finland which then belonged to Russia and caused widespread destruction. Under the leadership of Joseph Sturge food and clothing, seed corn, fishing nets and other supplies were sent to repair the damage. Whittier's poem on this event ends with the words

> The battle lost by England's hate
> By England's love is won.

thus indicating the main motive and result of relief work. In 1892 Friends distributed a fund of £40,000 in the famine-stricken parts of Russia.

When the great Irish Famine of 1846-47 occurred, Friends committees raised £200,000, largely from non-Quaker sources, and a group of English and Irish Friends distributed relief. In the American Civil War relief was administered and educational work done for the Negro freedmen as already mentioned. The Franco-Prussian War of 1870 wrought great devastation and misery in France. About forty English Quakers distributed relief supplies including seeds and cattle. At this time the red and black "Quaker star" was first used as a distinguishing mark. Today this emblem designates Quaker Service of all kinds all over the world.

In the Boer War of 1900 Friends sent a delegation to South Africa that succeeded in arousing British feeling against the crowded concentration camps in which Boer families were confined. This resulted in improved conditions. The subsequent relief included the restoration of the Boers' most treasured heirlooms, their family Bibles.

World Wars I and II witnessed an expansion of Quaker relief which eventually included work in all the countries affected by the wars. The introduction of universal military conscription into England and the United States led Friends everywhere into an effort to substitute relief work for military service. There was a general determination to make personal sacrifices as great as those made by persons who supported or took part in the war. This work began in England in 1914 with the "Emergency Committee for the Assistance of Germans, Austrians, Hungarians, and Turks in Distress," "The War Victims Relief Committee," and the "Friends Ambulance Unit" which took care of men wounded in battle. This Unit was too closely tied to the war effort to receive the official endorsement of the Society of Friends, but the larger part of its members were Friends. Soon after the United States entered the war in 1917 the "American Friends Service Committee" was formed to assist conscientious objectors and send relief workers abroad. Later, conscientious objectors were furloughed by the government to the Committee for relief work in France. The devastation caused by the war in France had already led English Friends to send workers there. These were joined by the Americans. This work consisted of relief and reconstruction operations of various kinds, including medical help and the revival of agriculture. At the same time a number of English and American Friends were sent to Russia to administer aid.

Such were the beginnings of a service which has continued to widen and has carried, and is carrying, Friends into many parts of the world on errands of mercy. At one time a million children were being fed in Germany. World War II added China and India to the countries assisted. Home service was begun in 1920 by the American Friends Service Committee. In the thirties Friends helped the stricken coal miners in West Virginia and elsewhere. This beginning has expanded into a great variety of undertakings, internes in industry, work camps, community integration of minorities, and, in the basic sense, adult education through institutes and seminars. Today in many parts of the world there are centers in which, by action and word, a spirit of reconciliation is demonstrated.

This long story of Friends Service has been told in many books and pamphlets. In all their work the Quakers have been supported and assisted by a much larger group of like-minded persons outside their membership for whom they have acted as instruments and with whom they have collaborated. The primary motivation of this relief work is humanitarianism, the removal of suffering and the repair of destruction. Secondarily, it is a form of preaching through action. War creates ill will which is the seed of more war. Relief work creates good will which is a seed of peace. War, unlike floods, earthquakes and famines, is a man-made evil which results in wrong human attitudes—hatred, greed and fear. These attitudes can be changed by a practical demonstration of their opposites—love, self-sacrifice and confidence. Friends may take their share of responsibility in repairing damages caused by the convulsions of nature, but their main concern is to create ties of good will and understanding in areas of conflict between nations, races and classes.

Another motivation of Quaker relief work is a sense of guilt. As an integral part of a society so constructed that war recurs, the Quakers must assume a share of responsibility for the causes of war. If this responsibility cannot be avoided, it may be partially atoned for by attempting to remedy the evils caused by war. A relief worker who believes in his own goodness because of his superior principles has not faced the real facts of the situation. Woolman deals with this problem:

> Where men profess to be so meek and heavenly minded and to have their trust so firmly settled in God that they cannot join in wars and yet by their spirit and conduct in common life manifest a contrary disposition, their difficulties are great at such a time.[21]

Quaker relief workers have received maintenance, but no salary. They are expected to live as near the standard of living of those whom they help as health and efficiency permit. They become, as far as possible, members of the community in which they find themselves and share in its problems and activities. In France, for example, the members of the Unit ploughed in the fields beside the peasants and built houses in cooperation with them. There is a consistent effort by such companionship to avoid the sense of help handed down, though this is difficult to avoid, especially in the distribution of food and clothing. Quaker relief workers are in the main nonprofessional, that is, they are not necessarily technically trained social workers. This helps to close the gap between them and those whom they help. They leave positions at home, spend one or two years in the field and return to the work they left. Thus the nonprofessional character of the religion of the Society of Friends is carried over, as far as possible, into its humanitarian work. Another policy which distinguishes the Quaker relief team is the effort made to be absolutely impartial and to distribute help regardless of race, nationality, religion or political opinion. Thus in the Spanish Civil War, help was given on both sides of the battle line in spite of private feelings which tended to sympathize with the Loyalists. Although many workers in Friends Service are not Friends, the Quaker type of meeting for worship and the Quaker method of arriving at decisions prevails.

Friends Service is a demonstration of all four of the primary social doctrines. It demonstrates community because it endeavors to unite the whole human race into one interdependent community; it demonstrates equality because of its impartiality; it demonstrates simplicity because of the standard of living required of its workers; and it demonstrates harmony by its main objective-the promotion of peace.

Notes

1. William E. Hocking, *Human Nature and Its Remaking*, 1918, p. 344.

2. See Howard H. Brinton, *Quaker Education in Theory and Practice*, 1940; rev. ed. 1949.

3. Albert Deutsch, *The Mentally Ill in America*, 1937, p. 58.

4. Deutsch, *The Mentally Ill*, p. 66.

5. Deutsch, *The Mentally Ill*, p. 63.

6. See Francis R. Taylor, "William Penn, Constitution Maker," in Howard H. Brinton, ed., *Children of Light*, 1938.

7. George Bancroft, *History of the United States*, II, 86.

8. See William Braithwaite, *Second Period of Quakerism*, Chaps. I-VII, for the story of the struggle for religious liberty.

9. Braithwaite, *Second Period of Quakerism*, p. 41.

10. Brooks Adams, *The Emancipation of Massachusetts*, 1887, p. 177.

11. William Dewsbury, *Works*, p. 45.

12. Joseph Hoag, *Journal*, 1861, p. 201.

13. William Penn, *A Weighty Question Concerning the Magistrates Protection of the Innocent*, 1661.

14. Henry Richards, *The Memoirs of Joseph Sturge*, 1864, p. 415.

15. William Penn, *Reflections and Maxims,* Pt. I, 1850, No. 537.

16. Thomas Chalkey, *Journal,* 1754, p. 207.

17. John Stoughton, *Howard the Philanthropist and his friends,* 1884, p. 296.

18. Alfred North Whitehead, *Science and the Modern World,* 1925, p. 161.

19. William Penn, *A Brief Account of the Rise and Progress of the people called Quakers,* p. 17.

20. Robert Barclay, *Apology,* p. 497.

21. John Woolman, *Journal,* edited by Janet Whitney, 1950, p. 70.

CHAPTER IX

The Four Periods of Quaker History and Their Relation to the Mystical, the Evangelical, the Rational and the Social Forms of Religion

The history of the Society of Friends falls into four periods which are marked, conveniently though only approximately, by the turn of the centuries. These periods can be designated as follows:

1. The heroic or apostolic period, about 1650-1700
2. The period of cultural creativeness, about 1700-1800
3. The period of conflict and decline, about 1800-1900
4. The period of modernism, from 1900 —.

These four periods represent four stages through which Quakerism in different areas has passed, is passing or will probably pass. The transition from one stage to the next takes place gradually. Changes occur in different places at different times and to different degrees. Some small areas of Quakerism are still in the second period which in their case can hardly be called creative, though it follows the form of the old creative epoch; others, more extensive, are still in the third period, the time of conflict and decline. Perhaps the dates suggested fit the Philadelphia experience more closely than that of any other area.

These four periods differ from one another primarily in the proportion in which four different elements or four different manifestations of religion are emphasized: mysticism, evangelicalism, rationalism and the activism of the social gospel. These four tendencies have been present in every period, but there has been considerable difference in the degree of attention and emphasis which each has received. The nature of the four forms will become clearer in the course of this chapter; suffice it to say here that mysticism is inwardly directed, evangelicalism is outwardly directed, rationalism is concerned primarily with a religion arrived at by the process of thought, and the social gospel is concerned with humanitarian service. These distinctions enter into both doctrine and practice. In terms of doctrine the mystic discovers religious and moral truth through inward feeling, the evangelical through Christian history which is an outward objective authority, the rationalist through logical thought, and the servant of humanity through practical efforts toward betterment in this world. For the mystic the primary religious practice is meditation and silent worship; for the evangelical it is study of the sacred record and proclaiming its message; for the rationalist it is the deduction of a right philosophy and theology; and for the activist the essential requirement is to help his fellow men.

It is probable that no living religion is without all of these forms, but there are wide differences in the degree of emphasis. Using these four types as our basis of comparison, we may estimate the ingredients in the four periods of Quaker history in some such way as this:

1. The synthesis or balance of mysticism and evangelicalism, about 1650-1700.
2. The period of greater mystical inwardness, about 1700-1800.
3. The conflict of mysticism and evangelicalism, about 1800-1900.
4. The rise of a paramount interest in rationalism and the social gospel, about 1900—.

1. The Heroic or Apostolic Period
The Synthesis of Mysticism and Evangelicalism

The first of these periods was marked by a deep spiritual inwardness which took precedence over the outward activity to which it gave guidance and power. It was also marked to an equal degree by a fervent zeal to spread the Truth in spite of violent and cruel opposition by both Church and State. In terms of practice there was, therefore, a living synthesis of mystical and evangelical religion. The same synthesis was achieved, though perhaps less completely, in the realm of doctrine. Much emphasis was placed on the significance of the historical events which gave rise to the Christian religion, including especially the life, teachings and sacrificial death of Christ. This emphasis was prominent in the writings by which the Quakers defended themselves against opponents who claimed they were not Christians because of their universalism, their opposition to the doctrine of imputed righteousness and their belief in the supremacy of the Light Within over the Bible. They based their stand on the New Testament, believing, in spite of all attacks upon their position, that Quakerism was "primitive Christianity revived."

The Quakers were, accordingly, at least in their own estimation, evangelical in doctrine, though leaning to what would today be called a "liberal" position. The inward side of religion was given precedence, though the outward was by no means ignored. Because of this, the setting up of meetings for worship for inward communion with God became the major objective in both England and America, and "the preaching of the Word" to assure a right belief—which was a major objective of Puritanism—was esteemed of less importance. The objective of the Quaker minister was not so much to teach as to direct his hearers to their Inward Teacher. It is natural, however, that historians of Quakerism should emphasize the more spectacular episodes in the lives of Friends who were preachers, since there is little of the dramatic in a silent Quaker meeting. The adventures of the so-called First Publishers of Truth in almost every accessible part of the earth in the face of relentless opposition are equal in dramatic quality to the more exciting experiences in the history of religion. There were no human beings whom the Quakers despaired of. A delegation was even sent to Rome to convert the Pope. They believed that the same Light of Christ could be appealed to in all men from the American Indians in the West to the followers of Mahomet in the East. Delegations sent to Mediterranean lands suffered more from the Christian Inquisition than from the heathen Turks. George Fox attempted to send letters by personal messengers to the King of Spain, the Pope, the King of France, the Czar of Russia, the magistrates of Malta, the Bey of Algiers, the mythical Prester John and, lest any be left out, "To all nations under the whole heavens." The bloody, cruel and finally victorious struggle to introduce Quakerism into Massachusetts resulted in floggings, imprisonments, banishment into the wilderness, and four deaths by hanging. Because shipmasters were prevented by severe penalties from bringing Quakers to America, a group of eleven sailed on their own tiny vessel guided by the Spirit. Joseph Besse in two large volumes, which constitute a kind of Quaker martyrology, records the sufferings and some of the adventures of twelve thousand Friends in the period prior to the Toleration Act in 1689. It is a record without parallel in religious history. In introducing the chapter on sufferings in Europe and Asia he speaks of the motives of these dauntless preachers:

> Their call to so extraordinary a service was grounded upon an assurance of faith in themselves, and a most clear and convincing evidence of a divine impulse upon their spirits and a necessity of obedience thereunto. This certain sense

of duty and the unspeakable peace of mind they found in the performance of it, which had supported them under many sufferings in their own country, led them to travel as with their lives in their hands to testify the Truth, even to the teeth of its greatest opposers, for, knowing that the cause was the Lord's, they were raised above the fear of man in publishing it, and the Presence of Him on whose errand they went did attend them through the greatest difficulties, enabling some of them cheerfully to lay down their lives in His service.[1]

Besse's account contains many sentences which end like the following:

The Man with the Black Rod and the Keeper took us and put us into an inner room in the Inquisition which had but two little holes in it for light or air but the glory of the Lord did shine round about us.[2]

It was this sense of a divine commission and a continued awareness of the divine Presence which made it possible for these often quite commonplace human beings to accomplish what otherwise would have been beyond human endurance.

A contemporary letter indicates the extent of the effort to publish the Truth. It is dated from the general meeting at Skipton in 1660 and is followed by a recommendation that a collection be taken in every meeting for the help of traveling Friends.

Dear Friends and Brethren,

We having certain information from some Friends of London, of the great work and service of the Lord beyond the seas, in several parts and regions, as Germany, America, and many other islands and places, as Florence, Mantua, Palatine, Tuscany, Italy, Rome, Turkey, Jerusalem, France,

Geneva, Norway, Barbadoes, Bermuda, Antigua, Jamaica,
Surinam, Newfoundland; through all which, Friends have
passed in the service of the Lord, and divers other countries, places, islands and nations; and among many nations
of the Indians, in which they have had service for the Lord,
and through great travails have published His name, and
declared the everlasting gospel of peace unto them that
have been afar off, that they might be brought nigh unto
God.[3]

During this active and vivid period the message was also spread
by a flood of books and pamphlets. Many of these were printed
secretly at great risk to the Quaker printers. By the year 1708 more
than twenty-six hundred books and pamphlets had been issued by
at least four hundred and forty different authors.[4] In 1672 a special committee was appointed by the Yearly Meeting to supervise
the printing and distribution of Friends books. This committee
saw to it that an answer was written to every anti-Quaker book.[5]
There were at least eight hundred of these. The pamphlets illustrate more clearly than the books the zeal and enthusiasm which
gave the Quaker movement such driving force in the face of
powerful opposition. While a few were ecstatic, and occasionally
almost incoherent, there were many reasoned defenses of Quaker
testimonies against oaths, tithes, hat honor and man-made social
distinctions in general.

This period was above all characterized by the power and
penetration of its vocal ministry. Of John Audland, twenty-two years
old, it was said, "Immortality shined in his face and his voice was as
thunder." When William Dewsbury came to Kelk it was reported
of his visit:

His testimony was piercing and very powerful, so as the
earth shook before him, the mountains did melt at the

power of the Lord, which exceedingly, in a wonderful manner, broke forth in these days in our holy assemblies, to the renting of many hearts, and bringing divers to witness the same state, measurably, as the prophet or servant of the Lord did in ancient times, whose lips quivered and belly shook, that he might rest in the day of trouble. Oh! It was a glorious day, in which the Lord wonderfully appeared for the bringing down the lofty and high minded, and exalting that of low degree. Many faces did gather paleness, and the stout hearted were made to bow, and strong oaks to bend before the Lord.[6]

When it was said of Thomas Relf that he had a "watering testimony,"[7] it meant that his ministry watered and made the Seed of God to grow in man. That many other Friends had such a testimony is shown by the great harvest that was gathered. The movement spread rapidly through England and America and in other parts of the world.

In this first period the emphasis was primarily on religious experience. The traveling ministers did not often give doctrinal sermons. They appealed to their hearers to seek and find the divine Light and Life within themselves. Theological opinions were not ignored but they were condemned as "airy notions" when unrelated to experience. Only for the sake of uninformed persons or in dealing with opponents who endeavored to prove that Quakers were not Christians, did members of the Society of Friends produce theological essays. They used the same words as did their opponents but not always in the same sense. In speaking of Christ it is sometimes difficult to tell whether they were speaking of the Eternal Christ, "the power of God and the wisdom of God" (I Cor. 1:24), or the historical Jesus of Nazareth. Often when their opponents were speaking of Jesus, the Quakers were using the same language to denote the "Word which was in the beginning with

God." It is as difficult to be specific about Quaker theology in this
first period as it is to be specific about Christian theology in New
Testament times. In *The Varieties of New Testament Religion* E. F. Scott
lists eight distinct points of view. Perhaps as many could be found
in early Quakerism. In seeking for differences of view among early
Friends, one has only to compare Penn's *Sandy Foundation Shaken*
which is highly mystical, with his own next book *Innocency with Her
Open Face* which is largely evangelical.

The Quaker religion of this period was a living union of the
mystical and evangelical aspects of Christianity as exemplified both
in doctrine and practice; in doctrine because no theological opinion was valid unless vitally related to religious experience; and in
practice, because outward activity was valid only in so far as it grew
out of inward spiritual guidance and power. C. G. Jung points out
that when the introvert and extrovert elements in human character are integrated, the strongest type of personality results. The
same is true of the balance and integration of the mystical or inward element in religion and the evangelical or outward element,
When either is developed at the expense of the other, some form
of disproportion—it may be fanaticism, or it may be formalism—
results. The peculiar power of the early Quakers was due, in
part at least, to the balance of the inward and outward aspects of
religion.

2. The Period of Cultural Creativeness and Mystical Inwardness

The period of creation was followed by a period of conservation.
No religious movement has ever maintained the fire, energy and
power which accompanied its formative period. The burning zeal
which flames out in the market place must sooner or later become
the warm glow of the household hearth. If religion is to become a
genuine part of life itself, it must enter the home as well as the

public square and become integrated with the routine affairs of family living.

This second period is referred to by all modern historians of Quakerism as the period of Quietism. This designation, while true, is not always correctly interpreted. It is not, as some appear to suppose, a term of disparagement. For the quietist, worship requires a passive as well as an active phase, a negative as well as a positive way, a time of receptivity and waiting for divine guidance as well as a time for action upon that guidance. The Quaker quietists were far from quiet once they were assured of the right word or deed. Their period of withdrawal was followed by a return to activity with an increase of insight and power. The leading spirits of this period, Anthony Benezet, Thomas Chalkley, John Churchman, Joshua Evans, David Ferris, Rebecca Jones, John and Samuel Fothergill, Catherine Phillips, Martha Routh, William Savery, Job Scott and John Woolman, to mention only a few, were all quietists, but every one of them traveled widely in the ministry and became an active agent in some social reform. In the so-called "quietist period" the Quakers governed three American colonies and were active in the politics of two more. In the technical meaning of the term, Quakers of the first period were also quietists, and all the usual phrases which signify Quietism, such as reference to the Light as "that which is pure" (or free from human contamination), can be found in their writings. In the transition from the first period to the second, there was no change in doctrine but there was an important change in behavior. The period following the end of persecution in England brought about by the Toleration Act of 1689 found the Quakers almost exhausted by the storm they had weathered. Most of the first leaders had died, many of them in prison, and a second generation was coming on who were not motivated by the blinding fire and acute zeal that comes from discovery of a new truth or from resistance to violent opposition. Many of the most active Friends had migrated to America where they were engaged in setting up a new society and a new way of life in a new world. The enthusiasm which accompanied the first revelation of the Truth was renewed in the enthusiasm with which the colonists set about creating a new commonwealth where Truth might reign. This was their Holy Experiment. They not only created governments conducted on Quaker principles, they created a distinctive Quaker culture, a unique way of life. The feeling engendered by this extraordinary opportunity in the new world is suggested in the early meeting minutes such as those of Chester (later Concord) Quarterly Meeting of Philadelphia Yearly Meeting whose Minute Book is described on its first page as

> Belonging to the People of God called Quakers of Chester County in the Province of Pennsylvania in America. Begun by Divers of those People who in great freedom of spirit left their native country of England and transported themselves and families to this Remote part of the world.

Philosophers have from time to time described their conception of an ideal commonwealth. Here was a vigorous group of ordinary people who not only dreamed of their utopia, but brought it into actual being.

The Golden Age of Quakerism in America was between 1700 and 1740. The first phase of the struggle to clear forests and build homes was then almost over, but material success had not yet become great enough to sap religious vitality. The French and Indian War which was to bring tension between Quaker rulers and the home government in England had not yet broken out. Pennsylvania under Penn's *Frame of Government* and a Quaker Assembly was the most prosperous of all the colonies and Philadelphia was becoming the center of culture in the New World. In Rhode Island half the population was Quaker and for thirty-six successive terms Quaker governors held office. The Quakers were the most important religious group in North Carolina. Under John

Archdale, a Quaker governor, they controlled at one time half the
seats in the Assembly. The Quakers had purchased New Jersey
before they acquired Pennsylvania, and, although they surrendered
their proprietary rights in 1702, they continued to wield a strong
influence in the management of the province. In Maryland, Virginia and New York, Quaker meetings were rapidly increasing in
numbers and membership due to the zeal of traveling ministers
and the ease with which a Quaker meeting could be set up.

In this period attention given to government sometimes interfered with religious duties as is shown in the minutes of Middletown
Monthly Meeting dated 1701:

> The greater part of the members of this meeting, being
> called away upon business relating to government, there-
> fore it is adjourned until tomorrow, being the fifth of this
> month.

John Kinsey (1693-1750) was at one and the same time clerk of
Philadelphia Yearly Meeting, Chief Justice of the Supreme Court
and Speaker of the Assembly. Others could be named, such as
Thomas Lloyd, David Lloyd, Isaac Norris and James Pemberton,
who combined religious with political responsibility in a way which
was characteristic of many leading Friends of the first half of the
eighteenth century.

But the most important product of the flowering of Quakerism
in the New World was the unique Quaker culture. By culture is
meant a clearly defined way of life with a spiritual basis. A true
culture affects every aspect of life. In the Quaker communities the
meeting was the center, spiritually, intellectually and economically.
It included a library and a school. Disputes of whatever nature
were settled in the business sessions of the meeting. The poor were
looked after, moral delinquents dealt with, marriages approved
and performed. There was little need for court or police force or
officials of any kind except a few whose function was to transfer

property and perform similar legal duties. Each group, centered in the meeting, was a well-ordered, highly integrated community of interdependent members. The charter of the community and the moral code which governed its way of life was written in the *Book of Extracts* which was not a depository of tradition, but a record, subject to constant revision, of enlarging moral insights. This flowering of Quakerism was not characterized by any outburst of literary or artistic production. Its whole emphasis was on life itself in home, meeting and community. This life was an artistic creation as beautiful in its simplicity and proportion as was the architecture of its meeting houses. The "Flowering of New England" has been described in terms of its literature, but the flowering of Quakerism in the middle colonies can be described only in terms of life itself.

During the second half of the eighteenth century in America forces and influences from within and without altered this favored condition. The French and Indian War flared out all along the frontier. Most of the Quaker members of the Pennsylvania Assembly resigned in 1756. The inhabitants of the Commonwealth feared the loss of Penn's charter if, because of the Quaker influence, they refused to co-operate in prosecuting the war. But this partial withdrawal from government was not followed by retirement within a shell of isolation. Work was urgent for Indians and Negroes. In 1758 peace was made with the Pennsylvania Indians largely through the efforts of the "Friendly Association for Gaining and Preserving Peace with the Indians by Pacific Measures." Friends who had refused to pay taxes to support the war gave lavishly to this organization in order to achieve the desired result and to demonstrate the adequacy of peaceful methods. Whenever the white man made a treaty with the Indians, Friends saw to it that a Quaker was present to defend Indian rights.

New efforts were made in the field of education. Monthly Meetings were required to report to the Yearly Meeting exactly what each was doing to educate its children. By the end of the century there were approximately sixty Friends schools in Pennsylvania and about half as many in New Jersey.

Of supreme importance was the strenuous effort which began about the middle of the century to reform the Society from within. There was great uneasiness about Friends in government who had shown a compromising spirit and about Friends who, having grown wealthy in business, were departing from simplicity. A new set of Queries, fourteen in number, to be answered in writing four times a year was devised in 1755 representing all the important testimonies regarding behavior. They constituted a powerful and inclusive check on un-Quakerly forms of behavior. Gradually the number of times on which the Queries were to be answered was reduced to once a year. The Discipline, as a moral code, took more definite shape and the means of enforcing it were increased. Many Friends were disowned for various types of delinquency, the most frequent being marriage with a person not in membership in the Society of Friends. Friends strongly believed in religious unity within the family. The loss from disownment was large though many disowned Friends later returned to their early allegiance. Throughout the century, in spite of disownments and rigid enforcement of the Discipline, the number of members increased. American Quakerism probably reached its numerical climax about 1800.

This century is here designated the "period of mysticism" because the conscious effort to follow divine guidance wherever it might lead was unusually strong. The first leaders had thrown themselves with such abandon and lack of self-consciousness into the task of spreading their message that they did not practice the continuous self-examination apparent in the more cautious and introspective members of the second period. There was a difference of degree not of kind. The *Journals* written by the leading Friends of the eighteenth century portray a humble, devout life guided from within, and a sense of peace and serenity resulting from aware-

ness that every task laid upon them by their divine Master had
been carried out according to the measure of Light and Power
which was given. The theological battles of the seventeenth century were over; the Quakers were generally accepted as Christians.
Less attention was paid to doctrine and more was directed toward
the cultivation of the right inward state. Theological opinion was
not absent, but it was in the background and seldom became the
subject of spoken or written discourse. Most sermons in meetings
for worship were appeals for obedience to the admonitions of the
Spirit made manifest within. Concerns for particular forms of social service were expressed in the meeting for business. Traditions
were growing up and exerting a strong influence. Whittier in "The
Pennsylvania Pilgrim" writes of a Quaker meeting of the period:

> The white, clear light, tradition-colored, stole
> Through the stained oriel of each human soul.

There was much traveling by the leading Friends, some of whom
were so continuously engaged in religious service that they were
seldom at home for any length of time. Several could say toward
the end of their lives that they had visited every meeting in the
Society of Friends. Individual journeys not infrequently occupied
as many as four years including crossing the Atlantic. Traveling
Friends held advertised meetings for addressing the general public, and meetings held in meeting houses were often attended by
many who were not Friends. The days of convincing the
unconvinced were by no means over. Great distances were covered by canoe or on horseback, sometimes along lonely frontier
trails. Martha Routh, an English schoolteacher in delicate health,
records that she traveled 11,000 miles in America in 1794-96.
Catherine Phillips records that she traveled 8,750 miles on horseback on an American journey in 1753-56. Meetings for worship
held with families were included on these itineraries sometimes
five or ten in a day. Traveling Friends were the links which bound

the widely scattered Society together, giving it coherence and insuring a certain degree of uniformity.

The most complete description of the Quaker cultural pattern of this period was written by Thomas Clarkson. Not himself a member of the Society of Friends, he had come into close contact with Friends in antislavery work and he admired their ways. Clarkson's *Portraiture of Quakerism* first issued in three volumes in London in 1806 became, in Quaker schools and elsewhere, the main source book for those who desired to preserve and perpetuate the Quakerism of the eighteenth century on both sides of the Atlantic. Clarkson observes in his introduction that there had been books written about Quaker history and principles but none, like his, about the manners and customs of the Society of Friends. But a living culture cannot be transmitted by a description, however exact. To be really understood, it must be felt and lived.

The Quaker way of life as developed in the seventeenth and eighteenth centuries survived in many places through much of the nineteenth century, and in a few areas it has persisted well into the twentieth. Friends now living, whose grandparents were examples of what Thomas Clarkson wrote about, comprehend and appreciate the inner significance of this thoroughly correlated system. They can, however, pass on only a faint impression of it to their children for whom the whole flavor and essence of the old Quaker life has become, if it is of interest at all, the object of antiquarian inquiry. Through such study the outward form is ascertainable, but the inner quality must be felt in order to be known.

3. The Conflict between Mysticism and Evangelicalism

During the larger part of the second period the mystical element in Quakerism took precedence over the evangelical. It was deemed essential that the outward should be a genuine and sincere expression of the inward. But gradually the elders and overseers who were guardians of the traditions governing "plainness in dress, speech and behavior" became dominant. The priestly type of mind took precedence over the prophetic type.

Friends do not have a testimony against forms as such. Inward feeling must inevitably find expression in outward form. Nor do Friends have a testimony against forms inherited from the past just because they come from the past. Action, in order to be based on as wide a range of experience as possible, must to some extent be governed by the wisdom of those who are no longer living. But it is possible for the past to exercise more weight than it should in determining the sense of the meeting. In the days following the American Revolution and the French Revolution there was much talk of freedom which had its influence on the Quakers. It is not surprising that there should arise in the first quarter of the nineteenth century considerable resistance in the Society of Friends to those who were enforcing very strictly a definite code of behavior. There were also many well-founded complaints by official Friends about looseness of conduct and the lowness of spiritual life. A conflict was brewing which first appeared as a tension between the rank and file and the Friends on the facing benches.

The conflict burst into flame when the elders, going beyond their accustomed prerogative as guardians of behavior, attempted to become guardians of the theological opinions of those who spoke in meetings for worship. This broke the Society of Friends in America into two parts. Those who were in favor of dictation regarding doctrine tended to be the more evangelical in belief, though there were many exceptions. Those who were opposed to dictation by the elders tended to emphasize the mystical side of Quakerism, though here also there were many exceptions. The tension increased from 1800 until it led to a separation which began in Philadelphia in 1827. Spiritual life was at too low an ebb to create the former synthesis of inward and outward. Edward

Hicks in his *Journal* calls it a "quibbling, scribbling age." The Inward Light, the source of unity, had become obscured. Worldly prosperity had taken the fortress which persecution had assailed so long in vain.

In England the tension between these two elements was, with the exception of two minor separations, kept within bounds with more mutual forbearance than in America. The evangelical party was generally dominant during most of the nineteenth century partly because, as is usually the case, it was more insistent on its principles than the mystical party. As each separation occurred in America, London Yearly Meeting always recognized the more evangelical party. English Friends traveling in America strongly supported that side and thereby increased the tendency toward separation.

The separations in America during the nineteenth century will be touched on here only in so far as they throw light on changes in Quaker ideas. Several factors conduced toward these changes. Friends were in closer contact with the outside world than they had been in the preceding century. Influences from two opposite directions were affecting them, the so-called evangelical awakening of the Methodist revival from the right and the rationalistic philosophy of the time, and the French Revolution from the left. The Methodists held that man was fallen and had no capacity for goodness. They stood for the plenary inspiration of the Scriptures, the Deity of Christ, His substitutionary death on the cross, and a personal religious experience which suddenly and miraculously converted the believer from a state of depravity to a state of grace. In their insistence on personal religious experience and in some of the social reforms which they advocated, they came close to Quakerism, and it is not surprising that some of the Quaker leaders of the early nineteenth century came to Quakerism as converts from the Methodist revival. No substantial portion of the Society of Friends was affected by the rationalism of Paine, Voltaire and

Hume or the popular deism which made God wholly transcendent. Paley's *Evidences* and Butler's *Analogy* were weak answers to deism, but the French Revolution appeared as a horrible outcome of free thought. The main result of the impact of rationalism on a part of the Society of Friends at that time was negative in supporting the reaction toward mysticism and against evangelical doctrines. The struggle both in the separation of 1827 and in that of 1845 was between those who emphasized the outward Scriptures and outward historical events recorded in Scripture and those who emphasized inward mystical experience.

In the heat of controversy each drove the other to extremes which later were somewhat modified. In Philadelphia the new evangelical emphasis came first to the city; the country, as usual, being more conservative, remained closer to the mystical emphasis of the eighteenth century. This was confusing. It meant that the conservative country Friends possessed a more liberal theology, while the radical city Friends held a more conservative theology. But country and city were at odds for another reason. City Friends could easily get together and attend committees. They were more wealthy and many of them more educated. They dominated the Yearly Meeting for Ministers and Elders and the Meeting for Sufferings, which was the Executive Committee of the Yearly Meeting. The country Friends could but seldom attend these important gatherings. They resented the domination of aristocratic, city Friends. For these reasons there were twice as many of the evangelical party in the city as there were of the liberal party. In the country, on the other hand, where the majority of Friends lived, this situation was reversed. Similar conditions prevailed when the separation spread to Baltimore and New York. In Ohio where there was no large body of city Friends, the two parties were practically equal.

The immediate cause of the separation was the attempt on the part of the Philadelphia elders to forbid Elias Hicks to preach. He was an aged and powerful minister who was then traveling with a minute from his home meeting in Long Island. A genuine mystic, sympathizing neither with evangelical doctrines nor with the type of rationalism which resulted in unitarianism, his whole religion was based on the Inward Light, yielding small place for the historical Jesus, the Bible, Christian tradition, or anything outward. Many who took his part did not understand or appreciate his extremely subjective type of religion, but they defended his right to preach and his concept of religious freedom. Others took his part because they disliked the aggressive heresy-hunting tactics of the evangelical Orthodox party. Samuel Janney, the leading historian of the Hicksite or liberal party, writes in his *Journal* for 1824:

> The doctrines I then held were those called Orthodox, but I could not endure the spirit of bitterness and party zeal by which those doctrines were too often accompanied.[8]

The Orthodox party claimed that the separation was due to doctrinal differences, but the Hicksite party denied this. The latter wrote to London Friends:

> We do not believe that the dissensions which have appeared amongst us had their origin so much in differences of opinion in doctrinal points as in a disposition, apparent in some, to exercise an oppressive authority in the church.

Doctrinal statements appearing in the Hicksite disciplines and elsewhere uphold this point of view.

When the separation finally occurred in 1827 both parties were to blame for their behavior: the Orthodox party for their belligerent attack on persons holding what they considered unchristian opinions, and for their disowning of all members of the Hicksite party; and the Hicksites for their impatience and unwillingness to wait, in the time-honored Quaker manner, for greater unity. They withdrew from what they called 'the scene of confusion." What had begun as a controversy over a problem of church government,

namely, the authority of the elders, now became a theological controversy between the followers of the historic Christ and the followers of the Inward Christ. This controversy much lowered the
general regard in which the Society had been held. *The Manifesto*,
the official organ of the Shakers, said that "when the Quakers so
far forgot their union as to wrangle about doctrine they sank into
worldlings." Both sides issued publications appealing to the writings of primitive Friends and both found much to support their
positions. What both overlooked was the fact that primitive Quakerism, like primitive Christianity, was a synthesis of mystical and
evangelical elements in which each modified the other. For primitive Quakerism the historical Christ and the Inward Christ were
one, the historical Christ having been the incarnation and complete revelation of the Inward Christ.

Since the Hicksite, or liberal Friends, had assumed a position
which allowed for a wide variety of theological opinion, no further
separations occurred among them. They reduced the authority of
elders and overseers so they did not continue to lay the same emphasis as did the Orthodox on time-honored Quaker traditions.
They emphasized democracy and tolerance. For a century their
discipline advised the meeting to deal with persons who denied
the divinity of Christ, which was defined as blasphemy.

The Orthodox wing adopted a more authoritarian position,
assuming greater control of the individual by the group. As a consequence, the old controversy between the mystic and evangelical
broke out again. This resulted in the Wilburite-Gurneyite Separation which began in New England in 1845 and gradually spread to
other areas. Joseph John Gurney's (1788-1847) name was attached
to the more extreme evangelical group, and that of John Wilbur
(1774-1856) to those who represented the older, more mystical
type of Quakerism which also contained definite evangelical elements. Gurney, an attractive, able and cultured member of a distinguished English family and a brother of Elizabeth Fry, spent

three years in a tour of American meetings in the years 1837-40. His devout life and powerful ministry made a profound impression. He was opposed by John Wilbur who claimed that he was preaching doctrines not in accord with primitive Quakerism, such as a belief in imputed righteousness through a profession of faith and in the Bible as the *only* source of Truth; *the* Word of God rather than *a* word of God. Later in his life Gurney denied having these opinions. Wilbur was of the prophetic type. His thought was closely in line with the Quakerism of the preceding century. He relied upon the Inward Light as the primary source of Truth, and the Bible as a secondary source revealing the same Truth. Gurney was a scholar, versed in theology, an advocate of higher education and particularly of Bible teaching to which the conservative Friends objected as a type of programmed religious service not inspired by the Spirit, and mere "head knowledge." At Oxford and elsewhere he had come under the influence of prominent English churchmen. Thomas Shillitoe, an active English opponent of Elias Hicks, criticized Gurney for being, as he said, "an Episcopalian, not a Quaker." Jonathan Evans, a leading opponent of Hicks in Philadelphia, was equally opposed to Gurney. When Wilbur expressed disapproval of Gurney in New England Yearly Meeting, the Yearly Meeting overwhelmingly supported Gurney, and by an irregular procedure brought about the disownment of Wilbur by overriding the support of his own Monthly Meeting. The adherents of Wilbur appealed to other Yearly Meetings, thus causing divisions in them. The Philadelphia Orthodox Yearly Meeting recognized the Wilburite Yearly Meeting in Ohio, but eventually, in order to appease their own small Gurneyite minority, withdrew correspondence, the usual form of recognition, from all other Yearly Meetings. Most members of Philadelphia Yearly Meeting at Arch Street continued to feel that they were a part of the Wilburite group, the recognition of which was never formally rescinded.

There were then in the second half of the nineteenth century in America three kinds of Quakers designated by the names of three persons. The Hicksites represented the more mystical, liberal, noncreedal branch; the Gurneyites, the more evangelical, authoritarian and theologically conservative branch; and the Wilburites, a branch whose position was between the other two. The doctrinal differences among the three were not clearly defined since they had no formal written creeds. It was more a matter of emphasis than of content. Among the Wilburites there was more opportunity than in either of the other two for a genuine synthesis of the mystical and evangelical elements in Quakerism. It was they who could most clearly lay claim to be the heirs of the original Society of Friends. But there was an important difference. The code of behavior which the first Friends arrived at through immediate experience of the Inward Light, the Wilburites, with many exceptions, tended to accept in large measure on the basis of tradition.

Again the more evangelical branch became subject to division. The history of religion has shown over and over again that creeds do not unite, they tend to divide. A group held together by a creed is more brittle and more subject to breakage than a more yielding organic group held together by the Spirit. Soon after the Civil War a great revival of evangelical religion, akin to Methodism, occurred, especially in the Middle West. It profoundly affected all religious sects, including the Society of Friends. Evangelists traveled from place to place, bringing multitudes to their knees crying for mercy and forgiveness. Quakers who had become evangelists or evangelists who had become Quakers held revival meetings in Friends meeting houses. This tendency generally showed itself first in the singing of hymns and proceeded finally to the taking over of the meeting by the evangelists. They preached a fourfold gospel of Justification, Sanctification, the Second Coming of Christ and Faith Healing. Many new members who were by this means brought suddenly into membership knew nothing of the Quaker meeting for worship. Meetings seeking to worship in silence were interrupted by impromptu hymns, calls to prayer, personal testimonies and shouts of hallelujah and amen. In order to care for the new converts and to bring order the evangelist was sometimes prevailed upon to remain and become a professional pastor, conducting a regular Protestant type of programmed service.* Through such influences a large proportion of the Society of Friends became removed from its foundation and brought into the full stream of Protestantism.

These changes brought in a new series of separations. Beginning in 1877 in Iowa and ending in 1904 in North Carolina, a number of meetings and individuals withdrew from those affected by these tendencies and affiliated with the Wilburites. They are now known as Conservative Friends. To them the evangelists appeared to be bringing in "strange fire,"[9] to be saying, "I converted these" instead of leaving it to the Lord, to be attempting to bring about suddenly by methods of high pressure the new life which can only grow slowly. In the *Journals* of the evangelists the pronoun "I" is used in a way in which it is not used in other Friends *Journals*. The Lord "gave *me* souls," writes Esther Frame,[10] an evangelist who joined Friends because of more opportunities for a woman to preach. When John Henry Douglas found his fervent

---

* Cf. George Fox's account of his visit to Rhode Island: "At another place I heard some of the magistrates said among themselves, 'if they had money enough, they would hire me to be their minister.' This was where they did not well understand us and our principles, but when I heard of it I said, 'It was time for me to be gone; for if their eye was so much to me or any of us they would not come to their own teacher.' For this thing [hiring ministers] had spoiled many, by hindering them from improving their own talents; whereas our labor is to bring all men to their own teacher in themselves."—*Journal*, 1891, II, 171-72

appeals in a Friends meeting unavailing, he cried out, "What shall I do with you?" A woman Friend then arose and said, "John, we own no man master in this assembly." This illustrates a fundamental difference between the new evangelist and the older Quaker preacher. For the evangelist the religious service was focused on himself; for the older type of minister the sermon arose out of the united life of the meeting. The evangelist kept careful count of the number of conversions he made. The older Friends did not pretend to know what changes the Spirit might be secretly making in the hearts of their hearers.

It has often been suggested that the pastoral system with its programmed worship came into the Society of Friends because of failure of the meeting based on silence and particularly failure of the older type of ministry. This may, in some instances, have been true, but in the great majority of cases it appears to have come, not because of absence of Life, but because of too much liveliness. The revival unsettled the meeting, produced a chaos of ecstatic testimonies and much running about, and the pastor was brought in to restore order. The more active, aggressive element also welcomed his assumption of responsibility to lessen the influence of the more pacific conservative element.*

Again the more evangelical party was subject to division. The Friends who had adopted the pastoral system became divided into a modernist wing with a somewhat critical attitude toward the Bible and a fundamentalist wing of Biblical literalists. The fundamentalists still depend on revivalistic methods. Their doctrine of sanctifi-

---

*English Evangelicalism produced a number of programmed meetings most of which have disappeared. According to the London Book of Meetings, the following religious community services were carried on in 1898: "24 First-day Evening 'Reading Meetings,' and 83 First-day Evening 'Mission Meetings.' "—*Friends Quarterly Examiner,* Vol. XXXII, p. 407 Seventh Month, 1898.

cation as a second experience following conversion has an affinity to the primitive Quaker doctrine of perfection though it is based on a different theology. The modernist Friends churches have largely given up revivalism which no longer exerts its former appeal. Their leading members today have been educated in Friends colleges and many have come into contact with other aspects of Quakerism. As a result there is a greater approval of the older way of Quaker worship. The pastoral Friends churches are frequently community churches which minister to a limited geographical area which includes persons with a variety of religious backgrounds. One of their main concerns is foreign missions.

This account, too brief to be wholly accurate, is intended to suggest the changes in Quaker ideas and the occasion of those changes. The clue to the tensions and cleavage is the inability of the more mystical and the more evangelical, the inwardly centered and the outwardly centered, the introvert and the extrovert to understand each other and to wait patiently enough in the Light for unity. The nineteenth century was a time of restlessness and division in all religious groups in America. The causes of disagreement were many, including migrations to new frontiers, civil war, and periods of transition in economic status as well as in scientific and philosophic thought.

A diagram will summarize graphically this period in Quaker history. Several minor separations are not included.

The Modernist Period: 1900-1950

The following description of this period concerns mainly that part of Quakerism in America which has continued the original way of Quaker worship and practice. It is to be observed, however, that the changes to be noted have taken place, in various degrees and forms, throughout Christendom.

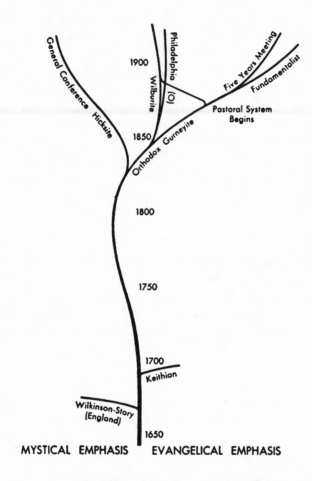

DIVISIONS IN AMERICAN QUAKERISM AS RELATED TO
MYSTICAL AND EVANGELICAL TRENDS

This diagram indicates only the beginning of separations which sometimes took place over a period of time. Tendencies toward unity in the
second quarter of the twentieth century and the growth of independent
meetings uniting all branches are not indicated.

During this period we can no longer refer only to conflict between the mystical and evangelical wings as the key to understanding Quaker history. The tension continued, indeed it must always be present, but other emphases were increasing. The Society of Friends was now wide open to outside influences. Rationalism and the religion of social service had always been present in Quakerism, but they were subordinate to the mystical and evangelical. Reason had been considered a reliable guide to moral and religious Truth if illumined by the Inward Light and checked by the New Testament. Social service was always held to be essential in Christian behavior provided that it arose from divine Leading. Barclay protests against the Protestant theology which enabled a man to be saved without good works. But subordination of the rational and the social to the mystical and evangelical did not continue to the same degree. Many Quakers became primarily intellectual and humanitarian in outlook. The searching for inner guidance in the heart and outer guidance in the Scriptures receded, though it never altogether ceased.

This change, which like all changes took place gradually, was due to several conditions. Chief among them was the general tendency toward secularization and humanism. All through the nineteenth century science had been coming forward as the most reliable guide to truth, and in the twentieth century it came to be revered as the most dependable source of knowledge. Rapid acceleration in the application of science had given to man an extraordinary control over nature. Reliance on the divine seemed less essential. Such reliance was sometimes considered a sign of weakness or ignorance. In cities little was in evidence that was not man-made or under human control. In earlier generations most Friends were farmers; now many were living in cities or suburbs where the mysterious and unpredictable aspects of the creation appeared at a minimum. Man seemed self-sufficient, victorious and without need of help from God or religion. Two world wars have since shown this victory to have been an illusion. Man's victory over nature was annulled by the fact that he had failed to triumph over himself.

Secularization and the tendency toward humanism was accelerated in the Society of Friends by higher education. In most colleges science took precedence and other studies employed the scientific method as far as was practicable. Even courses of study in religion and ethics sought for a scientific basis.

In the first half of the nineteenth century a strong religious atmosphere pervaded the Friends Boarding Schools. This was carried over to the colleges which developed in the second half of the century. But the Quaker colleges, like other denominational colleges, though they continued to emphasize religion, tended to satisfy an intellectual rather than a devotional interest. It is significant that the Wilburite Boarding Schools, Westtown, Barnesville and Scattergood, did not become colleges as did the Gurneyite Boarding Schools, Haverford, Earlham and Guilford. The Conservatives, being more inwardly directed toward the Light, did not feel so strongly the impulse toward higher education, but the Evangelicals, being more outwardly directed toward the Bible, Christian missions and evangelical beliefs, felt the need of Biblical study and theological preparation. The major concern of Joseph John Gurney in visiting Friends schools at Haverford and Guilford was to encourage Biblical study.

Through the early years of the twentieth century the Orthodox Yearly Meeting in Philadelphia still adhered to the Wilburite point of view based on a synthesis of mysticism and evangelicalism with a strong emphasis on the traditional Quaker pattern in "dress, speech and behavior." The shift to a more modern rationalistic point of view with a strong emphasis on social service occurred within a single generation. The Hicksite group, having less of an evangelical emphasis, had less of a tendency toward outward checks both in doctrine and in practice and so more readily permitted

their traditional mysticism to be replaced by the newer rationalism. At the middle of the twentieth century there is little to distinguish the majority of the Orthodox from the majority of the
Hicksites, though each group possesses a minority which perpetu-
ates older traits.

The most characteristic feature of this period was the initiation
of Conferences and Summer Schools both in England and in Eastern America. These were a new and effective means of adult education in the field of Quaker history and principles. In England
the Manchester Conference of 1895 marked a transition. In
America the Haverford Summer School of 1900 proved to be a
similar turning point. These schools were succeeded by similar
educational efforts all of which were expressions of renewed
interest in the past and a desire to learn from it. Included also
was a determination to come to grips with new trends in Biblical
criticism and scientific thought. Under the early inspiration of
John Wilhelm Rowntree in England, Rufus M. Jones in America
and many others, a new teaching ministry developed in both
countries. Theirs was the task of helping the Society of Friends
through the difficulties created by modern thought. It was discovered that, because Quakerism is based on immediate experience,
it had little to fear from the inroads of scientific or historical
research. The religion of the Society of Friends was shown to be a
faith which a highly educated modern mind could, without reservation, accept. Early Quaker history and thought which had become obscured and distorted by the conflicts of the nineteenth
century and the partisanship of those who still held extreme opinions, began to be set forth in adequate and readily available books
and periodicals.

A second important influence in this period in America was the
rise and growth of the American Friends Service Committee,
following the development of the Friends Service Council which
had functioned for some time in England. At the same time, Yearly

Meeting Committees were set up to deal with a great variety of social concerns.

In assessing the interplay of the four chief elements in every complete religion—mysticism, evangelicalism, rationalism and humanitarianism—it is clear that, in that area of Quakerism which is now under consideration and which has preserved the historic form of Quaker worship, the twentieth century has witnessed a growth of rationalism and humanitarianism at the expense of mysticism and evangelicalism. Mysticism, which is inward, tends to become rationalism, which is also inward; evangelicalism, which is outward, tends to become humanitarianism, which is also outward. It might appear that the evangelical interest in saving souls is very different from the humanitarian interest in saving bodies, but in so far as the first is concerned in improving living conditions in the next world and the second in improving living conditions in this world, there is an obvious parallel.

No doubt rationalism and humanitarianism were developed to a high degree at a time when they were urgently needed. It was necessary that Quakerism should have a rationalistic basis in order to cope with modern thought which more easily prevailed over faiths which had not clearly set forth their intellectual ground. A new outburst of social activity was indispensable to meet the tragic need of a world torn by two major wars. This activity has brought new life into the Society of Friends and many new adherents. As a result of the greater understanding of Quaker history and principles, and because of greater social activity, the decline in numbers of the nonpastoral Friends has been stopped and a steady, healthy increase is taking place. The migration from the country to the city has affected rural meetings adversely, especially those of the Wilburite Friends in the West, but this loss in the country has resulted in gains in the city. Migrating Friends today discover one another and form new meetings. Over one hundred and fifty such new meetings have been set up in various places in America since 1925. Many of these meetings have been started or carried on by workers or former workers of the American Friends Service Committee who have first learned about Quakerism while engaged in some project in this country or while working on a relief team abroad.

The growth of a rational religion with its teaching ministry and the growth of humanitarianism with its ministry of social service were favorable developments in the Society of Friends resulting in new life and increasing membership. In so far as they flourish at the expense of the older mysticism and the older evangelicalism, however, they may not in the end have proved entirely fortunate. The older social service, which still persists to some extent, originated in an individual concern and was solemnly endorsed by the meeting. It was a synthesis of the mystical and the humanitarian elements. The newer social service manifesting itself in the form of professional duties or appointments made by standing committees is frequently one-sided. The concern for service may be sincere, but it has originated outside the individual who carries it out. The older rationalism, which still to some extent exists, was tested and checked by the revelation of God in the heart of man and in the Scriptures. The newer rationalism has sometimes attempted to deduce Truth by reason alone with no premises based on historical events or inward feeling. Because of this origin, it is too often cold and impersonal.

Signs are now apparent in the Society of Friends that what has been called the modernistic period is drawing to an end. There is no reason why the growth of one or more of these four forms of religion should hinder the growth of the others. The most adequate religion is that in which all four are fully developed. But human nature is weak and it is easier to become one-sided than to achieve harmonious symmetry. Lack of balance in an individual may, however, be compensated by balance in the group. A group which contains the right proportion of prophets or mystics, evangelicals or priests, theologians or philosophers, and reformers or social workers may achieve more than a group in which such balance is lacking. But here we must remind ourselves again that, as Paul shows (I Cor. 12:28), gifts are not all of equal value; "Earnestly desire the spiritual gifts, especially that you may prophesy" (I Cor. 14:1).

Notes

1. Joseph Besse, *A Collections of the Sufferingsof the People called Quakers,* II, 1753, p. 391.

2. Besse, *Sufferings,* p. 400.

3. *Letters Etc. of Early Friends,* edited by Abram Rawlinson Barclay, 1841, pp. 292-93.

4. According to John Whiting's *Catalogue of Friends Books* (1708).

5. For the thoroughness with which this was carried out see Joseph Smith's *Catalogue of Anti-Quakeriana* which contains 461 pages of titles of anti-Quaker books and their answers.

6. *First Publishers of Truth,* edited by Norman Penney, 1907, p. 294; henceforth abbreviated F.P.T.

7. F.P.T., p. 49.

8. Samuel M. Janney, *Memoirs,* 1881, p. 21.

9. Frame, *Reminisiences of Nathan T. Frame and Esther G. Frame,* 1907 pp. 54, 80.

10. Frame, *Reminisiences,* p. 30.

CHAPTER X

Quaker Thought and the Present

THROUGH THE THREE CENTURIES of Quaker history the four primary elements present in all religions have at different times exerted their influence in varying degrees. During the first century and a half mysticism and evangelicalism were in balance in the group as a whole though many individuals tended to stress one or the other; during the nineteenth century mysticism and evangelicalism were in conflict, each pressing the other to extremes in the group as a whole, though in many individuals the two were in balance; and during the past half century rationalism and humanitarianism have assumed greater prominence, sometimes becoming dominant, though here again there are some individuals in whom the four tendencies are in balance.

The best type of religion is one in which the mystical, the evangelical, the rational and the social are so related that each exercises a restraint on the others. Too exclusive an emphasis on mysticism results in a religion which is individualistic, subjective and vague; too dominant an evangelicalism results in a religion which is authoritarian, creedal and external; too great an emphasis on rationalism results in a cold, intellectual religion which appeals only to the few; too engrossing a devotion to the social gospel results in a religion which, in improving the outer environment, ignores defects of the inner life which cause the outer disorder. In Quakerism the optimum is not equality in rank of the four ele-

245

ments. The mystical is basic. The Light Within occasions the acceptance or rejection of a particular authority, reason or service.

Mysticism and evangelicalism are directed toward the superhuman. Reason and good works are human. Yet man may let his attention slip below the human level. The three levels can be designated as follows:

	Inward	Outward
Superhuman	Mysticism	Evangelicalism
Human	Rationalism	Humanitarianism
Subhuman	Vitalism	Materialism

Let us first consider the inner three, even though they are so intimately related to the outer three that they cannot be fairly treated separately.

By vitalism is meant a religion which worships the life-force in its biological sense. This includes what might be called "tribal mysticism," the sense of kinship in a family, tribe, caste or race which finds expression in ancestor worship or worship of a tribal god. Included also is the cult of patriotism which, through symbols and rituals, worships the nation as a kind of pervasive personality. The Nazis, in their emphasis on "blood and soil," represent an extreme modern form of this type of mysticism. In the primitive fertility religions which worshiped the reproductive powers of nature we have older examples of mysticism on this level, the feeling which all persons have in some degree, that there is in man and nature an inner vital creative power which is worthy of reverence.

That the divine is immanent in nature is a creed not only of simple folk, but also of philosophers and poets, a creed which ranges all the way from primitive animism and magic to the highest flights of absolute idealism, finding the whole universe to exist only as a thought of God or as a body of which God is the universal soul. Hinduism today includes all these stages from animism to absolute idealism. Wordsworth expresses this nature mysticism in comprehensible terms in his "Lines, Composed a Few Miles above Tintern Abbey":

> . . . a sense sublime
> Of something far more deeply interfused,
> Whose dwelling is the light of setting suns,
> And the round ocean, and the living air,
> And the blue sky, and in the mind of man:
> A motion and a spirit, that impels
> All thinking things, all objects of all thought,
> And rolls through all things.

Nature mysticism, whether limited to the tribe or directed toward all nature, is a right beginning to religious progress; its limitation appears, however, if it does not grow into something higher. To center our worship on nature whether in whole or in part, or on family, race or nation, is to include the evil in these orders as well as the good. Nature "red in tooth and claw" is an incomplete expression of God. Loyalty to family, race or nation, while of value as far as it goes, is not good if the evils of these objects of loyalty and devotion are overlooked.

Nature mysticism or tribal mysticism runs the risk of leveling down instead of leveling up. By seeing God in all things we behold Truth, but that does not mean that all things should remain as they are, simply because God is immanent in them. God still creates and His presence, even in the lowest of His creatures and even in the most sensual desires, is evidence that His work has been begun, though not finished. Only as we turn our thoughts to God Himself do we find the Being worthy of our individual loyalty and worship. Christ, the revelation of God in human terms, is the culmination of the process of which nature is the beginning.

The Quakers believe that God is in nature and in all human beings, including what Robert Barclay called the "natural man," that is, man as a child of nature, an animal who is the descendant of a long line of animal ancestors. God, Barclay said, exists in "natural man" as a "Seed." This is a useful figure, for it implies growth. The Seed, or "that of God in every man" even the unregenerate, can be cultivated or "answered" and so started on a process of growth. As it grows man is lifted from the animal level to the human level and finally from the human to the divine.

The Seed will grow of itself if the soil is fertile and the surface not too hard or stony. The plant can be watered and nourished but its growth cannot be forced. The divine Life, like a plant, cannot be helped to grow by stretching or pulling. Finally it matures. It is interesting to notice that in the New Testament the word translated as "perfect" means also mature.* Perfection is the maturing of inner capacities, be they small or great; it is not the end of an infinite process but it is an attainable goal.

Continuing to fix our attention on the three levels as inwardly revealed, we find ample evidence in the Quaker *Journals* that these three actually exist in experience, however, they may be interpreted in theory. The journalists were extremely careful not to go beyond experience itself and to write down as truly as they could what their own experiences were without any attempt to adjust their descriptions to forms determined in advance by a creedal requirement. The spiritual journey of the writer was generally described in three main stages, the first in childhood, the second in adolescence and early adult life, and the third in full adulthood, though there was considerable variation in the age at which the turning

---

* Thus the word translated as "perfect" in the King James Version of the Bible is sometimes translated "mature" in the Revised Standard Version. "That we may present every man perfect in Christ Jesus" (Col. 1:28) becomes "That we may present every man mature in Christ."

points took place. The three sets of extracts that follow are examples taken from the *Journals* of each of the three centuries of Quaker history.

The first stage was a time of primitive innocence like that of Adam in Paradise. Like Adam, the writer sometimes heard the voice of God.

> While I was yet very young . . . being inspired with a divine principle, I did in those days sometimes feel the power of it overcoming my heart. [William Caton, 1636-65][1]

> In my early age I was sensible of the tendering impressions of divine love. [Mary Haggar, 1758-1840][2]

> I remember that at a very early age I experienced the operation of divine grace condemning me for evil and inciting me to goodness. [Samuel M. Janney, 1801-80][3]

These examples from many that might be given indicate a sharp divergence from the Calvinist doctrine of depravity. The young Quaker was a child of nature and as such felt in his soul the Word of God who had created and was still creating nature.

The second stage began with a period of juvenile frivolity which the journalist, writing of his experiences at a later age, looks back upon as vanity and a waste of time. A few typical expressions are:

> My mind was drawn out after the vain plays, customs, fashions and will-worships of the world. [James Dickinson, 1659-1741][4]

> I took great pleasure in airy and vain company. [David Ferris, 1707-79][5]

> The vivacity of my natural disposition often led me beyond due bounds. [Sarah Hunt, 1797-1889][6]

No *Journal* records more serious misdeeds than "frothiness of behavior" and fondness for various amusements, sports and games. The writer is still somewhat a child of nature but not entirely so, for soon an inner conflict begins. The divine voice is heard calling, not back to primitive unconscious innocence, for that is no longer possible, but up to the higher level of deliberate self-conscious obedience. There is a pull from above and a pull from below. The self is divided, a state well described by Paul when he said, "1 can will what is right, but I cannot do it" (Rom. 7:18).

Almost every journalist gives a vivid description of this stage of conflict.

> In this furnace I toiled and labored and none knew my sorrows and griefs which at times were almost intolerable. [Stephen Crisp, 1628-92][7]

> I never had before such a clear and undoubted sense of the two powers of light and life and of death and darkness. [William Evans, 1787-1867][8]

> I tried many ways to flee from him.... but he followed me up as he did the children of Israel in their travels. [Thomas Arnett, 1791-1877][9]

The intermediate stage of conflict was finally replaced by a complete willingness to follow the Light Within wherever it led. This third stage might come suddenly but more often it came gradually through a series of steps, one of which was the successful expression of a repressed concern to speak in a meeting for worship. When this occurred the family and friends of the speaker knew, sometimes to their astonishment, what had taken place secretly in the heart. Having made a public declaration, the speaker must now live up to it. He must adopt the plain dress and speech of the typical Friend as a way of showing the world where he stands. He has emerged on the level where his life is centered in the Light.

His inner tension and conflict is, for the present, no longer felt. Of course he may sometimes slip, indeed he generally does so. New periods of conflict and depression may occur, but on the whole his life is lived in a condition of inner peace and whole-hearted commitment to the will of God wherever it may lead. These journalists represent an achievement higher than average, but they were standard Friends in the sense that their *Journals* formed the basis of instruction in the Quaker way of life as read on winter evenings at the family fireside.

We find, then, three levels of human achievement which merge so gradually into one another that it may be difficult to tell where one begins and the other ends. The three are based on experience rather than on theory. Man actually finds himself poised between a world of darkness and a world of light. He can center his life in the dark world or in the flickering twilight of human reason or in the clear Light of the divine Presence. The dark world is not evil in itself. It forms the essential basis of our life on this earth. It is evil only when the soul becomes centered in it. The same may be said of the realm of reason. Without reason in control of sensual desires we could not rise to the level of men. Reason has lifted us up out of the world of sensuality into a realm where we have learned to a large degree how to control our instincts and our material environment. Through reason we have become human and through reason we defy the forces of nature which would otherwise overwhelm us. Through reason we have not only become lords over the beasts but we appear to have peculiar qualities and characteristics which distinguish us as beings different from them, not in degree only, but in kind.

But in the world of reason no ultimate goal is in sight. Neither the stars of night nor the sun of day shine clearly. Reason is baffled by insoluble problems. It can show the next step ahead but it cannot reveal man's destiny. Reason tries to construct a consistent system of ideas, an effort which is most ardently undertaken in later adolescence or in early adulthood. The college student of today is at the stage when rational consistency appears to be of supreme importance. He is determined to reconcile science and religion and when he fails he may throw away one or the other. Or he may attempt to find a rational solution to a problem like that of Job, the reconciliation of the justice of God and the suffering of the righteous. Or he may find himself baffled by the problem of freedom and determinism. When reason tries to achieve a consistent system of thought there is always some nonrational element left over which cannot be fitted into the system.

As a result, reason becomes humbled and submissive, and the human will finds itself ready to surrender to a greater Will. If this occurs, it need not be because of a belief that the universe is irrational and that there is, therefore, no consistent system of Truth. It should indicate the recognition that man's human mind is insufficient to know the ultimate consistencies which God knows. If the scientist by his experimentation discovers two facts which seem inconsistent, he does not discard science as irrational. He is confident that in the long run a greater knowledge will discover consistency. In the same way the seeker for ultimate religious Truth believes that in the mind of God Truth is a harmonious system. But the feeble light of human reason will not project its beams so far. Man must, therefore, seek in his soul the Light by which all things are seen as by the eyes of God. He must trust his feelings which go deeper toward the center of his being and of all Being than does even the most penetrating reason. He must, as far as he can, come into union with God, the ultimate spring of creative power and the final source of Truth. Man then finds that, through right spiritual development, he can center his soul in that world of Light which will enlighten reason, just as reason through right scientific processes enlightens nature.

In the twilight zone of reason the human being is a divided self. He tries to satisfy his desires by the accumulation of material possessions. But the more possessions he acquires the more he becomes possessed by them. His efforts to bring nature under his control make him a slave of nature. He constructs machines and then finds that his life is absorbed in serving them. The very science by which he controls nature reduces him to nature's level. He first discovered that his earth was not the center of the universe but a minute fraction of it. He then discovered he was descended from animals and concluded that he must himself be an animal. Later all his noblest emotions were interpreted in terms of his physical make-up and glandular secretions. His mind became reduced to a system of mechanical stimuli and conditioned responses. His religion was analyzed in psychological terms as the result of a father complex, a mother fixation, or some other psychopathic reaction. Finally, he invented instruments of warfare so destructive that he is now in danger of destroying his own species. No wonder he is in despair.

Man has wandered a long way from his primitive home. He has left behind his mother nature in whose shelter he was happy as a child, playing in the divine Presence. He cannot return because he is no longer a child. He must go forward and seek a new home for his spirit now that he has learned to reason, to compare, to test the present by some invisible ideal which he dimly sees glimmering ahead. Those who have already reached this goal tell him that there God's completeness will sustain his human incompleteness; the peace of God, which already exists as a Seed sown within his mortal being, will grow and flourish in his whole soul, even in the present world of strife and turmoil.

But to attain this peace, man need not withdraw from this world of strife and turmoil. The God whom he has found is not only a God of Peace who can receive him in "the everlasting arms." He is also, paradoxically, not only Truth, he is also Love. The Christ who said, "My peace I give unto you," was the same who suffered on the cross. This paradox brings us to a consideration of the three outer stages of the soul. That which is at peace within may be disturbed without. The wheel of social achievement can only turn if the axle in the middle is at rest. Man first finds God within and through that discovery he finds peace and strength. Then he can go out into this troubled world bringing with him peace and strength. This is the ministry of reconciliation by which man is reconciled to God and to his fellow men.

The three outer stages which we have rather inadequately called evangelicalism, humanitarianism and materialism, being respectively the superhuman, the human, and the subhuman, represent a different aspect of the same ultimate Reality as the three inner stages: mysticism, rationalism and vitalism. Thus matter is the outward appearance of inward life. By our scientific instruments we can only weigh, measure and time by clocks. Physical science can discover nothing but matter and its laws of motion. A living organism appears to science to be only an unusually complicated mechanism. For pure science there is no difference in essential nature between an automobile and a human body except that one is more complicated and difficult to understand than the other. Nevertheless, man feels a mystical intuition of that life within him which is beyond the reach of science. No scientific instrument can discover love, hate, joy or pain. It can only discover the currents along nerves or blood vessels which accompany such emotions.

Humanitarianism or social service is the outer and applied aspect of rationalism. Reason tells us that co-operation is better than conflict, that by helping others we help ourselves, and that by deteriorating our environment we weaken ourselves. We frame business contracts, laws, constitutions, rules of various kinds that help us to live with our fellow men on a basis of mutual helpfulness and with a minimum of conflict. The structure of the modern state, unlike that of the tribe or race, is largely a product of reason based on humanitarian interests. Even the totalitarian state makes this claim. It exists for the benefit of its citizens, and if some citizens are liquidated, even this is in the interest of the whole.

Yet humanitarianism based on reason is unstable. It assumes that man is wise enough to know that he ought to help his fellow men, but this knowledge does not always result in the right action. Men acquire power and use it for selfish interest. Modern democratic society is based on the theory that enlightened self-interest is able to create a peaceful, happy society. The "economic man" of the economists is a thoroughly selfish creature, but wise enough to see that selfishness can be carried too far for his own best interest.

A society based on enlightened self-interest is unstable and destined either to sink lower or to rise higher. It will either go down to the mechanical level where men are forced to work together by an authority acting from without, or it will rise into a religiously integrated group life where men co-operate because they are animated by an inner Spirit which is divine. In the latter case we have unity produced by the Light. Present-day democracies are devolving into the authoritarian state because human selfishness cannot produce its opposite which is human interdependence. Either we must have a greater degree of authority to hold men together from without, or a greater degree of religion to hold them together from within. There is no third choice.

That man can emerge to the third and highest level of group life which is integrated by religion has often been shown in human history. It occurred in early Christianity and early Quakerism and at many other times. I have called this achievement evangelical because it is a church in the best sense of that word, and in Christianity it is a church animated by the Spirit of Christ, the Word of God. The Christian Church was in intention a continuation of the Incarnation, the Incarnation as re-enacted in the life of the worshiping group when it realizes the divine Presence in the Midst.

But if we are to be truly evangelical we must realize the Atonement as well as the Incarnation. How can we today take up the Cross of Christ and follow him? How are we to share his suffering as well as his peace? If the Church is to be the continuation of the Incarnation it must also be a continuation of the Atonement. It must dare to live up to what it believes regardless of the suffering which this may entail. It must become a part of the Kingdom of Heaven rather than a compromise with the kingdoms of this world. It must take upon itself the world's suffering. Like a scouting party far in advance of the line of battle it may suffer many losses, but it will lead the way to victory.

Man in the middle zone of humanistic reason and humanitarianism will sink lower or rise higher, not so much through his own efforts, as because he submits to forces which either pull him down because he is a child of nature or lift him up because he is a child of God. The ancient expression, "We are saved by the grace of God," means that we cannot raise ourselves solely by our own efforts. Like a man climbing a ladder we must take hold of a rung above in order to ascend. Man cannot maintain himself as a man unless he is also more than a man. If he does not reach toward the superhuman, he sinks to the subhuman. When life becomes secular in the sense that it is centered only in the human, it becomes materialistic as is amply shown in our present-day industrial and scientific culture. In losing his hold upon divinity man loses his hold upon humanity as well. The Russian Communists illustrate this. In denying the truth of religion they have denied that which makes humanity worthy of reverence. The result is a subhuman, ant-heap type of community life.

The process of descent from the superhuman to the human and from the human to the subhuman has appeared in the declining stages of every great culture. Beginning with a primitive, tribal, nature religion, the culture reaches its height in aspiring toward the superhuman. As it begins to decline it passes through a humanistic period before entering the final materialistic stage, when it ceases to have life and creativity. In our Western Culture during the later Middle Ages man's attention was fixed on the superhuman. A typical achievement of this period was the cathedral with spires pointed toward heaven. Its stained-glass windows shut out all view of the world of nature. Everything within the cathedral reminded man of the supernatural. Encompassing society was the great Church, outranking the state, a supernatural, supranational community revealing supernatural truth beyond human reason and dispensing through its sacraments the supernatural grace. In the universities theology took precedence over all other studies and philosophy was its handmaiden.

There were, to be sure, few physical comforts, nor was there individual freedom. The most honored human being was the saint who possessed no property at all and might even have very little learning. Yet there was a vivid sense of the eternal impinging on this world of time. Great works of art and literature came into being. The City of God appeared in the dark world of nature to draw men up to a life above nature and the demonic powers within it.

But the zenith was passed, the Church became corrupt and the Renaissance, so-called because it appeared to be the rebirth of a like aspiration in the Graeco-Roman world, exalted the human spirit and the human body. Humanistic studies outstripped theological studies and began to dominate the universities. Slowly the great age of reason emerged when the philosophers of the Enlightenment felt that no problem was beyond solution by the human mind.

In the midst of this period two movements began which in many respects differed widely but which have shown a strong affinity for each other: the Protestant Reformation and the development of mechanistic science. This view of science reduced all things, including man, to mechanisms governed by the unalterable laws of nature. Predestinarian Calvinism, which largely dominated the later Reformation as its logical outcome, reduced man to a depraved status which was wholly subject to the unalterable decrees of God. In physical science man is moved by physical forces external to himself; in Calvinism man was saved by divine Grace external to himself. The Church as such was no longer looked upon by Protestants as the means of salvation. Man was an individual facing God alone. Science, in similar fashion, reduced him and the whole universe to a swarm of separate particles. Protestantism gave acceptance to the Bible record regardless of its rationality, and science accepted the so-called facts of nature however unreasonable they might appear.

Both Protestantism and mechanistic science weakened what might be designated as the religious horizontal component, the interhuman spiritual tie as a necessary factor in the process of what is called regeneration or salvation in religion and evolution in science. Protestantism kept the vertical relation between man and God as the one necessary factor. Catholicism and Quakerism emphasized the unifying power of the divine Spirit in the worshiping group as a kind of soul in the social organism. Catholicism gave less place to the individual than did Quakerism, which, having the Reformation as one parent, endeavored to preserve the individual.

Such a comparison is valid only as it refers to major historical trends in the past, the effects of which are still to some degree apparent in the present. Modern Protestantism contains a great variety of points of view covering the whole religious spectrum. Modern Quakerism also contains a wide variety of religious opinions, and even Catholicism, in spite of its exercise of hierarchical authority in matters of belief, exhibits variations. Every religion begins with a fairly homogeneous group. The longer it lives the more heterogeneous it becomes.

As a result of overemphasis on mechanistic religion and mechanistic science the great age of humanism is now drawing to a close. Humanistic studies still hold a place in colleges and universities,

but the physical sciences are dominant. Society is becoming increasingly individualized as the old bonds of group life, including
even the family, gradually weaken. Western man, having lost his
hold on the superhuman, is sinking below the human. The time
seems to be coming when only authority, exerted through force,
can enable men to co-operate. Democracies, based in theory on a
kind of humanism, are reverting to reliance on physical force. Wars
are increasing in number and violence. It may be that a dark age
looms ahead.

As Oswald Spengler points out in his *Decline of the West,* all great
cultures end with a godless religion. Our Western culture now tends
to support this observation as it proceeds toward materialism which
finds an extreme expression in Marxism. But Spengler does not
notice an important phenomenon which sometimes appears in
periods of decline. Small mystical groups come into being united
by an inner Spirit. They reject the degenerate culture around
them.[10] They believe that within themselves there germinates the
new and better society that is to be. Christianity appeared in the
declining stage of Graeco-Roman life as a new, vital upsurge of the
Spirit, preserving much that was good in the old culture and con-
veying it into the new. When Christianity was born the old forms
of community life based on tribal and civil loyalties were breaking
up and new associations of all kinds were being formed. The
Roman imperial system could maintain order by force but it
could not provide the communal life which the human soul
requires. The Christian Church met this requirement, and because
it was able to do so more fully than any of the many voluntary associations of the time, it increased while they decreased. Christianity
provided the religious basis which met the human need both for
community and for loyalty to a person. The invisible Christ Spirit
united the group into an organic whole. Beyond this, it provided
for participation in the first stage of the new and perfect order of
society, the Kingdom of God which would replace Caesar's empire.

A declining culture may give birth to something which, being independent of temporal forms, is derived from the super-temporal nature of Reality. Christianity began in a Hebraic culture, was carried throughout the Graeco-Roman world, and was then infused into Europe. While it has taken on cultural forms from all of these areas, Christianity is rooted in elements which are independent of all three. Quakerism, in considering itself to be "Primitive Christianity Revived," was not actually the revival of the earlier movement. It omitted many Hebraic traits in early Christianity and attempted to emphasize only the timeless elements at the heart of the original gospel. Among Hebraic elements which were eliminated were water baptism, the concept of a blood-sacrifice and the coming of the Messiah in clouds of glory. These characteristics do not appear in John's Gospel and Epistles nor in the later letters of Paul which served as the primary sources of Quaker theology. It was John and Paul who contributed to the timeless element in Christianity in an effort to enable the new religion to grow out of its Jewish swaddling clothes.

Early Quakerism, unlike early Christianity, appeared at a time of upsurging activity in religion, politics and science. As an integral part of that activity it made contributions in all three of these fields. On its active, outward side, Quakerism was fully in line with the trend of the times, but on its mystical, inward side it was not in accord with the times. In spite of the belief that a return to the world must follow every withdrawal, the past three centuries have not been propitious for a doctrine of withdrawal, even in this form. Quakerism at first made a strong appeal by its subtraction of the forms which had accrued in the course of Christian history and which by this time appeared to obscure the original message. Many were attracted by the attempt to have a religion of honesty and sincerity. But when the Friends spoke of an inward experience which was above all outward forms, few could follow. The new science was just beginning to open the wonders of the world without. Newton was a contemporary of Fox. This science the Quakers accepted as eagerly as any others, for it was based on genuine firsthand experience and it revealed the ways of God in nature. For example, Thomas Lawson, a Quaker schoolmaster of the early period, writes in his scientific textbook which appeared in Latin:

> His works within and His works without, even the least of plants, preach forth the power and wisdom of the Creator and eyed in the spaces of eternity humble man.

Only later did it become evident that science could exalt as well as humble man.

Vast geographical areas were opening in the New World. There was much work to be done on the frontier. Men were too tired to espouse a religion which could not be administered by men who made it their professional responsibility and too preoccupied to wait in silence upon the Lord. The Puritan type of activism was more congenial to the mechanical age than the Quaker cultivation of the inward life. As a result of these conditions, Puritanism waxed while Quakerism waned, although in the early colonial days in America Quakerism was ahead. In the eighteenth century Quaker energy was largely used up in holding the ground it had already gained, while in the nineteenth century a large section of Quakerism gave up the endeavor and settled down into a type of life and worship close to that of Protestantism.

But the middle of the twentieth century presents a different picture. Men are beginning to realize that pure activism does not lead them anywhere. Much of it appears more like the convulsive jerks of epilepsy than a journey toward a definite goal. The cry of the day is motion and more motion, faster and faster, but there is little said about where this motion takes us. Numberless gadgets make life physically easier, but not more important. A long series of books have appeared lamenting the decline of our Western culture. They are skillful in diagnosing the disease, but they offer no cure.

In science something new has come about which may forecast the character and direction of a change just as the mechanistic science of Galileo and Newton forecast the character of the last three centuries. To many scientists the structure of the physical world now appears more organic than mechanistic. The conception of a soul, so prominent in the science of the Middle Ages, has come back, though in a different form, Some scientists who have turned philosophers conceive objects such as atoms, molecules, cells and animal organisms to have parts which are so united from within that the whole is greater than the sum of its parts. In a mechanism the whole is equivalent to the sum of its parts. In an organism a part is what it is because of its relations to the whole; in a mechanism a part is the same outside the whole as it is within. As a result, when electrical particles form atoms, atoms form molecules, molecules form cells and cells form animal organisms, integration occurs in such a way that something new has come into existence which cannot be discovered or predicted by an examination of the parts. On each level a new integrating factor exists which creates a new type of unity and co-ordination. It is, therefore, impossible to explain the higher in terms of the lower.

What is the source of this unity? To say that it comes from below is to hold that it results from a happy accident. There is, however, one level in this evolutionary process at which we can view it from within as well as from without. That is the level on which we ourselves are. According to our own inner feelings as expressed in our highest insights, the integration of man and the integration of society is due to power which comes down from a superhuman Life outside ourselves. The man whose personality has become divided so that he does that which he would not, becomes united and at the same time elevated to a higher level by the Light Within.

That is how it feels. Such feelings are like those of an astronomer who plots the trajectory of a comet and finds that it comes from outside the solar system. The divided, disintegrated group is united by divine Power from above, as the history of religion from the most primitive times to the present has so often shown. Perhaps we can say that the summit of the evolutionary process of higher and higher types of integration is a Church, a body whose soul is the Eternal Christ, the Word of God which, as John says, creates the world and produces unity in it (John 17:21). The process by which a Quaker meeting comes into unity may be typical of the whole evolutionary process through which God creates. This evolution proceeds not by competition but by co-operation.

But these theoretical speculations do not bring home to us the great truths of our religion. We cannot worship an impersonal Integrating Factor, though it is helpful to know that such exists. The new science, however, offers us a universe more congenial to an inward, mystical type of religion than a universe explained largely in terms of mechanics, which deals only with external, measurable quantities. Perhaps this new science reveals merely a few straws which show the direction of the wind. For example, in the theory of relativity, action at a distance, characteristic of Newtonian mechanics, has disappeared. This may forecast the disappearance of the doctrine that God acts upon man only from without. The principle of indeterminacy in physics may foreshadow the disappearance of a religion which still preserves in some form the doctrine of predestination. The hypothesis that the Power comes from above which creates organic unity in all stages of the evolutionary process from atoms to the Church Universal leads directly to the concept of the Light of Christ as the source of unity. Paul's words that "He is before all things and in him all things hold together" (Col. 1:17) may be not only a religious insight but even a scientific hypothesis.

Whatever comfort and support we may be able to derive from this form of present-day science and philosophy—and it is too early to know exactly where it is leading us—the fact remains that failure to find happiness and security in the outer world will turn some men to look for help from within. The failure of materialism and humanism will lead some to seek that which is above both. The doctrine of inevitable progress through scientific knowledge which so dominated the thought of the nineteenth century is no longer held to be valid. Science is not the Messiah that will bring in the Kingdom of God. Engineers and scientists are not, as H. G. Wells supposed, our seers and prophets. The material world of physical science cannot satisfy the human spirit. Unless modern man learns to sit loose to the world without, through greater dependence on the Life Within, he will be overwhelmed by the very environment which he has fashioned.

Perhaps we are on a spiral movement in history which is bringing us around to a point of view which resembles that of the medieval world as it developed in the springtime of European culture, a season which in many respects had a primitive nature religion though it inherited, through the Catholic Church, a legacy from the advanced stages of Greek and Hebrew thought. The feudal system of that time produced a closely integrated community life, but on a low, preindividual level. Today the disintegration of the older forms of group life and the gradual atomization of our social structure, especially in cities, have performed a service in destroying what was outworn and in developing the individual as a unique, free personality. But many are dissatisfied. An indivdualistic religion provides no home for the spirit and a religion which preaches perpetual struggle offers no peace or security. The result is nervous tension pervading all life. A multitude of clubs and other kinds of associations have come into being to meet the needs of the lonely, insecure individual. They minister to a part of man, but not to his whole nature. A type of group life is needed which creates social relationship on all three levels—the spiritual, the intellectual and the economic, or what we have called the super-human, the human and the subhuman. This took place in the Middle Ages, through an all-inclusive Church, but we cannot go back to an older, more primitive pattern. Having won freedom and individuality, we must center our lives in the superhuman.

Our current religious organizations to some degree meet the requirements for the spiritual as an essential element in the highest and most satisfying type of group association. But, as has been pointed out, this highest level has both an inner and an outer side, it is both mystical and evangelical. Most modern religious organizations meet the need on the outer or evangelical side more fully than on the inner or mystical side, though the inner is never entirely neglected. A Christian church today, however it may be defined, is generally a group held together by a common faith and a common way of worship. The form of worship does not specifically provide for dependence on the Presence in the Midst to unite the group from within. Modern movements in Protestant theology are going back to the older Protestantism with its exclusive evangelical emphasis. Liturgical tendencies in public worship are reviving elements from a still older pre-Protestant and even pre-Christian ritual. Though there is a widespread interest in mysticism, it is, with some important exceptions, largely academic and antiquarian. The mysticism of the medieval saints and the mysticism of the Hindu Vedanta are being examined and in some instances revived, but they fit with difficulty into our modern Western life. Though much can be learned from them it is impossible to transport such spiritual exercises in their entirety from one culture to another.

Unless man can develop his interior dimensions in such a way as to form a dyke against the floods from the world without, he will become engulfed in the world of nature and sink back to the subhuman level whence he long ago emerged. His Protestant individuality and freedom, won at great sacrifice during the past three centuries, is being lost to the increasing domination of the state and the military establishment. Protestantism has demonstrated an ability to serve as the religion of a rapidly developing scientific and industrial culture in a free society, eager to control the world of nature. That culture is now declining because man, in learning to control the outer world, has neglected his own inner world. A new and vital materialistic philosophy hovers on the outskirts ready to flood in and fill the vacuum created by the retreat of the Spirit. When man is not guided by the divine Spirit within he must, to avoid chaos, submit to an outer control. Gradually we are coming to a time when we are presented with the choice between a totalitarianism based on the control of man by man or a religion based on the uniting power of the Holy Spirit.

It is not probable that multitudes will forthwith select the second alternative. Some will try to save society as a whole. Others in despair of salvaging the ship will take to the lifeboats, land on another shore and build another ship of state. This happened in the declining days of the Graeco-Roman world when small communities of Christians adopted a wholly new way of life. This can happen again. It may be that these small units will grow into large communities and give their character to the rising culture of a new world. Such pioneering societies may not be called Quaker, but their religion will resemble that of the Society of Friends and they will be able to learn something from the failures and achievements of three centuries of Quaker experience.

Notes

1. Richardson, *Journal,* in *Friends Library* IX, 435.

2. Richardson, *Journal,* VII, 432.

3. Samuel M. Janney, *Memoirs,* 1881, p. 6.

4. *Friends Library,* XII, 370.

5. David Ferris, *Memoirs,* p. 18.

6. Sarah Morey Hunt, *Journal,* 1892, p. 3.

7. *Friends Library,* XIV, 139.

8. William Evans, *Journal,* 1870, p. 17.

9. Thomas Arnett, *Journal,* 1844, p. 19.

10. This is pointed out in Howard H. Brinton's *Religious Solution to the Social Problem,* 1934, and also in his *Divine-Human Society,* 1938.

An Historical Update
1950 - 2003

by

Margaret Hope Bacon

WE LIVE IN AN AGE of accelerating change. In the fifty years since Harper & Row published Howard Brinton's classic, *Friends for 300 Years*, many things have changed in the world, in the culture, and in the Religious Society of Friends. While the pages he wrote fifty years ago about the birth of the Quaker movement, the role of Quaker thought and belief and its place in the history of religious thought, Quakerism as understood as group mysticism, the meaning of Quaker ministry, the functioning of the Quaker meeting and the larger Quaker community all remain timeless, as fresh today as they were fifty years ago, some of the changes of the past half century need to be considered as we contemplate *Friends for 350 Years*.

As Brinton wrote, "If Quakerism is to remain a vital religion, it must come to terms with the thought of each succeeding epoch." Whether the twenty-first century, bringing to culmination the technological revolution, can be viewed as the introduction of a new epoch remains to be seen.

But the past fifty years have seen not only the beginnings of a technological society, but a turning away from the totalitarianism

which would have been impossible to predict in 1950. Instead of
the fear of a totally controlled society, as predicted in Aldous
Huxley's *Brave New World,* and George Orwell's *1984,* we have
seen the overthrow of dictatorships and oppression in Russia and
its satellites, in Spain, in the Philippines, in Latin America, in
many of the nations of Africa, including South Africa. Many of
these revolutions, such as in Yugoslavia and South Africa, were
accomplished essentially by a democratic uprising of the people,
using nonviolent means. There remain many totalitarian societies
but, speaking very generally, the state is no longer considered
all powerful in the twenty-first century. Instead, humans are
wrestling with how to control terrorist groups that know no
national boundaries and multinational corporations which are
beyond the control not only of individual states but of such
conglomerates as the European Union or the United Nations as
currently organized.

Although there have been many small wars since 1950, we have
seen no more world wars. Interest in peaceful solutions to conflicts has increased on many levels. United Nations troops study
methods to reduce conflicts and the United States now has a Peace
Institute. Methods of conflict resolution are being taught not only
in the schools, colleges, and the prisons, but also to soldiers and
police, and are used by armies of occupation. Sweden, Austria,
and Denmark are studying the use of nonviolence as governmen-
tal policy to deal with situations of conflict. At the time of the Vietnam War there were more conscientious objectors in the United
States than at any other time in history.

Along with war protest, the 1960s saw the development of two
movements with close ties to Quakerism: the concern for civil
rights which led many young people to go South to work on voter
registration and school integration while others began to confront
racism in their schools and churches; and the development of what
was called the women's movement, with its emphasis on the

equality of all persons regardless of gender. Both movements had deep Quaker roots, although the forms they assumed in the 1960s were not necessarily Quaker.

Brinton ends his 1950 book with the prediction, common to his day, that individuals will have a choice between the authority of the totalitarian state or the authority of religion, and while most would choose the former, a small number would "take to the life boats" and create a new society based on a religion resembling that of the Society of Friends. This way of thinking continued to be general through the 1950s and 1960s, coming to a head at the time of the Vietnam war, or just after it, when a number of those caught up in the Youth Revolution chose to establish communes or other alternative societies, often in country settings. But as it began to become clear that the long-predicted coming of the totalitarian state was not going to materialize, this movement waned, and those so led often turned their interest to the ecological movement, a new development of the past fifty years.

Along with the wave of interest in alternative communities there arose an interest in alternative religions. Some of these were charismatic and fundamentalist, but others were forms of Asian or Middle Eastern religions stressing mysticism and contemplation. Emphasis was placed on achieving peace of mind and personal integration, rather than on doing God's work in the world. Some could be defined as cults which sought to control the minds of participants. Even within main stream religions, there developed new variations, such as the charismatic movement widespread in the Catholic church.

Brinton wrote of the threat to religion of scientific and rational thought. But in succeeding decades many scientists have found that new insights into the make-up of the universe, its basic building blocks, provide room for a vitalistic rather than mechanistic understanding of matter and the evolution of life.

Nor have the last fifty years been dominated by the rule of reason, as Brinton feared. Instead, there has been a shift in popular American culture away from exclusive reliance on reason and toward the rule of self-expression and feeling. Young people, and not so young people, jog, exercise, eat organic foods, and meditate because it is good for them and because it makes them feel good. Many seek religious expression on the same basis.

This form of self-centeredness, resulting in the development of what has been called the "Me Generation," can be considered more inimical to religion than either scientific or rational thought. Most religions, as Brinton points out, rest on some basis of authority and demand some discipline.

Both authority and discipline seem contrary to the demands of self- actualization. Thus we have seen a slow decrease in membership in the main line churches and denominations, along with the rise of alternatives, from Fundamentalist to Eastern to goddess worship, many promising instant gratification and "feeling good."

Several times in *Friends for 300 Years* Howard Brinton mentions his hope that the times might be ripe for the reemergence of Quakerism as an important answer to the needs of the day, illustrating this point by mentioning the growth of new meetings in the period 1925-1950. Such hopes have not been realized. Membership in Quaker meetings and churches has at best held its own in the past fifty years, while many congregations have shrunk. In 1950 there were approximately 120,000 Friends in the United States against a total population of 151,000,000; in 2000 the figure was 103,000 against 265,000,000. There has been growth in several new unprogrammed yearly meetings, mainly in the west, and in independent unprogrammed meetings, while many of the established eastern meetings, such as Philadelphia, have seen a decline.(There is some indication that in the past five years this trend is reversing itself slightly.) Friends United Meeting membership has been diminished by the number of Quaker churches deciding to affiliate with the Friends Evangelical International. Only in third world countries in Africa and South America are meetings growing, as the result of the work of pastoral and evangelical Friends.

With the increasing move to the cities, there are today fewer rural Quaker meetings and Quaker churches in the United States, Canada, and Great Britain than in 1950. More and more, Friends are collected in and around urban centers, especially university centers. As a result, the Society of Friends is becoming increasingly oriented to the middle and upper middle class. Gone are the days when its membership rested mainly in farm and artisan families. This change in orientation is not always recognized, and leads to misplaced efforts to "reach out" to minorities and other disadvantaged persons who are apt to be put off by the presence of unconscious class rituals among Friends.

Howard Brinton wrote his book from the point of view of the silent worship tradition in which he grew up, in general, and Philadelphia Yearly Meeting in particular (See page 213).To write about the Religious Society of Friends from the vantage point of either Philadelphia Yearly Meeting or London Yearly Meeting in 1950 was not regarded as remarkable. Today, most Friends strive to be far more inclusive. Through the Friends World Committee for Consultation (FWCC) there has been a growing interest in bringing Friends from the silent meeting, pastoral, and evangelical backgrounds together on common ground. All are interested in preserving their common Quaker history, and in joint action in support of the historic peace testimony. Meetings of all Friends in 1970 gave birth to a Faith and Life Movement, and later to Turn Toward Peace, an effort to bring all branches of Quakerism together in a common search for peace. FWCC has regularly brought Friends from all over the world together in triennial conferences, and Youthquake has served the same purpose for Young Friends. The Friends Committee on National Legislation, which has become increasingly active in the years since 1950, has striven to be inclusive of all branches of Quakerism. Friends in the silent tradition, particularly a group from Great Britain, have taken an interest in the growing development of Evangelical Friends in Bolivia. Coupled with the effort to be more inclusive has been a major effort of the past fifty years, running through all branches of the Society of Friends, to open Quaker schools, meetings, and churches and organizations to persons of other racial and ethnic backgrounds. When Howard Brinton wrote *Friends for 300 Hundred Years*, some Quaker schools had attempted to realize racial equality, mainly by admitting one black student, but others had not yet made this step. Today Quaker schools and colleges are interracial, and many meetings and churches have achieved this goal, though others are struggling. In turn, the presence of persons of darker complexion within the previously all-white institutions of the Society of Friends has made many Quakers more sensitive and more interested in reaching out to third world Quaker churches.

The past fifty years has seen an explosion of interest in Quaker history by scholars in all branches of Quakerism. One conclusion from this work, led by such scholars as Hugh Barbour and Geoffrey Nuttall, is that Quakerism can no longer be considered an outgrowth of European mysticism, but rather an aspect of the Puritan movement itself, with its own tradition of mystic experience of the Holy Spirit. This discovery has encouraged theological dialogue between the various branches of modern Quaker thought, through such organs as *Quaker Religious Thought.*

Interest in breaking down barriers that separated Friends in the past has led to some major changes in the past fifty years. In 1945 the two branches of New England Yearly Meeting, the Gurneyite and Wilburite, came together. In 1955 New York, Canada, and Philadelphia Yearly Meetings experienced reunions of the Hicksite and Gurneyite wings, and in 1966 Baltimore Yearly Meeting followed suit. Even the Conservative Friends have held gatherings, beginning in 1965, though they have chosen not to affiliate. In 1965 the Five Years Meeting, made up of Gurneyite Yearly Meetings, became the Friends United Meeting. That same year the Evangelical Friends Alliance was born. (It changed its name to Evangelical Friends International in 1989.) In 1978 London and Ireland Yearly Meetings united their service wings into Quaker Peace and Service.

On the local level, many new and united meetings have been created, ignoring the divisions of the past, while older meetings have healed old divisions and come together, such as Twelfth Street Meeting in Philadelphia, a bastion of Gurneyite Quakerism, and Race Street Meeting, a strong center for Hicksite Friends for many years. Because of the large number of new and convinced Friends it is sometimes hard to find members who are quite clear about what the separations of the nineteenth century were all about.

Even within Philadelphia Yearly Meeting the past fifty years has seen many changes. When Howard Brinton wrote, many meetings still maintained the tradition that a child born to meeting members was automatically made a member, the so-called birthright member. Today this practice is largely abandoned. In 1950 some meetings still recorded ministers, those especially gifted in the ministry. Today the ministry is regarded as the obligation of every membership, although a committee on Worship and Ministry continues to function in most meetings.

Connected with the ending of the concept of the birthright has been a move away from an older practice of carrying members who were born into the meeting but no longer attended or supported the meeting. At one time several of the larger city meetings had a number of such nominal Friends on their lists. The increasing cost of carrying individual members, coupled with a growing belief that membership demands certain obligations, has led to a winnowing out of such nominal members. This has accounted for some of the drop in membership.

Attracted by the Quaker peace testimony, by the growing emphasis on inclusiveness, and by the mysticism at the heart of the silent Quaker worship, many young people have come into Quakerism in recent years. There are now far more convinced than birthright members in the Religious Society of Friends. Philadelphia Yearly Meeting, which once had the appearance of a reunion of one vast family, is now diverse in appearance. There appear to no longer be the number of weighty Friends who once swayed decision making.

In some individual meetings, these changes have triggered a search for new ways to arrive at the sense of the meeting. The use of the clearness committee, once employed only to allow marriages or to release Quaker ministers for travels beyond the verge of the meeting, has been explored to help individuals understand to what form of ministry they are being called, and to determine whether this ministry should be supported by the meeting. Individuals have also used the clearness process to decide on such matters as job and/or location change, going to graduate school, getting divorced or accepting overseas service of some nature.

The influx of these many new Friends has forced meetings to adopt new strategies for the teaching of Quakerism and Quaker history. A Quaker Studies Program was initiated in 1981 in Philadelphia Yearly Meeting, and subsequently a series of courses in Quakerism—Quakerism 101, 201, 301, etc.—was developed and is now widely used among silent meeting Friends. New writing on Quaker history, as well as new scholarship by Quaker historians, has emerged. At Earlham College the increased need for studies in Quakerism resulted in the establishment in 1960 of the Earlham School of Religion, which prepares men and women to be pastors in the Quaker churches, and others to take leadership roles in Quaker institutions. Among evangelical Friends, the development of the Quaker Theological Discussion Group in 1957, followed by the publication of the journal, *Quaker Religious Thought,* begun in 1959, has stimulated a reexamination of the Quaker past.

Among the new recruits to liberal Quakerism in the past fifty years have been a number from the Catholic tradition who have brought with them the concept of the role of the spiritual director, or of spiritual friendships. Closely tied to Pendle Hill, a School of the Spirit was developed in the late 1980s, and there is a movement called Spiritual Formation throughout the meetings in the silent tradition. Brinton always believed that Quakerism was as close to Catholicism as to Protestantism, and would have been interested in this turn toward a more disciplined spirituality.

Along with the interest in new forms of spiritual expression has come a renewed interest in the relation of artistic expression to religion. Friends have felt for some time that the turning away from all art, music, and literature by earlier generations of Friends was in a sense a historic mistake, understandable in the times at which it arose, but no longer applicable today. At present there is a Friends Fellowship in the Arts which publishes a newsletter, holds regular exhibitions, and offers prize to beginning artists.

Among other new interests to have arisen among Friends in the past fifty years, is the ecology movement, finding expression in a nationwide organization, Friends of the Earth, and a closely allied interest in simple, non-destructive patterns of living. There is even a Quaker Luddite movement which has held several annual meetings at Sweetwater Friends Meeting in Barnesville, Ohio

The women's movement, arising in the 1970s and 1980s, has had an impact on all branches of Quakerism, reminding Friends of their 350-year-old testimony on the spiritual equality of women. Scholars have studied Quaker women and have published the early journals and seventeenth- and eighteenth-century writings. At the Earlham School of Religion, many women have prepared for service as Quaker pastors. The use of gendered language has changed. In liberal meetings many have explored feminist theology. Woodbrooke College in England hosted the first world con-

ference of Quaker women in 1990, bringing together women from
Latin America, Africa, Europe, England, and North America, and
bridging all present-day varieties of Quakerism.

Among some Evangelical Friends there has been a trend toward
embracing models from the larger evangelical world, including
increased emphasis on missions and the concept of developing
mega-churches, holding services which sometimes utilize rock
music and sports ministries to attract the unconverted and build
congregations of one thousand or more, just as early Friends managed to attract large crowds. Especially in the eastern regions and
southwest yearly meetings these trends are notable.

Efforts toward rapprochement between liberal Friends on the
one hand and pastoral and evangelical Friends on the other have
been dampened by the rise of concern about gay and lesbian
Friends, a matter never considered an issue for most Friends in
1950. Starting with the publication by a committee of British
Friends of *Toward a Quaker View of Sex* in the early 1960s, discussion
of the issue of recognizing Friends with a different sexual orientation rose in many of the liberal meetings, as more and more
members so identified themselves to the meeting. A fellowship
of Gay and Lesbian Friends was formed in the early 1980s, and
a few such Friends began to ask to be married under the care of
the meeting. The issue was widely discussed within several of the
eastern yearly meetings, though no action was taken. Several constituent meetings, however, decided to take such marriages under
their care.

All this has been disturbing to more biblically oriented Friends,
who believe scripture forbids such relationships, and are worried
that the general public will believe that liberal Friends speak for
all Friends when they recognize such marriages. This schism was
compounded when the American Friends Service Committee an-
nounced that it was including gay and lesbian persons in its affirmative action program.

A similar concern dividing liberal and conservative Friends has been the issue of abortion.

In 1969 the American Friends Service Committee published a book, *Who Shall Live: Man's Control over Birth and Death,* written by a committee of Quaker doctors and ethicists, including Henry Cadbury, arguing that abortion in the first trimester is acceptable, as well as that persons had the right to choose their own time of death. Later, with the rise of the women's movement, many Quaker women of liberal persuasion advocated a woman's right to choose, and participated in public marches and organizations taking this position. Some liberal Friends, male and female, objected, feeling that the concept of life as sacred, so essential to the peace movement, should not be compromised. But to the evangelical and biblically oriented Friends, the issue was absolute, and the actions of liberal Friends deeply distressing.

A third source of tension between liberal and evangelical Friends has been the growth of Quaker universalism and the creation of a Quaker Universalist Fellowship. Most of the universalists say that Jesus was divine, but so were other prophets. They believe in the eternal, not the historical, Christ. Many scholars feel that this source of tension within the Society of Friends has been present from the very beginning, Fox's belief in the primacy of the Spirit, or Inward Christ was at war with his own reliance on scripture and his unquestioned belief in the risen Christ. Today it worries not only evangelical but many liberal Friends that there is a turning away from the Christian roots of the Quaker movement.

Still another source of tension has been changes in the American Friends Service Committee. Created in 1917 by Rufus Jones, Henry Cadbury, and others in an effort to bring Friends of all persuasions together in "a service of love in wartime," AFSC has been controversial from its earliest days. Although the Board was composed of even numbers of Orthodox, Hicksite, and Five

Years Meeting Friends, it was felt that the Orthodox had the greatest influence. Evangelical Friends originally hoped that AFSC workers would preach the gospel in the communities they served, whereas local governments often specifically denied entrance to relief workers who sought to proselytize. Many Friends hoped that AFSC would concentrate on providing service opportunities for Quakers, whereas AFSC, from the early years on, was more focused on getting the job done efficiently.

All these tensions were exacerbated in the 1960s when AFSC gave up its popular summer work camp program, in part because it could no longer serve in loco parentis to teenagers now affected by a new spirit of rebellion, and in part because it sought to serve young people in the poor communities to which it had formerly brought white affluent young people. Quaker schools and families accustomed to the AFSC providing opportunities for summer service to their young people were unhappy with this change.

In addition, as AFSC began to develop its present affirmative action program, designed to make it an organization which shared power with the minority communities it sought to aid, Friends felt excluded from the possibility of spending a sabbatical year in service, or becoming a staff member. These changes, which have been called professionalism but which AFSC regards as empowerment, served to antagonize some liberal Friends, while evangelical and pastoral Friends objected to the public statements of the AFSC which seemed to imply (despite the best efforts of the staff) that the Committee spoke for all Friends.

The relationship between Pendle Hill, when Howard Brinton taught and wrote, and the American Friends Service Committee, which he had served and in which his wife Anna played a prominent role, was very close in 1950, so that Howard could write about humanitarian service for Quakers as though it were service primarily through the AFSC. In recent years that relationship has not been so close, as Pendle Hill has turned more deeply toward new forms of spiritual development, and the AFSC has offered fewer service opportunities to Friends, as a result of its affirmative action program.

When Brinton wrote, he feared that rationalism and humanitarianism were becoming the dominant factors in the Society of Friends. Today, these tendencies no longer appear to be the threat. Rationalism seems to be being replaced by new forms of mysticism; humanitarianism appears to have given way to interest in more inward turning. What is missing to many observers and critics of present-day Quakerism is the acceptance of any form of authority either of past religious truths or present testimonies. In some meetings it appears that individuals are left free to decide what, if anything, they believe.

Brinton wrote that "religion needs a consistent system of ideas, without which it is vague, and incapable of propagating itself." While Quakerism has given primacy to the Light Within, instead of demanding adherence to a single creed, it maintained a consistent system of ideas throughout three centuries. Today, as we appear to be wandering far afield, it is good to return to Brinton's exposition of the ideas on which Quakerism has been based, as seen from the point of view of a Christian mystic, and to discover how we can reinterpret them for the twenty-first century.

Page and Line Notes

Introduction

Page xiv, Line 21-24. Today, historians regard this statement as over-simplified. It also implied that Friends maintaining the silent tradition were not affected by other religious influences. They were.

Page xv, Line 19-20. This is the first of many places where Howard Brinton speaks of "God and man." In 1950, both men and women understood "man" as a generic word, encompassing both men and women. Were he writing today, Brinton would probably say "God and the human race," or "God and humans."

Chapter I. "To Wait Upon the Lord"

Page 3, Line 1. What Brinton says is true for Reform Jews, but not Hasidic Jews.

Page 5, Line 9. Studies of Puritanism since Brinton's time have shown that it was neither dry nor formal.

Chapter II. The Light Within as Experienced

Though an excellent chapter, this might have been strengthened by supplementing the quotations from George Fox with those of other founding Quakers, both men and women.

Chapter III. The Light Within as Thought About

Page 62, Line 1. Quaker historians today believe that Calvin was more of a humanist than Brinton paints him.

Chapter IV. The Meeting for Worship

Page 88, Line 26. Brinton overemphasizes the role of the Catholic mystics on Quakerism. Probably only a few Quakers ever read the works of Madame Guyon, Fénelon, and Molinos.

Pages 98-99. In the Whittier poem, the lines 4-5, the image of the black boy is rather racist. Though an abolitionist, Whittier maintained some of the current stereotypes. Probably today Brinton would not use this poem.

Chapter V. Vocal Ministry

Page 103, Line 14. "The first person singular is seldom heard in Quaker ministry." If this were true in 1950, it is not today.

Page 104, Line 23. Similar experiences were reported by other Quaker ministers, men and women. Brinton might have drawn on the journal of Elizabeth Hudson, a contemporary of Job Scott.

Chapter VII. The Meeting Community

Page 148, Line 5. During the period known as Quietism, Friends did not judge decisions by their apparent outcome. Both William Allen and John Woolman belong to this period. Brinton might also have cited the journal of Ann Moore. This attitude is less prevalent today.

Page 156, Line 10. Quaker historians today question Brinton's assertion that only those invited attended business meetings in the eighteenth century.

Page 159, Line 10. There is no historical evidence that Quaker soldiers were dismissed for refusing to treat their officers as superiors.

Page 160, Line 5. There is no evidence that servants and mistresses ate together and called each other by their first names. It may have been true at Swarthmoor Hall.

Page 160, Line 18. Race was not an issue in seventeenth-century England.

Page 162, Line 9. There is no evidence for the statement that Quakers treated their slaves with respect, though we would hope so, and none that they allowed children of slaves to attend Quaker schools. Instead, Friends established separate schools for blacks.

Page 167, Line 6. Historic evidence shows that many Quaker tailors, silversmiths, and the like did sell what might be termed superfluities.

Chapter VIII. The Meeting and the World

Page 178, Line 14. It is hard to prove historically that no Quakers suffered injury during the French and Indian war.

Page 178, Line 29. Recent scholarship has shown that Quaker Indian agents appointed by President Grant were not as successful as previously thought.

Page 179, Line 30. The paragraph beginning "Friends in the South." was true for Friends in North Carolina, but not necessarily elsewhere.

Page 180, Line 6. More recent scholarship has shown that only a few Quaker homes participated in the underground railroad. These escape routes were generally managed by blacks themselves, with help from such individual Friends as Thomas Garrett, Levi Coffin, Isaac Hopper, and others.

Page 180, Line 27. It is questionable that racial problems are today less serious in the West Indies.

Page 182, Line 21. Scholars in Quaker schools, however, had to memorize Barclay's catechism.

Page 185, The Pennsylvania prisons became models only in the late eighteenth and early nineteenth century. Quakers are incorrectly credited with the system of solitary confinement, which was first developed by an English penologist, John Howard.

Page 186, Line 7. The reforms in Newgate Prison may not have been as sweeping as stated. Fry also inspired a group of American women who worked on penal reform throughout the nineteenth century.

Page 189, Line 12. The concept of arriving at a consensus, or sense of the meeting, predated the concept of pacifism, which is comparatively recent.

Page 189, Line 21. Billings, not Penn, probably wrote the *Concessions and Agreements* for West Jersey.

Page 189, Line 28. Modern scholarship has revealed there were several *Frames of Government*. Brinton probably means the 1702 frame, which, according to J. William Frost, Penn hated. For more up-to-date information on the Frame of Government see *The*

Papers of William Penn, edited by Mary Maples Dunn and Richard S. Dunn, (Philadelphia: University of Pennsylvania Press, 1981).

Page 196, Line 7. The expectation that members would not fight was probably less common in the seventeenth century than here stated.

Page 202, Line 12. This discussion of the anti-pacifist position of the so-called Neo-Calvinists is somewhat dated.

Page 203, Line 17. Brinton may be overstating the optimism of the New Testament which encompasses the Book of Revelation.

Page 203, Line 25. Christians expected Christ's imminent return, not a new social order.

Page 210, Line 8. Some AFSC overseas workers now receive a salary, though not in Brinton's time.

Page 210, Line 18. In recent years, AFSC has employed more local workers and sought skilled professionals for such work as prosthesis.

Page 210, Line 28. In the Spanish Civil War, recent research reveals, more help went to the Loyalists than the Republicans. It should also be mentioned that Friends were unable to assist both sides during World War I and World War II.

Chapter IX. The Four Periods of Quaker History

Page 213, Line 6. The decline was primarily in the Philadelphia Yearly Meeting, not in the Midwest. As Brinton states on line 16, these are dates in Philadelphia Yearly Meeting's history.

Page 216, Line 25. It may be an overstatement to say that the sufferings of the Quakers were unparalled in religious history.

Page 222, Line 30, and Page 223, Line 1. Modern historians think it is an overstatement to say that half of the population of Rhode Island was Quaker, or half the legislators in North Carolina were Quaker.

Page 223, Line 19. David Lloyd should not be included in the list of those exercising religious and political responsibility.

Page 223, Line 28. Many early meetings did not establish schools for many years.

Page 224, Line 18. Some Quakers resigned in 1756, but not the majority. Resignation of Quakers was a more gradual process.

Page 224, Line 24. The conquest of Pittsburgh also played a role in establishing peace with the Indians.

Page 224, Line 30. Often, but not always, Quakers were present at treaties with the Indians.

Page 232, Line 16. In fact there were divisions among Hicksite Friends, leading to the creation of such groups as Congregational Friends, Progressive Friends, Anti-Slavery Friends

Page 232, Line 21. Hicksite discipline advised disowning Friends who denied the divinity of Christ.

Page 234, Line 12. Though Wilburite Friends lay claim to being the heirs of the original Society of Friends, other Friends' group just as legitimately make this claim.

Page 234, Line 32. By the inclusion of faith healing, Brinton has telescoped two evangelical movements, the Holiness and the Pentecostal, into one.

Page 235, Line 1. Many of the revival meetings were not regular meetings for worship, but specially called ones.

Page 236, Line 6. It is an overstatement to say the revivalist minister focused on himself. He believed his techniques helped but God did the saving work.

Page 236, Line 15. More recent scholarship suggests that the revivals were not all spontaneous, that individual Friends planned to promote them. *See* Thomas Hamm, *The Transformation of American Quakerism: Orthodox Friends, 1800-1907* (Bloomington: Indiana University Press, 1988)

Page 237, Line 2. Modern scholars question Brinton's statement that the revivalists concept of perfection was based on a theology different from that of early Friends.

Page 239, Line 5. Historians feel that Quakerism has been open to outside influences long before the twentieth century.

Page 240, Line 17. Swarthmore College is omitted.

Page 242, Line 27. Unfortunately, the healthy increase that was taking place in 1950 has not continued.

Page 260, Lines 11-15. Recent scholarship suggests many early Friends expected the Second Coming. Some Evangelical Friends use water baptism, and speak of salvation through the blood of the Lamb.

APPENDIX I

The Philadelphia Queries of 1955

I. Meetings for Worshiip and Business

1. Religious Meetings

Are your meetings for worship and business held in expectant waiting for divine guidance?

Is there a living silence in which you feel drawn together by the power of God in your midst?

Do your meetings give evidence that Friends come to them with hearts and minds prepared for worship?

Are your meetings a source of strength and guidance for daily Christian living?

2. Ministry

Is the vocal ministry in your meetings exercised under the direct leading of the Holy Spirit, without prearrangement, and in the simplicity and sincerity of Truth?

Do you foster the use and growth of the spiritual gifts of your members?

3. Participation in Meeting

Do your resident members attend meetings regularly and punctually?

To what extent are your meetings for worship attended by persons not in membership and are they welcomed and encouraged to continue attendance?

Are your meetings for business held in a spirit of love, understanding and forbearance, and do you seek the right course of action in humble submission to the authority of Truth and patient search for unity?

II.. FRIENDS' CARE OF ONE ANOTHER

4. Unity within the Meeting

Are love and unity maintained among you?

Do you manifest a forgiving spirit and a care for the reputation of others?

When differences arise, are endeavors made to settle them speedily and in a spirit of meekness and love?

5. Education

Do your children receive the loving care of the Meeting and are they brought under such influences as tend to develop their religious life?

What efforts are you making to educate all your members in the knowledge of the Bible, of Christianity and of the history and principles of Friends?

Do you maintain schools for the education of your youth under the care of teachers of Christian character in sympathy with the principles of Friends and supervised by committees of the Meeting?

Do you encourage members to send their children to Friends' schools and do you give such financial aid as may be necessary?

6. Oversight of the Membership

What is being done to draw members together into a spirit of fellowship?

Does the Meeting keep in contact, either by visits or personal letters, with all its members?

Are Friends in material need assisted as their circumstances require?

Do you counsel with those whose conduct or manner of living gives ground for concern?

III. RESPONSIBILITIES OUTSIDE THE MEETING

7. Social and Economic Relationships

What are you doing as individuals or as a Meeting:

To aid those in need of material help?

To encourage total abstinence and remove the causes of intemperance?

To insure equal opportunities in social and economic life for those who suffer discrimination because of race, creed or social class?

To create a social and economic system which will so function as to sustain and enrich life for all?

8. *Civic responsibility*

What are you doing as individuals or as a Meeting:

–To understand and remove the causes of war and develop the conditions and institutions of peace?

–To carry your share of responsibilities in the government of your community, state and nation, and to assure freedom of speech, and of religion and equal educational opportunities for all?

9. *Extending Our Message*

What are you doing as individuals or as a Meeting:

–To interpret to others the message of Friends and to cooperate with others in spreading the Christian message?

IV. PERSONAL LIVING

10. *The Home*

Do you make a place in your daily life for inward retirement and communion with the Divine Spirit?

Do you make your home a place where friendship, peace, and refreshment of spirit are found, and do you have regular periods of family worship?

Do you frequently and reverently read the Bible and other religious literature?

Do you choose those recreations which will strengthen your physical, mental, and spiritual life and avoid those that may prove a hindrance to yourself and others?

11. Self-Discipline

Do you keep to simplicity and moderation in your speech, your manner of living, and your pursuit of business?

Are you careful to keep your business and your outward activities from absorbing time and energy that should be given to spiritual growth and the service of your religious society?

Are you punctual in keeping promises, just in the payment of debts, and honorable in all your dealings?

Are you free from the use of judicial oaths, from betting and gambling and from practices based on the principles of gambling?

Are you free from the use and handling of intoxicants and the misuse of drugs?

Do you take your right share of responsibility in work and service for the Meeting?

12. Human Brotherhood

Do you live in the life and power which takes away the occasion of all wars? Do you seek to take your part in the ministry of reconciliation between individuals, groups, and nations? Do you faithfully maintain our testimony against military training and other preparation for war and against participation in war as inconsistent with the spirit and teaching of Christ?

In all your relations with others do you treat them as brothers and equals?

APPENDIX II

The Philadelphia Queries of 2000

F RIENDS HAVE ASSESSED the state of this religious society through the use of queries since the time of George Fox. Rooted in the history of Friends, the queries reflect the Quaker way of life, reminding Friends of the ideals we seek to attain. From the Christian tradition, Friends have taken as a standard the life and teaching of Jesus, not only as recorded in the New Testament, but even more importantly as revealed inwardly, as we seek God's truth and its expression through our lives today. Friends approach queries as a guide to self-examination, using them not as an outward set of rules, but as a framework within which we assess our convictions and examine, clarify, and consider prayerfully the direction of our lives and the life of the community.

Over the years, the content of the General Queries has changed, as each generation finds its own voice. The earliest General Queries of London Yearly Meeting asked for specific facts and figures: which Friends imprisoned for their testimonies had died, which present prisoners there were, and what sufferings. Even in the more abstract question, "How does Truth prosper among us?" there was an expectation of a quantifiable answer—in this case, the number of new Friends. Today, queries that are looking for specific factual answers are not included in the General Queries. Rather, they are considered supplementary to the queries and their focus is the "right ordering" of the monthly meeting organization.

The language of the General Queries today is language that encourages the probing-in-depth of an issue or a concern. While changes in specific focus and language are inevitable over time, the queries have been marked by consistency of convictions and concerns within Friends testimonies—simplicity, peace, integrity, stewardship, equality and community—as well as by strength derived from worship, ministry, and social conscience.

Meetings consider the General Queries in a variety of ways. Some Meetings value the preparation of written answers; some use them as an aid to inward reflection; some make them part of the meeting for worship, some of the meeting for business. Friends may consider each in turn, or may consider several together that meet a current need. There may be times when a Meeting will reword a query or contemplate a new one to meet its particular situation. Friends will benefit from review of the full cycle of queries over a year or two. It has been common practice to use the responses to the queries addressed to Meetings as a basis for reports to the quarterly meeting. Whatever the approach, Friends' faithful attendance to the queries in openness to the Spirit enriches the life of the Meeting.

The following General Queries are arranged with a set for the Meeting and a set printed in italics for the individual. In addition, within the section of *Care for One Another* there is a set for the family to consider. While some Meetings read aloud and consider both the corporate and individual sets, others consider only the corporate sets, leaving the individual set for personal reflection and response.

General Queries

1. MEETING FOR WORSHIP

Are our meetings for worship held in stilled, expectant waiting upon God?

As we worship is there a living silence in which we are drawn together by the power of God in our midst?

Is the spirit of our worship together one that nurtures all worshipers?

How does our Meeting respond when the vocal ministry seems inappropriate, or when the meeting for worship is consistently not gathered?

Do I faithfully attend meeting with heart and mind prepared for worship, clear of any predetermination to speak or not to speak, and expecting that worship will be a source of strength and guidance?

Does worship deepen my relationship with God, increase my faithfulness, and refresh and renew my daily life, both inwardly and in my relationship with others?

Have I experienced in worship that direct leading to listen or to speak, and have I been faithful to my own experience?

2. MEETING FOR BUSINESS

Is our meeting for business held in the spirit of a meeting for worship in we seek divine guidance?

Are we careful to keep in the spirit of worship each of the concerns that emerge, whether of nurture, of Spirit, of social concerns, of property, or of finance?

Are Meeting decisions directed by prayerful consideration of all aspects of an issue and are difficult problems considered carefully with patient search for truth, unhurried by the pressures of time?

How do we respond if we notice the meeting has lost an understanding of the presence of God?

Do we recognize that we speak through our inaction as well as our action?

Do I regularly attend meeting for business and in a spirit of love and unity? If unable to attend, how do I attend to my responsibility?

Do I consider prayerfully the many concerns that are lifted up on any issue, acknowledging that the search for truth in unity involves what God requires, being open to personal transformation as the community arrives at the sense of the meeting?

3. SPIRITUAL NURTURE, MINISTRY, AND RELIGIOUS EDUCATION

Does our Meeting encourage the ministry of both word and deed? How does our Meeting recognize, develop, and nurture the gifts of our members and attenders of all ages?

Does our Meeting prepare all its members and children for worship and for a way of life consistent with the principles of the Religious Society of Friends? How do we teach about Quaker practices in business and worship and their importance to the functioning of our Meeting community?

In what ways do we support each other in order to seek God's will and act upon our understanding of truth? Is there opportunity in our Meeting to share the excitement of religious discovery and the possibility of religious transformation?

Does our Meeting provide opportunities for all in the Meeting to learn about:

    – the Inner Light, the living Christ within, the Bible, the writings of Friends, our Christian heritage, other religious traditions and their respective roles in the history and formation of Friends' principles?
    – the common testimonies Friends declare?
    – the variety of expression Quaker faith takes today?

Do I maintain as part of my personal and family life those daily practices that focus on continued spiritual growth, with disciplined worship, inward retirement, and communion with the divine spirit?

Do I frequently read the Bible and other religious literature, including the records of the lives and experiences of Friends? Do I take the time to explore these resources with others, and likewise encourage my children?

Do I share my own faith and spiritual journey, and encourage such sharing within my family?

4. CARE FOR THE MEETING COMMUNITY

Care for one another

Are love and unity maintained among us? When conflicts exist, are they faced with patience, forbearance, and openness to healing? Are avenues for exploring differences kept open? To what extent does our Meeting ignore differences in order to avoid possible conflicts?

Is the Meeting a safe, loving place? When we become aware of someone's need, do we offer assistance? Are the meetinghouse and the Meeting property physically accessible to all?

Do all adults and children in our Meeting receive our loving care and encouragement to share in the life of our Meeting, and to live as Friends? Do we truly welcome newcomers and include them in our Meeting community?

When a member's conduct or manner of living gives cause for concern, how does the Meeting respond?

How does our Meeting keep in touch with all its members?

Am I ready to offer assistance as part of my religious community serving its members? Am I equally willing to accept graciously the help of others?

Do I recognize and face disagreements and other situations that put me in conflict with others? Do I manifest a spirit ready to give or receive forgiveness?

Do I treat adults and children alike with respect and without condescension? Is my manner with visitors and attenders to my Meeting one of welcome?

Care in my home

(This set of personal queries may be helpful for the family to consider within the family setting. Families may also wish to explore other General Queries as part of regular family worship.)

Is my home a place where all members of the family receive affection and understanding, and where visitors are welcome? Do I choose recreation and a manner of living that enriches the body, mind, and spirit; and shows a high regard for family, community, and creation?

Is our family prepared to discuss such sensitive topics as death, faith, money, even sex and drugs, in a manner that allows openness and honesty, and also direction?

How do I help to arrange life at home so that there is an opportunity for all to learn and absorb by example what it means to live a life of Spirit-led commitment?

5. EDUCATION

What is our Meeting's role in the life and support of Friends' education? If supporting or maintaining a Friends school, have we developed an appropriate relationship of Meeting and school? What is our role in the spiritual life of the school and its maintenance of Friends' principles?

What does our Meeting do to support education in the wider community?

What help do we provide for the children and adults in our Meeting to pursue the education they seek, whether academic, technical, or vocational? Do we make provision for children in our Meeting to attend a Friends school?

How do I show my concern for the improvement of public education in my community and in the world?

Am I aware of what Friends schools are doing and of their plans for the future? How do I show encouragement and support?

6. EQUALITY

How does our Meeting help to create and maintain a society whose institutions recognize and do away with the inequities rooted in patterns of prejudice and economic convenience?

Is our Meeting open to all regardless of race, ability, sexual orientation, or class?

What steps are we taking as a Meeting to assure that our Meeting and the committees and institutions under our care reflect our respect for all and are free from practices rooted in prejudice?

Do I examine myself for aspects of prejudice that may be buried, including beliefs that seem to justify biases based on race, gender, sexual orientation, disability, class, and feelings of inferiority or superiority?

What am I doing to help overcome the contemporary effects of past and present oppression?

Am I teaching my children, and do I show through my way of living, that love of God includes affirming the equality of people, treating others with dignity and respect, and seeking to recognize and address that of God within every person?

7. SOCIAL RESPONSIBILITY AND WITNESS

How does our Meeting work:

 – to overcome social, legal, economic, and political injustices, locally and in the wider world?

 – for the funding of community services that does not rely on gaming income?

Does our Meeting serve the community through action on concerns for civic improvement? What actions are we taking to assure everyone equal access to education, health care, legal services, housing, and employment as well as equal opportunities in business and in the professions?

When a member has lifted up a concern, how does our Meeting respond?

Does our Meeting encourage those seeking clearness for their convictions of conscience to hold up such convictions with prayerful openness to the Light?

Am I mindful of how my lifestyle and my investments can contribute to the improvement of the human condition, or to the exploitation of others?

Am I open to seeking clearness on matters of conscience and to assisting others in doing so? How do I respond and support one who acts out of a clear leading when I am under the weight of another?

What am I doing to work for the betterment of my community to assure the maintenance of effective public services which do not rely on funding from gaming?

Do I fulfill my civic responsibilities when they do not conflict with divine leadings?

8. PEACE

How does our Meeting act to advance peace, to oppose violence, and to support the constructive use of authority in our community, our nation, and the world?

What are we doing as a Meeting:

    – to free our nation from militarization, so evident in our society and in its economy?

    – to understand the causes of war and violence and to work for the development of the attitudes and institutions of peace?

    – to recognize and correct the causes of violence within our communities, and to work toward overcoming separations and restoring wholeness?

    – to increase the understanding and use of nonviolent approaches for the resolution of conflicts?

Do I live in the power of that Life and Spirit that takes away the occasion of all wars?

How do I maintain Friends' testimony that military training and all participation in war and its preparation are inconsistent with the teaching and the spirit of Christ?

Do I work for the establishment of alternative ways of settling disputes? Am I aware that to build a world community requires that we all face our differences honestly, openly, and in trust?

Do I treat conflict as an opportunity for growth, and address it with careful attention? Do I seek to recognize and respect the Divine in those with whom I have a basic disagreement? Do I look for ways to reaffirm in action and attitude my love for the one with whom I am in conflict?

9. MINISTRY OF OUTREACH

Outreach

What are we doing as a Meeting to communicate our presence and our principles to the community around us? Does our Meeting's ministry of outreach lead Friends to share their spiritual experiences with others?

What are we doing to invite persons not in membership to attend our meetings for worship and to encourage their continued attendance? How does the Meeting welcome visitors? Are we sensitive to the needs and hesitations of each visitor?

Are we tender to the needs of isolated Friends and Meetings, and to nearby Meetings seeking support?

How do I ground myself in the understandings of my faith? Am I clear about my beliefs? How do I prepare myself to share my faith and beliefs with others?

Does my manner of life as a Friend attract others to our religious society?

Do I seize opportunities to tell others about the Religious Society of Friends and invite them to worship with us?

Is my manner with visitors and attenders to our Meeting one of welcome?

Collaboration

In what ways does our Meeting respond to opportunities to join with other faiths in worship, in social action, and in spiritual dialogue?

How does our Meeting encourage its members to seek opportunities to meet and work with Friends world wide?

What opportunities have I taken to know people from different religious and cultural backgrounds, to worship with them, and to work with them on common concerns?

What opportunities have I taken to know, to work, and to worship with Friends outside of my own Meeting?

10. Stewardship of the Environment

Is the Meeting concerned that human interaction with nature be responsible, guided by a reverence for life and a sense of the splendor of God's continuing creation?

Are the decisions of the Meeting and its committees relating to the uses of property, goods, services, and energy made with sensitivity toward the environmental impact of those choices?

How does our Meeting learn about environmental concerns and then act in the community on its concerns?

How am I helping to develop a social, economic, and political system which will nurture an environment which sustains and enriches life for all?

Am I aware of the place of water, air, and soil in my life? Do I consider with care the necessity of purchasing substances hazardous to the environment? Do I act as a faithful steward of the environment in the use and disposal of such hazardous substances?

Do I choose with care the use of technology and devices that truly simplify and add quality to my life without adding an undue burden to essential resources?

11. STEWARDSHIP OF RESOURCES

Does our Meeting serve social and economic justice in its uses of property and money?

How does our Meeting engage its members in the support of the Meeting's work, its ministry, and the upkeep of its property?

How does our Meeting engage its members in the support of the quarterly and yearly meetings and other Quaker organizations?

To what extent does our Meeting rely on current members for financial support, and what role does endowment income serve? Does the Meeting consider carefully the appropriate role of invested funds?

Am I clear that I am the steward, not the owner, of property in my care?

Do I simplify my needs, making choices that balance self-sufficiency (to avoid unnecessary dependence on others) and fair sharing of resources? Do I make choices as a consumer that support the equitable distribution of income?

Do my employment and other activities allow for use of time and energy in spiritual growth and in service to the Religious Society of Friends?

Do I contribute generously within my means to the funding of the work of Friends in my Meeting, in the yearly meeting, and in the wider world of Friends?

12. INTEGRITY AND SIMPLICITY

What does our Meeting understand to be the meaning and implication of our testimonies on simplicity and integrity?

How do our Meeting's actions demonstrate this understanding?

As a Meeting, what are we doing to encourage members to embody integrity and simplicity in their everyday lives?

How do I strive to maintain the integrity of my inner and outer lives in my spiritual journey, my work, and my family responsibilities? How do I manage my commitments so that overcommitment, worry, and stress do not diminish my integrity?

Am I temperate in all things? Am I open to counsel and advice on overindulgence and addictive behavior, such as gambling? Do I take seriously the hazards associated with addictive and mood-altering substances?

Am I careful to speak truth as I know it and am I open to truth spoken to me? Am I mindful that judicial oaths imply a double standard of truth?

Do I refrain from membership in organizations whose purposes and methods compromise our testimonies?

INDEX

Action, Activism, 75-76, 82, 228, 261

Adam, 48, 249; fall of, 27, 39, 46, 61-63, 110

Adams, Brooks, 193

Advices, 126, 127, 161

Affirmation, 106, 171, 172, 190

Agape, 135

Allen, William, 97, 148, 162, 169, 185

American Friends Service Committee, ix, 162, 181, 208-09, 241, 243, 278-81

Anabaptists, xviii, 14, 15

Anarchy, Anarchism, xviii, 14, 17, 42, 123, 129, 137, 199

Aquinas, Thomas, 69

Arbitration, 205; mediation, xvi

Archdale, John, 222-23

Aristotle, 69

Arnett, Thomas, 250

Atonement, 50-55, 58, 66, 79, 250

Audland, John, 10, 218

Augustine, 47, 66, 166

Authority, 146, 147, 245

Baily, Joshua L., 174

Balby letter, 122

Bancroft, George, 191

Baptists, xviii, 13, 14

Barclay, David, 204-05

Barclay, Robert, xiv, xv, 39, 40, 198, 205; Apology, xvii, 23, 33, 41, 44, 47, 59, 62, 63-66, 80, 88, 95, 100, 110, 112, 160, 161, 195, 196, 198, 205, 239, 248

Barthianism, 64

Baxter, Richard, 192

Bellers, John, 162, 205

Benezet, Anthony, 180, 207, 221

Benson. Cervase, 31

Bernard (of Clairvaux), 88

Besse, Joseph, 217

Bhagavadgita, 41

Bible, xv, xvii, xix, 12, 16, 20-23, 45-49, 74, 91, 96, 97, 104, 109, 138, 148, 182, 195, 215, 230, 233, 236, 239, 240, 243, 248, 258; Quaker attitude toward, 40-43

Blood of Christ, 4, 51, 52, 53, 54, 86

Bloomingdale Asylum, 188

Body of Christ, the Church as, 4, 17

Books, pamphlets, 218

Braithwaite, William Charles, xv, 63, 64

Brayshaw, A. Neave, xv, 65

Bright, John, 205

Buddhism, xx, 61, 102

Burnyeat, John, 54

Burrough. Edward, 9

Business, limitation of, 167, 168

Calvinism, xv, xvii, xix, 13, 62, 64, 65, 66, 69, 257

Camm, John, 10

Camm, Thomas, 10
Capital punishment, 185, 186
Catholic, Catholicism, xvi, xvii, 3,
    4-5, 13, 14, 17, 55-56, 61, 69,
    73, 88, 103, 105, 258, 264
Caton, William, 6, 249
Chalkley, Thomas, 141, 199, 221
Christ, 3, 11, 20, 22, 25, 27, 28,
    29, 30, 32, 36, 43, 45, 46, 47,
    48, 49, 50, 51, 52, 54, 55, 56,
    58, 59, 61, 63, 81, 86, 93, 100,
    105, 107, 116, 122, 165, 195,
    197, 198, 201, 202, 203, 229,
    232; the eternal, and the
    historic Jesus, 39, 45-46, 48-50,
    56, 219; blood of Christ, 4, 51,
    52, 53, 54, 86; see also Jesus
Christology, 49
Church of England, xviii, 13, 16,
    192
Churchman, John, 221
Civil disobedience, 204, 206
Claridge, Richard, 195
Clarkson, Thomas, 163, 227
Claypole, Lady, 108
Clement, 47
Clerk, 130, 131-32
Cloud of Unknowing, 94
Coale, Josiah, 47, 116
Coffin, Levi, 180
Community, 145, 153-57, 176, 211
Compromise, 60, 61, 133, 146, 256
Comstock, Elizabeth, 180
Concern, 124, 126, 131, 163, 173,
    250

Conscience, 35, 39, 43-44, 52, 59,
    83, 128, 136, 146-47, 150, 177,
    183, 195
Conscientious objectors, 189, 191,
    208 see also War, Non-violence,
    Pacifists
Consensus, 141
Conservative (Wilburite) Friends,
    232-34, 240
Constitution of the United States,
    190-91
Contemplation, 70, 76, 78, 88, 89
Conventicle Act, 16, 123, 192
Conversion, 9, 13, 237
Convincement, 9
Creaturely activity, 77-78, 82
Creed, 19, 70, 117, 138, 245, 248
Crisp, Stephen, 250
Cromwell, Oliver, xviii, 1, 12, 108,
    185, 194
Cross, crucified, 24, 51, 56, 161,
    195, 253, 256

Dark world, 30
Darkness, ocean of, 33; power of,
    141
Davies, Richard, 7
Deceit, 31, 32, 37, 69, 79
Delaware, 189, 193
Dewsbury, William, 11, 115, 121,
    159, 218
Dickinson, James, 249
Discipline, 127, 128, 157, 178,
    179-225; Book of Extracts, 224

Disownment, 112, 127, 159, 225
Divine-human, 142, 177
Divine and human, 53; relation between, 63-69
Doctrinal sermons, statements, 219, 231
Doctrine, xvii, 32, 40, 58, 61, 138, 140, 183, 221, 226, 231
Douglas, John Henry, 235
Dymond, Jonathan, 170

Eddy, Thomas, 188
Education, xvi, 110, 118, 121, 144, 153, 156, 170, 176, 181-84, 224; schools; for Indians, 179; for Negroes, 180; Boarding Schools, and Colleges, 181-84; adult religious education, 182, 241
Eldering, 113-14
Elders, 13, 113-15, 117-18, 227-29, 230-31
Ellwood, Thomas, 162
England, Mary, 107
Equality, 145, 159-63, 176, 211
Evangelicalism, 213, 215-20, 227-37, 240, 242-43, 254, 265
Evangelism, (see Evangelicalism)
Evans, Jonathan, 233
Evans, Joshua, 111, 221
Evans, William, 168, 250
Evil, 57, 69, 79, 92, 93; in man's nature, xv, 55; man's responsibility for evil and good, 55-59

Fathers, Church, 23, 148, 195
Feeling, as guide to action, 147, 148-50
Fell, Margaret (Fox), 9, 15, 165
Fénelon, 88, 99
Ferris, David, 221, 249
Fifth Monarchy Men, 194
First Publishers of Truth, 5-9, 59-60, 216
Fisher, Mary, 160, 194
Fisher, Samuel, 41, 195
Fiske, John, 185
Follett, M. P., 132
Forster, William, 185
Fothergill, John, 205, 221
Fothergill, Samuel, 95, 115, 221
Fothergill, Susanna, 201
Fox, George, xiii, 8, 9, 10, 19, 26-28, 33, 36-37, 49, 52, 59, 65, 69, 119, 123, 124, 140, 159, 178, 179, 183, 185, 194, 216, 261; Epistles, quoted or referred to, xv, 17, 23-26, 28-31, 33-37, 39, 44, 52, 81-82, 85, 93, 94, 109, 110-11, 129, 132; Journal, quoted or referred to, 34, 45, 47, 52, 59, 82, 108
Frame, Esther, 235
Frankford Asylum, 188
Franklin, Benjamin, 187, 205
Free Produce Association, 179
Freedmens Association, 181
French and Indian War, 178, 201, 206, 222, 224
Friendly Association, 224

Friends Ambulance Unit, 208
Friends Service Council, 208-09, 241
Friends War Victims Relief Committee, 208
Frost, Bede, 94
Fry, A. Ruth, 170
Fry, Elizabeth, 186, 232
Fundamentalists, 236

Galileo, 139, 262
Garrett, Thomas, 180
Garrison, William Lloyd, 177, 180
Gentile Divinity, 46
German Quakers, 179
Grace, 55, 61, 66, 85, 229, 249, 256, 258
Graham, John William, xv
Gratton, John, 14-16
Greek thought, 26, 49, 64, 220, 221; compared with Hebrew thought, 67-70
Grellet, Stephen, 108, 162, 185
Grubb, Edward, xv
Guidance, 103, 124, 148, 150, 177
Gurney, Joseph John, 163, 232-33
Gurneyites, 232-34
Guyon, Madame, 88, 99

Haggar, Mary, 249
Hall, John, 167
Harmony, 145, 157-59, 176, 211
Hebrew thought, 26, 49-51, 53,

55, 56-57, 58, 260; compared with Greek thought, 67-70
Hegelian idealism, xv, 64
Henderson, James, 97
Hicks, Elias, 82-83, 230, 233
Hicksites, 231-33, 234, 240-41
Hinduism, xx, 61, 246, 265
Hoag, Joseph, 196
Hocking, William E.,176
Holy Experiment, 222
Holy Wisdom, 88
Hopper, Isaac T., 180
Howgill, Francis, 9-10
Humanism, 256-57, 264
Humanitarianism, 245-46, 254-56
Hunt, Sarah, 249

Ignatian system of meditation, 88
Ignatius, 116
Incarnation, 58, 61, 68, 69, 80, 203, 255
Independents, Congregationalists,xvii-xviii, 13, 14, 60, 192
Indians, 36, 47, 141, 150, 176, 194, 216, 218, 224
Inquisition, 139, 216

Janney, Samuel, 231, 249
Jesus, xxi, 30, 40, 48-50, 52, 53, 58 86, 106, 195-96, 219; the Christ of history, 108, 202, 247; see also Christ, Christology, Atonement

John, Evangelist, xix, 22, 23, 40, 47-48, 54, 67, 79, 81, 86, 135, 136
Jones, Rebecca, 221
Jones, Rufus M., xv, xxi, 65, 241
Jordan, Richard, 98, 102, 104
Journals, Friends, 7, 14, 67, 98, 99, 104, 149, 167, 201, 225, 235, 248-51
Jung, Carl G., 147, 220
Justification, xvii, 55-56, 215-16, 232, 234
Justin Martyr, 47

Kinsey, John, 223
Koran, 194

Lamb, Charles, 103
Lao-Tse, 200
Law, 62, 136, 137; Mosaic, 137, 195
Lawrence, Brother, 67
Lawson, Thomas, 261
Lettsom, Dr. John C., 199
Light, Inward, as experienced, Chap. II; as thought about, Chap. III, Children of Light, 2, 20, 122; as unity, xxii, 25, 26, 27, 37, 93, 113, 129, 140, 196, 229, 239, 255, 262, 263; as power, 34; names for, 25, 45; as Substance, 28, 29; its contrary, 30, 31; as "blood," 52; as above, 27, 140-41; measure of, 34, 35, 198; universality of, 20, 36, 37,
45-48; and Scriptures, 40-43, 215; and Christ, 50; and the Seed, 61; and reason, 44-45; and conscience, 43-44, 183; as related to man, 63-70; as Father, Son and Spirit, 23, 79; and worship, Chap. IV, 108; as pure, 83-84; as guidance in ministry, Chap. V; as Love, 137; as source of social concern, 144; see also Truth, Spirit, Christ Within, Mysticism
Lilburne, John, 159
Lloyd, David, 223
Lloyd, Thomas, 223
Locke, John, 190
Logan, George, 205
Lucas, Margaret, 97
Lundy, Benjamin, 180
Luther, 69
Lutherans, xvii

Mahomet, 194-95, 216
Manchester, Conference at, 241
Materialism, 246, 254, 256, 264
Measure, 23, 34, 35, 43, 47, 49, 50, 93, 122, 178, 198, 226
Meditation, 88, 90 95, 96, 102, 214
Membership, 102, 130, 146, 153, 155; birthright, 153
Mental hospitals, 176, 177, 187-89
Methodists, 229
Ministry, Chap. V, 19, 36, 234, 250; in the early meetings, 5-17

Minutes, 130, 131, 172; a minute, 231
Missions, foreign, 176n., 237, 240
Mohammedanism, xx
Molinos, 88, 99
Montanist Movement, 116
Moses, 53, 54, 138
Mott, Lucretia, 180
Motze, 141
Mysticism, defined, xviii, 32; Quaker type of, xix-xx, 78-82, 259; Catholic, 88-89, 103, 264; and evangelicalism in the Society of Friends, Chap. IX; nature mysticism, 247; as contact with the superhuman, 250-52, 264; and the new science, 262, 263, 264

Natural man, 62, 66, 248
Naylor, James, 123
Neo-Calvinism, xv, 202
New England, 12, 36, 155, 193, 216, 232
New Jersey, 189, 223, 225
New Testament, xix, 12-13, 22, 51, 58, 202, 239, 248
Newport, Elizabeth, 47, 101 (n. 26)
Newton, Isaac, 140, 261, 262, 263
Non-violence, 184-206; see also War, Conscientious objectors, Pacifism
Norris, Isaac, 223
North Carolina, 189, 222, 235

Oaths, 170-72, 190, 218
Obedience, 61,66, 68, 136, 206, 226
Old Testament, 21, 22, 32, 49, 56, 116, 195
Opportunities, 98
Ordained, 117
Ordination, xvii, 109
Orthodox party, 228-37, 240-41
Otto, Rudolf, 86
Overseers, 13, 118n., 151, 173, 228

Pacifism, 60, 157, 176, 189, 194-95, 196, 198-203; vocational, 198; see also War, Non-violence, Conscientious objectors
Pastoral system, 235-37
Paul, Apostle, xix, 22, 41, 45, 49, 54, 56, 67, 69, 79, 116, 135, 137-38, 144, 202, 244, 250, 260, 263
Peace, inner, 1, 26, 27, 29, 37, 59, 60, 79, 81, 93, 104, 136, 150, 167, 201, 217, 251, 253, 256; and unity, 17; peace-creating, 54, 186; international, 193-206, 211
Pearson, Anthony, 32
Pemberton, James, 223
Pemberton, John, 201
Pendle Hill, 182
Penington, Isaac, 29, 30, 42, 69, 95-96, 99. 104, 105, 195, 197, 198

Penn, William, 39, 40, 46, 80, 95-96, 114, 119, 137, 141, 163, 164, 166, 171, 178, 185, 192, 195, 198, 201, 205, 220; Frame of Government, 189, 222, 224
Pennsylvania, 136, 185, 188, 189, 193, 222, 223
Pennsylvania Hospital, 187
Pentecost, xix, 3, 110, 203
Perfection, perfectionism, xv, 55, 59-61, 66, 202, 237
Perrot, John, 123
Philadelphia Yearly Meeting, 173-74, 207, 222, 230, 233
Phillips, Catherine, 43, 142, 221, 226
Philosophers, 244
Philosophy, 18, 26, 29, 214, 264
Plato, 46, 67, 69
Plotinus, 4, 27, 46, 69
Police power, 198
Pope, the, 13, 162, 216
Poulain, A., 89
Pragmatic test, 103-04, 147-48
Prayer, 88-91, 97, 99-100, 107, 109, 140
Presbyterian, xvii, xix, 13, 14, 64
Price, fixed, 169
Priest, xviii, 4, 12, 20, 45, 117, 244
Prisons, 184-87
Prophets, Old Testament, 2, 20, 32, 68, 70, 109, 116, 117; New Testament, 116, 117, 243; Quaker, 13, 26, 112, 116, 117, 228

Protestant, Protestantism, xvi, xvii, xviii, 3, 5, 17, 20, 40, 42, 45, 46, 55, 56, 59, 61, 69, 73-74, 137, 138, 193, 195, 201, 202, 235, 261, 265
Proud, Mary, 99
Public Friends, 8, 9, 19, 21
Pure, 25, 34, 83, 84-85, 90, 93, 148, 221
Puritan, Puritanism, xviii, xix, 1, 13, 17, 136, 159, 165, 183, 188, 215, 261

Quaker Act, 191
Queries, 99, 126, 127, 151-52, 155, 157, 162, 169, 173, 225
Quietism, xiv, 63, 81, 221

Racial discrimination, 163; see also Indians, Slavery
Ranterism, 14, 137
Rationalism, xvii, 118, 213, 214, 229, 231, 239, 240, 242, 245, 254
Reason, xvii, xxi, 44-45, 62, 118, 146, 147, 251, 252, 258
Reconciliation, 51, 79
Redemption, 51, 56, 58, 79
Reformation, xviii, 23, 257
Regeneration, xv, 66, 81, 258
Relief, Relief Work, xvi, 155, 206-10; Irish wars, 206; Acadians, 206; Revolutionary War, 205;

Napoleonic Wars, 207; Balkan
    Wars, 207; Crimean War, 207;
    Irish Famine, 207; American
    Civil War, 207; Franco-Prussian
    War, 207; Boer War, 208; World
    Wars I and II, 208; Spanish
    Civil War, 210
Religious liberty, 176, 190, 191-93
Renaissance, 55, 257
Resurrection, 58
Retirement, 95-96, 97, 107, 149
Retreat, York, 188
Revelation, xxi, 40, 48
Revolutionary War, 158, 205, 207,
    228
Rhode Island, 169, 189, 222
Richardson, Tohn, 114, 141
Rivers, W. H. B., 141
Robinson, William, 8
Routh, Martha, 168, 221, 226
Rowntree, J. W., xv, 241
Russia, 96, 205, 207, 208
Rutty, John, 97, 115, 168

Sacrament, Sacramental, 4, 13,
    66, 67, 74, 77, 85, 86, 117, 257;
    Baptism, 52, 85, 86, 138, 260;
    Communion, 45; The Last
    Supper, 53, 86-87, 117
Sacrifice, 51, 53, 57-58
Salvation, 5, 21, 32, 39, 45, 46, 56,
    64, 74, 104, 136, 258
Savery, William, 221
Science, xx-xxi, 44, 45, 73, 106,

139-40, 169, 170, 183, 239, 252,
    254, 257-59, 262, 263, 264
Scott, Job, 59, 96, 104, 221
Scriptures, 40-43; see also Bible
Seekers, xiii, 11
Sense of the meeting, 130
Separations: Wilkinson-Story, 128;
    American, 228-30; Hicksite-
    Orthodox, 230-34; Wilburite-
    Gurneyite, 232-35; Pastoral
    -nonpastoral, 234-36; Funda-
    mentalist-Modernist, 236-37
Sewel, William, 116
Shadow, 28-30, 32, 35, 69, 79 see
    also Substance
Shakers, 232
Shillitoe, Thomas, 149-50, 168,
    185, 233
Shipley, Catharine, 199
Shipley, Thomas, 180
Silence, 6-12, 21-23, 26, 70, 73, 86,
    90, 92, 96, 97, 98, 102, 103,
    104, 107, 109, 112, 126, 129,
    166, 182, 235, 236
Simplicity, 145, 148, 152, 163-74.
    176, 182, 183, 211, 228
Sin, 51, 55, 57, 61, 65, 66, 68, 74,
    93, 108; Original, 59, 201
Skipton letter, 122, 217
Slavery, 85, 127, 130, 144, 151,
    162, 176, 178-81; Underground
    Railroad, 179; Emancipation,
    180
Spirit, Inward Light referred to
    as, xxii, 5, 19, 21, 27, 28, 40, 98,

106,107, 119, 138, 142, 216, 236; in early Christianity, 3, 13, 21, 25, 46; of Christ, 10, 15, 16, 22, 138, 203; in Hebrew thought, 68; as creative, 30, 35, 36, 94

Spiritual director, 88, 103, 105

Stacy, Thomas, 6

State, 44, 156, 189-91, 199, 215, 254, 266

Stephenson, Marmaduke, 8

Story, Christopher, 6

Story, Thomas, 7, 129

Stubbs, John, 6

Stubbs, Thomas, 6

Sturge, Joseph, 199, 205, 207

Stuyvesant, Peter, 160

Substance, 28, 37, 49, 69, 79; *see also* Shadow

Sufis, xx

Swarthmore Hall, 9

Symbol, symbolic, xix, 41, 42, 53, 57-61, 91, 107, 161, 246

Synagogue, 3

Taoists, xx

Temperance, intemperance, total abstinence, 127, 173, 176

Teresa of Avila, 89, 92

Theology, theologians, theological opinions, xix, 23, 26, 39, 42, 49, 59, 63, 70, 90, 214, 219, 228, 230, 232, 237, 244, 257

Thoreau, Henry David, 204

Tillyard, Aelfrida, 95

Toleration Act, 191, 216, 221

Toynbee, Arnold J., 75

Tradition, xvii, 21, 28, 118, 163

Trinity, 22

Truth, early name for Quakerism, xiv, 2, 5, 7, 19, 35, 36, 63, 122, 215, 217, 222; as name for the Inward Light, 25, 30, 34, 40, 41, 85, 123, 129, 137, 226, 253; tests of, 146-49, 239, 243, 252; and simplicity, 169-170; Quaker method of arriving at, 132-33, 137

Tuke, Samuel, 188

Underhill, Evelyn, 83

Union with God, Unity with God, xv, 66, 68, 89, 91, 92, 93-94, 133, 136; Union or fellowship, 87, 94-95

Unitarianism, 231

Unity, 129, 130, 132, 134, 137, 139, 140, 142, 158, 231, 237, 263

Universalism, 215

Utopia, Utopian, Utopianism, 61, 202, 222

Vote, 130; method of voting, 133-34, 141, 142

Walser, Frank, 132

War, 35, 60, 127, 155, 165, 196, 198, 202, 204; violence, 37; *see also* Non-violence, Conscientious objectors

Waugh, Dorothy, 160

Wells, H. G., 264

West Indies, 180

Westminster Confession of Faith, 65

Wheeler, Daniel, 90, 96, 167

Whitehead, A. N., 139, 200

Whittier, John C., 81, 98, 119, 180, 207, 226

Wilbur, John, 232-33

Wilburites, 232-35

Wilkinson, John, 6

Will, 49, 66, 68, 81-82, 85, 88, 89, 91, 106; of God, 61, 77, 92, 109, 136, 138, 202; froward, 150

Williams, John, 115

Withdrawal, 70; and return, 75-88

Winstanley, Gerrard, 159

Witchcraft, 188

Women, 31, 109, 110, 124, 141-42, 156, 160, 183, 186; Women's meetings, 124, 172; Daughters, 45, 110

Woodbrooke, 182

Woolman, John, 83-84, 87, 104, 148, 150, 162, 164, 165, 180, 194, 210, 221

Wordsworth, William, 247

Work Camps, 162, 184, 209

World Council of Churches, 204

Worship, in the early meetings, Chap. I; theory and practice of Quaker worship, Chap. IV, 102, 129, 145, 226, 242; and ritual, 16, 32, 86; private retirement, 96, 97, 107; opportunities, 98; and the meeting for business, 130, 145; and ministry, Chap. V; and social concern, 145; and the pastoral system, 236-37

Yogis, xix

Zen, xix, 102, 103

FRIENDS FOR 350 YEARS

was composed on a Power Macintosh 7600 computer using Adobe Pagemaker 6.5 and the ITC New Baskerville typefaces from the Adobe Type Library. Seven thousand copies were printed in the United States of America by Haddon Craftsmen—a division of R.R. Donnelley, Bloomsburg, PA in October 2002. The book was printed on 55# Boise Wyoming Book Antique paper.

History of the Typefaces

British printer John Baskerville of Birmingham created the types that bear his name in about 1752. This version of Baskerville was designed for Linotype-Hell by George Jones in 1930. The International Typeface Corporation licensed it in 1982. This Baskerville design has a delicacy and grace that come from long, elegant serifs and the subtle transfer of stroke weight from thick to very thin. ITC New Baskerville is well-suited to longer texts and display uses.

Book design by

Eva Fernandez Beehler and Rebecca Kratz Mays